A
SANKOFA
MOMENT

A
SANKOFA
MOMENT

The History of
Trinity United Church of Christ

Rev. Dr. Jeremiah A. Wright, Jr.

A SANKOFA MOMENT: The History of Trinity United Church of Christ

SAINT PAUL PRESS, DALLAS, TEXAS

First Printing, 2010

Cover design by LaShaunn Tappler of LT ComDesign, LLC
Edited by Jeri Wright of The Grace of God, NFP

The Bible quotations in this volume are from the New Revised Standard Version of the Bible.

The name SAINT PAUL PRESS and its logo are registered as a trademark in the U.S. patent office.

ISBN-13: 978-0-9826196-2-9

Printed in the U.S.A.

Contents

Acknowledgements

*T*his is my fifth book. My first four books were collections of sermons. I owe the publication of those books to Reverend Jini Kilgore and to Dr. Colleen Birchett. It was their idea to publish my sermons. They took the tapes of my sermons, edited them and then "shopped around" for publishers.

This is my first attempt at writing a book, however, that is not a collection of sermons. This book was forced on me by my daughter, Jeri! I am really grateful to her and I will say more about that later on in this acknowledgement section. For now, I just want to take a stab at acknowledging all of those who have made this book possible.

I first want to thank my grandparents, Reverend Hamilton Martin Henderson and Mrs. Mamie Henderson. I learned what being a pastor in a rural setting and in a small church meant while watching my grandfather serve two different, small, country churches: the Gravel Hill Baptist Church in Surrey County, Virginia, and the Jerusalem Baptist Church in Temperanceville, Virginia. His wife, my maternal grandmother, taught me how to read before I got to kindergarten. I owe my understanding of pastoring a small church, and my ability to read, to those two giants in my life.

My "Grandpa Jim" taught me what integrity was. Grandpa Jim was my father's father. He was a tobacco farmer in Caroline County, Virginia. He was also a deacon at the St. John Baptist Church in Caroline County, Virginia. His honesty and his desire to have his son get the education that he could not get are gifts that helped make the writing of this book possible.

My paternal grandmother was killed long before I was born. She was killed when my dad was in his early teens. My father's aunt, Mrs. Hattie Sharp, however, became a surrogate mother for my dad and she became my sister's and my, "Aunt Hattie." We never thought of her as a "Great Aunt." She was our aunt and her love for learning in spite of the racist environment in which she was nurtured have helped me to keep my eye on the academic prize when forces around me could have very easily distracted me and kept me from reaching my goal.

My mother and father, Dr. Jeremiah A. Wright, Sr., and Dr. Mary Elizabeth Wright, are giants in my life. My father's forty-two years of pastoring the Grace Baptist Church of Germantown in Philadelphia not only taught me all that I knew about ministry and being a pastor "up close and personal," his model of ministry also gave me the paradigm that I tried to follow for thirty-six years as the Pastor of Trinity United Church of Christ.

My mother, being the financial secretary of our church, taught me church administration when I was still a teenager. I owe them a debt I can never repay.

My mother and father stood behind us at Trinity Church when we were under one hundred members. They made the first pledge for our Building Program when we started to grow. They continued to pay their Building Fund pledge long after both buildings were up and they showed me through their constant prayer life what it means to be a loving parent even when your child is acting a fool! (Yes! I acted a fool many times.)

My mother's siblings are also persons to whom I owe a great debt and without whom this book would not have been possible. Her brother, Dr. Thomas Howard Henderson, was the Dean of Virginia Union University when I started my undergraduate studies there. His friendship with Sam Proctor is legendary. His succession of Sam Proctor as the first non-minister to be the President of Virginia Union University was history-making! His PhD from The University of Chicago and his taking the time to talk to me as if I were his private mentee helped shaped my love for learning and my keen awareness of the necessity of academic excellence.

My mother's brother, Dr. John B. Henderson, the Pastor of the Bank Street Baptist Church of Norfolk and the Pastor of Samuel DeWitt Proctor's family, taught me what unconditional love meant as he adopted his wife's niece, Joyce, and raised her as if she were his own child. His "pastor-to-pastor" advice in my early years as Pastor of Trinity United Church of Christ is advice that I will go to my grave treasuring.

My mother's baby brother, Welton Henderson ("Uncle Shorty"), taught me what academic excellence and perseverance meant. He served as the principal of an inner city school in the racist South and he never gave up on his desire for excellence. He demanded excellence from his faculty and from his students.

My mother's sister, Pearl Henderson Wood, became my "other mother" when I went away to college at Virginia Union University. She opened her home to me as if I were her own blood son and she nurtured me through a very difficult period of adjustment in my life. She pushed me to become both pastor and professor. I had shared with her as a teenager that, that was my life's goal. She never let me abandon that dream, that goal and that hope. I owe a great deal to Aunt Pearl and without her this book would never have come into being.

My sister, LaVerne, is someone whose presence in my life I must acknowledge. She pushed me to be the best student I could be. She pushed me to be honest and to be true to myself. She held me to a standard of excellence for which I will always be grateful. Her husband, my brother-in-law, Bill Miner, was a support to me when I was a teenager, when I was in the military and all throughout my ministry. I acknowledge his gifts to my life and to my ministry and I thank him for helping this book be birthed.

My mother and my father had play daughters and sons all throughout my life. My mother's first play daughter, however, was Aunt Peggy. Aunt Peggy and her husband, Uncle Rudy, became my big brother and my big sister. Their constant support helped me to write this book even when I did not feel like it!

Dr. Samuel DeWitt Proctor is a man whose presence in my life I acknowledge with gratitude to God and with eternal thanksgiving! Dr. Proctor was my first professor of preaching. Dr. Proctor was the President of Virginia Union University when I started at Virginia Union University. Dr. Proctor used to teach me Homiletics as he drove me from Richmond, Virginia, to Philadelphia, Pennsylvania, on the weekends when he was preaching there.

Ten years after my leaving the PhD program in the History of Religions Department at The University of Chicago Divinity School, Dr. Proctor called me. He told me it did not make any sense for me to have put all of those years in while trying to earn a PhD. (I was at the Divinity School for six years!) He told me to come on in to a program that he was starting and finish up my doctoral work under him.

I started my higher education under Samuel DeWitt Proctor. I had known him all of my life. I finished my Doctoral degree under Dr. Proctor and it is because of him that this book has been written.

My wife, Ramah, has been a constant source of support. Ramah has stood by me when people were singing my praises and Ramah was always there for me as people dragged my name through the dirt, the mud, the muck and the mire of their negative assessments of me and my ministry.

Ramah was more than the "*wind beneath my wings.*" Ramah was a suffering spouse who always put my ministry above her own personal feelings and asked for God's strength in helping her to be the mate that God would have her be in my life. Without Ramah, this book would never have been written.

In acknowledging the generations before me and beside me, however, I have to acknowledge the generation behind me. My oldest daughters, Janet and Jeri, came to Trinity Church when they were seven years old and six years old. They grew up in Trinity Church. They have stood beside me, walked beside me, prayed for me and picked me up when I was beaten down. I am forever grateful to God for them and for their presence in my life.

My daughter, Janet, served as my Executive Secretary for a decade and a half. She became my "alter ego." She helped to shape my pastorate in a way that was a blessing in the lives of the people I was trying to serve and I will go to my grave thanking her for her love and her devotion.

My daughter, Jeri, is the reason you are holding this book in your hands! During my sabbatical leave right before I retired, Jeri asked me to write a *"brief history"* of Trinity United Church of Christ. She gave me the impression that I was writing it for the Web site. I wrote what Jeri asked for and Jeri kept asking me for more!

Jeri kept telling me to add a little bit more in terms of the Bible Study Development Program. She told me to add a little bit more in terms of the second decade of my ministry. She kept saying. "Add a little bit more! Add a little bit more!"

By the time we got down to the Fall of 2008 (after my retirement), I told Jeri that what she was asking me to add was making my "*brief history*" too long for the Web site. It was then that she told me that I was not writing it for the Web site. I was writing a history of the church and it would be a book that she was taking orders for in December when I preached for the 47th anniversary of our congregation!

On the first Sunday of December of last year, Jeri started taking orders for this book that you hold in your hand. All I had written at the time, however, was what I wanted to go on the Web site, or what I thought was going on the Web site. It is because of Jeri's pushing me that I went on and wrote the volume you now hold. Thank you, Jeri.

Nathan and Nikol came into my life when they were six years old and ten years old. Nathan and Nikol became a part of my family when they were eight years old and twelve years old. I have never called them "stepchildren." They have never been "step" children to me. They have always been my children and it is because of their support that this volume came into being.

My baby daughter, Jamila, is the child to whom I can never say "Thank you" enough. Jamila did without a daddy and a mommy while her mother was in seminary and her daddy was "on the road," and Jamila never gave up on us! Jamila went through hell as the media crucified her father, yet Jamila kept on loving me. Thank you, Jamila, for making this book possible.

My grandchildren, Jeremiah, Jazmin and Steven are an inspiration to me and were three more reasons that I kept on writing this book that I did not want to write. I kept hearing a voice that said, "*You owe it to your grandchildren!*"

I am working on an autobiography. I am working on my book on Black Sacred Music. I am working on another book that will chronicle what it was like being the Pastor of the first African American President of the United States.

While working on those books, however, the voice that prompted me to keep on writing this volume helped me to see how my grandchildren needed to be able to read about the church that was the church into which they were born, the church which nurtured them, shaped them and gave their grandfather a reason to hold on when the world wanted him to let go! I owe them that story and it is because of them that you now read that story.

I must acknowledge the members of Trinity United Church of Christ who made this volume possible. From the charter members of our church down to the newest members of our church, I owe you a great debt.

This book could never have been written had it not been for Reverend Barbara Allen and S.L. Allen, Jeffrey Radford, Manford and Cherribelle Byrd, Shelby and Doris Grant, Rupert and Gwen Graham, Val and Ethel Jordan, Blaine and Doris DeNye and all the other members who were here in March of 1972. This book would not have been possible had it not been for all of those who caught the vision and who helped me to be the Pastor that I tried to be for thirty-six years.

I acknowledge each member of our congregation and I thank God for all of the members of our congregation.

This volume would not have been possible without my personal staff: Ivey Matute's patience and kindness; Charles Lofton's diligence and faithfulness; and my diligent transcriptionist, Cynthia Gibson, who also became an editor pointing out to me things that I was leaving out of this volume. Those three have helped come into being what it is you hold in your hand and to them I acknowledge my gratitude and my debt.

Most of all, my beloved, I thank God. I thank God for the way in which God never gave up on me even when I am sure He must have wanted to give up on me! I know I let God down many times. God's love is unconditional, however. God's grace and mercy have followed me, fed me and kept me.

I thank God for making this volume possible. I hope you will be blessed by the experiences captured in these pages.

Reverend Dr. Jeremiah A. Wright, Jr.
Pastor Emeritus
Spring 2009

Introduction

*T*he Akan people have an important symbol known as Sankofa. It is expressed in the Asante Adinkra symbols as a bird whose body is heading in one direction, but whose head is turned in the opposite direction. What the symbol is teaching is that we cannot go forward without first going back to our past to understand how it is we got to where we are.

Put another way, Sankofa means that if we do not know from whence we came, we will forever be heading in the wrong direction. The African concept of recognizing the past, honoring the past, knowing our past, embracing our past and learning from our past is found not only among the Akan people. It is found all across the Continent of Africa.

In Chancellor Williams' book, **Destruction of Black Civilization,** Dr. Williams tells the story about the young traveler in Africa who asks the old man, "'*Whatever happened to the people of Sumer? Legend has it that the people of ancient Sumer were Black!'*

"The old man stopped and thought for a moment. Then he softly said to the young traveler, 'Ah! They forgot their story

and so they died!"'

Any people who forgets their story, any people who does not remember their history, any people who ignores their past, are people who are on their way to death. Psychologists call it social death. Theologians call it spiritual death!

We pause for a "Sankofa moment" to look back at our history as a congregation, to understand our story and to tell our own stories, so that future generations can know the way over which we have come. That is why my daughter, Jeri, chose to give this book the title *A Sankofa Moment*.

I give you in the pages that follow a history lesson that is much, much more than history.

I offer to you "our story" as seen from the vantage point of one who pastored this congregation for thirty-six years. It is my hope that in reading our story you will see (in the words of James Weldon Johnson) how *"we have come over a way that with tears has been watered."*

Chapter 1
The Beginnings

*T*he story of Trinity United Church of Christ is a fascinating story, a powerful story and a story that must never be forgotten.

About twenty years ago I went to preach at the church where my father served in Philadelphia. The host Pastor there, Dr. G. Daniel Jones, had a session where I sat with the seminarians of that church to talk with them about ministry, theological education and the Black Church in North America. During the question and answer period one of the seminarians asked me, *"How is it that you were raised American Baptist and ended up in the United Church of Christ?"*

Because they also wanted to know the difference between the American Baptist denomination and the United Church of Christ, in my response to that student I shared with the seminarians at my "home church" the rich and powerful history of this denomination we call the United Church of Christ. It is helpful to know that history in order to understand how Trinity United Church of Christ came to be started by the Chicago Metropolitan Association of the Illinois Conference of the United Church of Christ in 1961.

The United Church of Christ is made up of four predecessor denominations˜the Evangelical church, the Reformed church, the Congregational church and the Christian church. The Evangelical church and the Reformed church are churches that came out of German and Dutch countries. They had no Africans in their congregations and their primary contact with Africans in the United States of America was through healthcare and the Settlement House Movement during the Great Migration.

The Congregational church and the Christian church, however, have very different histories. Their involvement with Africans goes back into the 1600s for the Congregational church, and to the 1800s for the Christian church. First, a word about the Christian Church.

The Christian church is primarily a denomination whose congregations are heavily populated throughout the states of North Carolina and Virginia. When I came into the denomination in 1972, there were 288 African American congregations in a denomination that had over 6,000 congregations! Of the 288 Black congregations, 200 of them were out of the Christian tradition and found in North Carolina and Virginia.

Dr. J. T. Stanley writes about those churches in his very important book, **The Afro-Christian Tradition.** Because those churches were in the South where agriculture shaped the context in which they were founded, Africans were allowed to worship by themselves and they were able to retain African elements in their worship services that congregations north of the Mason-Dixon Line were not allowed to maintain. I never will forget my first visit to one of the churches out of the Christian tradition.

I was invited to preach at the Wesley Grove Christian Church in Newport News, Virginia, in the late 1970s. The only exposure I previously had to UCC churches outside of Trinity in our denomination were the churches in Chicago: Lincoln Memorial Congregational Church, Good Shepherd Congregational Church, the Congregational Church of Park Manor and South Shore Community Church. Those churches had worship styles that were similar to the Congregational Church of New England.

You can imagine my surprise, therefore, when I walked into Wesley Grove and saw the Mothers Board dressed in white with white doilies on their heads and tambourines in their hands! The worship that Sunday morning (and for the rest of the week) was cut from the same cloth as the black rural worship styles that I had seen in my daddy's home church, St. John Baptist Church in Caroline County, Virginia, and the worship I had grown up seeing in my grandfather's churches in Surrey County, Virginia, and in Temperanceville, Virginia.

The same hand-clapping, foot-stomping, floor-jumping exuberant worships that I experienced at my grandfather's churches (Gravel Hill Baptist and Jerusalem Baptist) and the St. John Baptist Church in Ladysmith (Caroline County), Virginia, was what I found at Wesley Grove Christian Church in Newport News, Virginia. That worship at Wesley Grove was typical of the worship engaged in every week in the 200 Black Christian churches out of the "Old Convention of the South."

The worship styles in the Christian church and African American congregations in the Christian church were very different from the worship styles of the Congregational Church of New England and the churches started *for* Africans by the Congregational church.

One important difference to note in addition to the worship style, those two styles of those two denominations, is the fact that assimilation and acculturation were the norms for the Congregationalists and for Africans who were a part of the Congregational Church of New England. Claiming an African heritage and an African identity was the "strong suit" for the Black churches in the old Convention of the South. In the 1830s those churches proudly called themselves "Afro-Christian!"

In stark contrast to the Afro-Christian tradition, however, the Congregational Church of New England is a different story altogether. The Congregational Church is the same denomination that founded Harvard University, the same denomination that most Americans know about because of Plymouth Rock and the Mayflower Compact, and the same denomination that also founded Yale University and Howard University! We will come to the founding of Howard University and the other 500 Black schools set up by the Congregational churches in just a moment.

The Congregational church's commitment to Africans, to the Anti-Slavery Movement, to the Abolitionist Movement, and to the plight of Africans in the United States is one of the outstanding aspects of Congregationalism and is an important part of our "Sankofa moment." Not all white members of the Congregational church were believers in equality for Africans, however.

Congregationalists as famous as Cotton Mather were against slavery, but were in no way persons who believed that Blacks were equal to whites. This is one sad aspect of our "Sankofa moment."

Cotton Mather's catechism for Africans is an excellent example of the racism that was commonly found among New England Congregationalists. The fact that many of the rich white New England businessmen who were slaveholders and who were involved in the Transatlantic Slave Trade were also members of the Congregational church is yet another sad aspect of our "Sankofa moment."

Though social equality and racial equality may not have been the primary agenda of white congregations in the denomination, the ending of slavery and the evils of slavery were two of the important aspects of the Congregational church that helped shape their involvement with Africans as far back as the 1600s.

At the annual meetings of individual congregations, Associations and what today can be called "Conferences," the Congregational Church of New England, resolution after resolution was passed condemning slavery and the evils of the Transatlantic Slave Trade. While the African Americans in the Christian denomination were calling themselves "Afro-Christian" in the 1830s, the European American Christians in the Congregational church were actively engaged in the Underground Railroad!

Harriet Tubman is known as the "Black Moses of our race" in that she made over nineteen trips back into the South to free enslaved Africans. Not as well known as Harriett, but persons who were responsible for freeing thousands of Africans, were the members and ministers of the Congregational Church of New England. Several of their churches became stations of the Underground Railroad. Several ministers and leading members of the Congregational church acted as Conductors on the Underground Railroad.

Unlike Harriet Tubman who risked her life as a Conductor, the white members of the Congregational church could pose as slave-drivers and/or merchants carrying their cargo from one point to the next. The ways in which members of the Congregational church engaged in this subterfuge is absolutely fascinating. On some trips the Conductors would have forged manifests pretending to be transporting their "cargo" from one slave owner to the next.

In other instances the Congregational church that was a station on the Underground Railroad would go to great lengths to hide the Africans running away from slavery. Those congregations went to great lengths to feed the runaways, to provide them with a change of clothes and to throw the slave patrols completely off of the track.

Some of the churches that were used as stations in the Underground Railroad had false floors. The members of the church who were aiding the Africans to escape to freedom would pull back the floorboards, let the Africans go beneath the floor of the Sanctuary where they could rest, eat and hide from the slave patrols that were looking desperately to recapture the fugitive slaves.

The white members of the church would then put a carpet over the trapdoor and little old ladies quilting comforters would put their rocking chairs on top of the carpet (over the trapdoor) and assume their positions there whenever a slave patrol would come by the church.

Remembering that there was no television or radio in the 1830s and 1840s, one can see how important a change of clothes was for the Africans in the escape process. All the patrols had to go on in looking for the fleeing Africans was what the flyers said the runaway slaves were wearing at the time of their escape. At each stop on the Underground Railroad they would be provided with a change of clothes, however, which would make the description on the flyers null and void.

In the midst of being actively involved in the Underground Railroad and working as an integral part of the Underground Railroad, in 1841 the Congregational church took its involvement in the lives of Africans a notch higher!

In 1841, Africans aboard the slave ship *Amistad* revolted, took over the ship and tried to sail back home to the West Coast of Africa. They knew that Africa was where the sun came up. Their spiritual ("Let Us Break Bread Together On Our Knees") from the period of African enslavement says, "When I fall on my knees with my face to the *rising sun*." Since Africans knew that "home" was where the sun came up they held a sword to the helmsman's throat and commanded him to sail toward the sun. Sailing toward the "rising sun" meant that they were on their way home.

The helmsmen of the *Amistad*, however, would only sail east during the day. At night they would slowly turn the ship around and head back toward the United States Coast. That zigzag motion caused the *Amistad* which had set sail in Cuba to end up off of the coast of Connecticut!

Spotted by the United States Coast Guard, the ship was boarded by the United States Coast Guard outside of the three-mile limit and the slaves were put in chains while the surviving slave traders were treated as freed persons who had been illegally imprisoned by Africans. The slave traders were set free by the United States Coast Guard.

The celebrated *Amistad* case went all the way to the Supreme Court and the Congregational church paid for the defense of the Mende people (the Africans who had revolted aboard the *Amistad)*. When the story of the *Amistad* is told, the crucial role of the Congregational church is left out in most instances. It certainly was left out of the movie **The Amistad**.

Members of the Congregational Church of New England felt that slavery was wrong. They felt that slavery should be abolished. They worked desperately to end slavery and to set Africans who were enslaved free. They did not think, however, that Africans were equal to them. They just thought that slavery was wrong!

After the Civil War, the Congregational church stepped it up yet another notch! A massive refugee problem had been caused with the release of four million Africans who could not read or write. They were left stranded in the South as easy prey to their former slaveholders and to the racist whites in the South who did not think that they should have been freed at all in the first place.

They had no skills because it had been against the laws in the British colonies to teach Africans how to read and write, so it seemed as if they were headed for a "second slavery" either in the Convict Lease System or in sharecropping. To address this "refugee problem," the Congregational church sent missionaries into the South by the thousands and set up over 500 schools for the freed Africans.

The schools were both a "blessing and a curse." They were a blessing in that their establishment produced hundreds of thousands of black school teachers, trained clergy, physicians, surgeons, attorneys, judges, master's degree recipients and PhD's!

My own maternal grandparents were blessed by one of the schools set up by white missionaries from the North after the Civil War was over. They were graduates of Virginia Union University¯a school set up by Baptist missionaries.

Blacks who had no future and no possibility of hope found themselves academically equipped to enter into occupations they had never dreamed of prior to the missionary effort on the part of the New Englanders. Some of the schools were set up by the Presbyterian Church (Johnson C. Smith University in North Carolina), and some were set up by the Anglican (Episcopal) Church (St. Paul College in Virginia).

Some were set up by the Baptists (like Virginia Union and Morehouse) and over 500 were set up by the Congregational Church of New England. The schools were a blessing in that they provided a "closed campus" environment where students could learn unimpeded by the hatred of whites who were against Black education. The missionaries lived on the campus. The campuses were "self-contained."

Most of the campuses were either built on the water or next to a body of water, so that food could be grown, animals could be cared for, irrigation could take place and adequate water for bathing, for washing clothes and for preparing meals would be in abundant supply for the students, the missionary teachers and all those who ran the schools and lived on the campuses of the schools.

The missionaries lived on the campus and the students also lived on the campus from the beginning of the academic year until graduation the following spring. The dormitories and the faculty housing were home for the teachers and the students. The missionaries also had a chapel on the campus where the students could worship daily and the people from the surrounding communities could worship on Sundays.

A typical day in the school set up by the American Missionary Association of the Congregational Church of New England included morning devotions, academic subjects such as English, Math and History, and a lunch break. An afternoon session would consist of Home Economics, "practical subjects," plus Literature, World History, Geography and a foreign language; and then the day would close with evening vespers.

As those boarding schools, those "normal schools," those agricultural and mechanical schools, continued to turn out graduates, there were thousands of Africans who joined the Congregational Church of New England that had given them a quality education. J.T. Stanley's son, A. Knighton Stanley, writes about the American Missionary Association (AMA) schools set up by the Congregational church in his book, **The Children Is Crying.**

Rev. Susan Mitchell (a minister produced by Trinity UCC) and Joyce Hollyday, within the past decade, have done an awesome job of capturing the stories of children whose parents attended those schools right after slavery. Their work, **On the Heels of Freedom,** gives the reader an inside glimpse of what it was like to attend those schools set up by the missionaries. It is an excellent companion book to Dr. Stanley's **The Children Is Crying**. The genius that those mission schools uncovered, cultivated and developed was "the blessing" of those mission schools.

"The curse" of the mission schools, however, was that Africans were taught how to be New Englanders. Africans were taught how to assimilate and to acculturate to white New England

Congregational culture. Africans were taught that the way Congregationalists worshipped was the *only* proper way to worship.

Africans were taught that the way Africans worshipped, the way Africans had been worshipping, the way those black students' parents, grandparents and family members had been worshipping, was ignorant, heathen, bordering on paganism, too emotional and unworthy of a student at or a graduate of one of the mission schools set up by white missionaries from the North. In other words, Africans were taught that European culture and Christianity were synonymous! That was the curse. The mission schools were both a blessing *and* a curse!

The African students were taught that the only proper singing worthy of a worship service at one of the mission schools was the singing of European anthems, European hymns and concertized, anthemically-arranged "Negro spirituals." There could be no more African singing.

There could be no more "fist and heel" rhythm-keeping. There could be no more washboard, tambourines, banjos and drums. There could be no more bodily displays of emotion and there could be no more Africanisms in the Worship Service.

Dr. Stanley's book raises an important question in terms of the "blessing and the curse." He asks rhetorically why is it that over 500 of those schools were set up by the missionaries after slavery and yet there are less than ten that exist in the 21st century? The obvious answer, he suggests, is that Europeans denigrated African culture and African worship. They tried to make Africans into Europeans (or white New Englanders) and they failed.

They tried to stamp out the African culture and the African ways of being in the world, the African ways of honoring God and worshipping God, and as a result their schools have died because Africans remained African or returned to their African roots once they graduated from schools that had taught them how to be white and taught them how to look down on their African ways.

Of those 500 schools that were set up by the American Missionary Association of the Congregational Church of New England, there are eight still in existence today: Fisk University, Dillard University, Tougaloo College, Talladega College, Huston-Tillotson College, LeMoyne-Owen College, Howard University and Clark-Atlanta University. The School of Divinity at Howard University was started in the Sanctuary of the First Congregational Church of Washington, D.C. Hundreds of thousands of graduates of those Historically Black Colleges and Universities (the AMA schools started by our predecessor denomination) became members of the Congregational church because that was the church that had given them their "start" in life!

The racial problem caused by the miseducation of the Blacks who attended those AMA schools, however, was as follows: *Where was an African supposed to worship upon graduation from one of the AMA schools?* He or she had been taught that Black worship was ignorant and that New England worship was the only proper way to worship, but there were no "New England" churches in the South that were going to welcome Africans in the 1860s, the 1870s, the 1890s or even the early 20th century. The problem of where do Africans worship became a real problem for the graduates of the AMA schools, especially now that they had been trained "away" from their people, their culture and Black worship.

If the graduate of a mission school stayed near the campuses of Howard University, Atlanta University, LeMoyne-Owen College, etc., he or she simply could go back up on the campus on Sunday and attend Worship Services at the school. The chapel of LeMoyne-Owen College, for instance, is the Sanctuary of the Second Congregational Church of Memphis, Tennessee.

Howard University still has its "Friends of the Chapel" and those persons are members of the Howard University Chapel who worship on Howard's campus fifty-two Sundays a year.

If, however, the graduate moved away from the city in which the campus was situated, there was a problem. If you finished Fisk University, for instance, and moved up to Chicago there was no way you could attend or join the First Congregational Church of Chicago as an African in the 1800s or the early 1900s! Racism was still real in this country—I do not care how much "Jesus" you had or how saved you thought you were! You could not worship in a white church as a Black Christian!

The Congregational church was thereby forced to start churches for the graduates of their AMA colleges, universities and normal schools. They started those churches in cities where large numbers of graduates were congregating. That is how we got our first church in the state of Illinois.

The Congregational denomination started the Emmanuel Congregational Church in the city of Chicago in the 1880s. It was specifically started for graduates of the schools that Congregational missionaries had set up and run. Please note that the Emmanuel Congregational Church was not set up for "whosoever will." It was set up for graduates of the AMA schools only!

The race riots at the turn of the century in the city of Chicago resulted in two striking realities that need further study! Rioting whites burned down Emmanuel Congregational Church. They did not touch the historically Black churches like Quinn Chapel African Methodist Episcopal Church or Olivet Baptist Church, however. Those churches were churches for Blacks who "knew their place."

Emmanuel, however, was seen as the church for the "uppity Negroes," and rioting whites on the rampage were not about to let that church building stand. Those Negroes had to be put back in their place; and so the church was burned to the ground.

In 1909, the Congregational church in the state of Illinois tried again. They started another church for the graduates of the AMA schools. They started the Lincoln Memorial Congregational Church in memory of Abraham Lincoln who had started this whole problem by freeing the Negroes, but not taking into account that once they got educated they could no longer worship with their own people.

In Chicago, Lincoln Church sits today at 65th and Champlain. It did not sit there in 1909. Blacks were not allowed east of State Street in 1909.

In the 1920s we got the second Black Congregational church in the state of Illinois. Members of Lincoln split out of Lincoln because of the "color problem." One of our charter members at Trinity, Mrs. Cora Bowman, used to belong to Lincoln Congregational Church. She told me that there were too many dark people joining Lincoln in the 1920s, so the light-skinned Negroes pulled away and started the Congregational Church of Good Shepherd.

Good Shepherd Church sits today at 57th and Prairie. It did not sit at 57th and Prairie in Chicago in the 1920s. Blacks were still not allowed east of State Street in the 1920s!

If you read (or remember) Richard Wright's **Native Son**, you will remember how Bigger Thomas was afraid of being caught east of State Street after sunset. Prior to the 1950s Chicago was as segregated as Johannesburg, South Africa. Just as Blacks could not be caught inside the city of Johannesburg after dark, unless they were live-in servants, the same held true for Blacks on the Southside of Chicago and the rigidly enforced racial boundaries that separated Blacks and whites in the first half of the 20th Century.

In Johannesburg, those Blacks who worked in Johannesburg lived in the southwest township (Soweto). In Chicago, those Blacks who worked in the white neighborhoods lived in strictly defined Black communities inside the "Black Belt." Just as long as they were not caught on the other side of State Street after dark they were in good shape or relatively safe.

In 1931, the Congregational church merged with the Christian church and became the Congregational-Christian denomination. In 1934, the Evangelical church merged with the Reformed church and became the Evangelical and Reformed denomination.

In the early 1950s, Blacks began moving east of State Street. They moved into what was then the posh neighborhood of Chicago called Park Manor. The Congregational-Christian denomination decided a church was needed in the upper middle-class Negro section of the city for persons who could afford to live in those two-story brownstones and those mansions along South Parkway. It is for that reason that the Congregational Church of Park Manor was started by the denomination.

Please note, once again, that Park Manor was not started on any principle remotely resembling anything that Jesus said. It was only started for a "certain kind" of Negro.

The housing projects of Robert Taylor Homes, Ida B. Wells, Washington Gardens and Princeton Park were all in place in the 1950s. The Congregational-Christian church in the state of Illinois, however, did not try to start any churches for "the masses." The congregation it did try to start was for the "classes!"

It is also interesting from a church history perspective that no other Black churches were started by the Congregational-Christian church in the state of Illinois anywhere else in the state of Illinois! It was as if Blacks did not live in Rockford, Rock Island, Peoria, Champagne, East St. Louis or any other city in the state of Illinois.

The thinking behind this strange behavior was that the graduates of the AMA schools, the Negroes who had college degrees, the Negroes who were intelligent, the Negroes who knew how to worship properly and the Negroes who did not have "niggerisms" in the worship style, would be found in a city like Chicago and not in the rural areas or smaller town areas. One of our Congregational pastors, unfortunately, said publicly from his pulpit that he would *not tolerate any niggerisms in his worship services!*

In the early 1950s the Congregational Church of Park Manor was started and it was established at 70th and South Park Avenue. South Park Avenue is today called Dr. Martin Luther King, Jr. Drive. It sits right across the street from Kelly United Methodist Church.

The United Methodist church as a denomination was also trying to start a church in the "middle-class Negro" section of the city for a certain class of people also. The Disciples of Christ also started the Park Manor Christian Church in the same era and in the same neighborhood, 73rd and St. Lawrence.

In 1954, the landmark *Brown v. Board of Education* decision was rendered and "integration" became the goal and the model for public education in the North and for the formation of Christian congregations in the North. Many Blacks and many whites thought that there would be an "integrated church" in the North following that 1954 Supreme Court decision. They were wrong.

In 1955, one year after the Supreme Court decision, the Montgomery Bus Boycott began and the "Civil Rights Movement" of the 20th century was underway! In 1957, the Congregational-Christian church and the Evangelical and Reformed church merged and became the United Church of Christ!

In the late 1950s, Blacks started moving into the far South corridor of the Southside of Chicago and the Chicago Metropolitan Association of the Illinois Conference of the United Church of Christ decided that it was time to start a church for the homeowners who were moving into that far Southside corridor.

There were two schools of thought during that era. One was that a congregation for the middle-class, home-owning Blacks would meet a need for those intelligent, college-trained and professional Negroes who could afford to live on the far Southside of Chicago.

The other school of thought was that the church should be built near Halsted Street because Halsted Street was the dividing line between the Black community and the white community; and with integration now being the goal, whites would flock to join this new "integrated" United Church of Christ where Negroes knew how to worship God properly! They were wrong too!

The Illinois Conference of the United Church of Christ talked to the Assistant Pastor of the Congregational Church of Park Manor, the Reverend Dr. Kenneth B. Smith, and asked him if he would be interested in being the Pastor of a new church start on the far Southside of Chicago.

(Almost a half century later, the Illinois Conference of the United Church of Christ used practically the same methodology in selecting the Reverend Dr. Ozzie Earl Smith to head a new church start in the far south suburbs of Chicago, the Covenant United Church of Christ.)

When Dr. Kenneth Smith said yes, a parsonage was purchased at 9704 South Emerald Avenue and meetings began to be held in the homes of persons who had once been members of Lincoln Memorial Congregational Church, Old South Congregational Church, the Church of the Good Shepherd and the Congregational Church of Park Manor who now lived in the 95th Street community.

The attraction for many of the founding members of Trinity United Church of Christ was that they would no longer have to drive back up on the Southside into those neighborhoods that were now changing and becoming "the ghetto."

After a series of house meetings and meetings at the new parsonage, the first Worship Service of Trinity United Church of Christ was held at the Kipling School on the first Sunday in December in 1961. From the second Sunday in December of 1961 until the new church had its first building in 1966, the congregation of Trinity United Church of Christ worshipped in the Shedd School at 98th and Forest.

Worship services were held in the school each week. All of the meetings of boards, councils, officers and church members were held either at the church parsonage at 9704 South Emerald or in the homes of the founding members and the charter members. The church was chartered in June of 1962.

Please remember that the church was started by a white denomination for Negroes who knew how to worship properly. Please remember that many of the founding members thought that whites who lived across Halsted would be joining the church and making it an "integrated church." Especially did they think that would be the case after the first sanctuary was put up on property purchased by the denomination at 95th and Parnell Avenue.

The worship services of Trinity United Church of Christ were not designed for "all kinds of people." The services were designed to be like the services in white churches. Their attempt was to attract educated, middle-class, middle-income and upwardly mobile Negroes and whites who were "our kind of people." That part of our "Sankofa moment" is an important part of our story.

The new Black congregation in the Illinois Conference of the United Church of Christ was the first Black church started by the denomination after we had become the United Church of Christ (UCC). Trinity UCC was never a part of the Congregational church because the Congregational church had merged with the Congregational-Christian church in 1931 and then merged with the Evangelical and Reformed church in 1957 to form the United Church of Christ. Our church's charter reads: "Trinity United Church of Christ."

To keep from attracting the "wrong kind of people," however, when our first sanctuary was put up in 1966, the leaders of the church did not want to put the words "United Church of Christ" on the church bulletin board. Those words would have attracted the wrong element.

In 1966, when the first sanctuary was built, the words that were outside on the bulletin board read: "Trinity United Church of Christ (Congregational)." That wording was purposely chosen to make sure that passersby, visitors and potential members knew that we were not an ordinary Black church. We worshipped in the congregational style of New Englanders. We did not have Black worship and we were not the Church of Christ or the Church of God in Christ (Pentecostal)!

Trinity United Church of Christ grew by leaps and bounds from that first Sunday in December 1961 until 1966. No whites joined the congregation, however. What the church planners thought would happen did not happen. Our membership went up to over 400 adults. Our small Sanctuary only sat 200 people (with chairs down), but most members do not come to church every Sunday, so we could comfortably seat 200 every Sunday in what was becoming an attractive "alternative" to typical Black worship.

Our Pastor was college-educated (Virginia Union University) and seminary-trained! His sermons made sense. His sermons spoke to the realities of the day. Our Founding Pastor marched with Dr. King. He was active in the Civil Rights Movement. Our church was socially-focused on the plights of Blacks in the South, on ending segregation, ending discrimination and bringing about "integration."

Our music, however, made an even louder statement to any potential would-be members. Our music stated that we were not the kind of church that they could find at Fellowship Baptist Church or at St. Paul Church of God in Christ! No whites joined the church, but we kept up the hope of integration as we sang along with Dr. King, "Black and white together someday!"

In 1966, Dr. Smith left Trinity United Church of Christ to take a position with the Community Renewal Society. (He subsequently went on to become the Pastor of the Congregational Church of the Good Shepherd and then the President of Chicago Theological Seminary!)

Our second Pastor, Reverend Willie Jamerson, started in 1967. He kept up the strong social focus of our ministry and kept our church on the "cutting edge" of social issues as we attempted to be an alternative church that was concerned about the plight of African Americans in the 1960s after Malcolm X was killed and Blacks were becoming more and more "radicalized."

In 1968, however, things changed. In 1968, Dr. King was murdered and in the words of Lu Palmer, *"Negroes turned Black!"*

In 1968, Black Gospel music was sung on Black college campuses for the first time since the founding of those colleges in 1865! Negroes not only turned Black in Chicago; they turned Black all over this nation!

From 1865 until 1968, no authentically Black music was allowed on most of the Historically Black Colleges and Universities (HBCU's) in the country. Remember! Those colleges were started by white missionaries from New England. New England had taught the Africans that they had no culture; they had no music; they had no "sacred music"; and they had no ways of worshipping that were worthy of intelligent and educated people.

I sang as a soloist in the choir at Virginia Union University. We were not allowed to sing Gospel music in the 1950s or the early 1960s. We were only allowed to sing European anthems, hymns and arranged "Negro spirituals." We were not allowed to sing common meter, short meter, long meter, hymns or "Dorsey music." "Dorsey music" was the term given to Gospel music because of its founder, Thomas Dorsey.

The same was the case at all of the historically Black colleges and universities—especially those founded by the Congregational Church of New England. There was no Black Gospel music sung or taught at Howard University, at Fisk University, at Dillard University or any of the Black United Church of Christ schools.

There was no Black Gospel music sung in any of the Black UCC churches in the North that were on the Congregational side of the "merger." Remember to hold that point in contrast with the worship services described already in the Christian churches in North Carolina and Virginia!

In 1968, Black Gospel choirs were started at Howard University and dozens of the 117 Black colleges and universities across this country. The Howard University Gospel Choir was started in 1968 by Richard Smallwood! I was there! I was at the founding of that choir and was subsequently elected to be the National Chaplain of the Howard University Gospel Choir.

As Black Gospel music hit the Black college campuses, Black Gospel music also hit the mainline churches in America. Black

Gospel music started to be sung in Roman Catholic parishes, in Anglican parishes, in Presbyterian churches, in United Methodist churches and in the mainline, old line white denominational churches where Black people worshipped!

Because the music department of Trinity Church would not budge on that issue, however, the membership started dwindling. There were actually two factors that caused the membership to start dropping from the 400 numbers that we were enjoying in the mid '60s. The first, obviously, was the change in pastoral leadership.

Reverend Willie Jamerson walked into the same kind of problem that Ralph David Abernathy walked into, that Lyndon Baines Johnson walked into and that Otis Moss III walked into.

After Dr. Martin Luther King, Jr. had held the leadership position in the Southern Christian Leadership Conference, had made his famous "I Have a Dream" speech and had received the Nobel Peace Prize, when he was assassinated the public could not fathom the Reverend Dr. Ralph David Abernathy as being their new "leader." He had more pastoral experience than Dr. King had and he had his earned PhD long before Dr. King did, but he was not Dr. King. It was that simple (and that complicated).

Black America did not look to Ralph David Abernathy as its leader (as it had looked at Martin Luther King). Black America did not even look to Dr. Abernathy as King's successor. Even Reverend Jesse Jackson, who was working for the Southern Christian Leadership Conference, did not see Ralph as his boss or his supervisor. It was that simple and it was that complicated.

What was true on the issue of leadership at the Civil Rights level saw a similar scenario played out on the political level. Lyndon

Baines Johnson was a seasoned politician. John F. Kennedy was a freshman senator from Massachusetts. The similarities between President Barack Obama and President John F. Kennedy are striking!

President Kennedy chose Lyndon Baines Johnson as his running mate because Johnson was perhaps the most powerful Democrat in the United States Senate. He had longevity. He had relationships "across the aisles." He knew all of the senators and most of the congressmen by their first names. He knew their families.

With my having served as a cardiopulmonary technician who worked up close on President Johnson, I can tell you this. He also knew their business! (Their private business!)

With that kind of clout, President Johnson could get legislation passed that President Kennedy would never get passed. President Johnson, however, did not have the "charisma" nor did he have the mystique of the "Camelot era" that John Kennedy had.

When John Kennedy was assassinated in Dallas, the politicians may have had to accept Johnson as their new leader. The American public never did, however! It was that simple and it was that complicated.

What took place in the areas of Civil Rights leadership and political leadership also takes place in the area of congregational leadership. After thirty-six years of serving as a Pastor and after bringing in my successor two years before I retired, I saw the same thing happen at our church! Those who had known only my pastorate, my pastoral leadership style and those who had known only me as their Pastor had a difficult time accepting Reverend Moss as their new Pastor. Many of them walked away.

Many of them joined other churches. Many of them stopped going to church. Many of them stopped giving.

It was not so much that they did not like Pastor Moss. The fact was a simple fact. Pastor Moss was not Jeremiah Wright. It was that simple and it was that complicated. Reverend Willie Jamerson ran into the same ecclesiastical buzz saw! He was not Ken Smith.

Ken Smith had been our Pastor when we had no building. Ken left, as a matter of fact, shortly after we got our first building. Many of our church meetings used to be held at Ken Smith's parsonage at 9704 South Emerald. The members knew Ken. The members knew Ken's wife. The members knew Ken's children. Now Ken was gone and they did not want to hear anything that Willie Jamerson had to say.

Was he saying it incorrectly? Was he saying it ineffectively? No. The problem was that he was not Ken Smith! It was that simple and it was that complicated.

Add to that a change in the mood of the country, a change in the understanding of Black Sacred Music and the desire to embrace African culture, African songs, African hairstyles, African names while holding on to the faith delivered by Ma'Dea and others—all of which were met with fierce resistance by the leadership of Trinity United Church of Christ—and you can begin to understand why the membership dropped from 400 members down to eighty-seven adult members by the fall of 1971.

Reverend Jamerson, however, was a faithful Pastor. Though confronted with two absolutely insane sets of obstacles to clear, Pastor Jamerson did an excellent work as our second Pastor. He continued to lead the congregation of Trinity United Church of

Christ and a ministry that focused on both Arms of the Cross -
- both aspects of the Gospel of Jesus Christ!

The vertical Arm of the Cross was (and is) a symbolic artifact
which points to our relationship with God. The congregation
since its inception had stressed the strengthening and deepening
of the relationship between the members of the congregation
and God.

There are two Arms to the Cross, however. The horizontal Arm
of the Cross was (and is) a symbolic representation of how we
are to reach out into the culture and into the society in which
the church of Jesus Christ is planted to make a positive difference
in the world in which the members lived. That had been one of
our "strong suits" from the day that we were founded as a United
Church of Christ congregation, given our denomination's deep
roots in the Social Justice Gospel.

Pastor Jamerson kept the congregation active in the fight for
equality that erupted in 1968 and spilled over into what has been
called "The Black Revolution" in the years following Dr. King's
assassination and Malcolm X's murder.

Reverend Jamerson led the congregation in its fight against
discrimination as the Chicago Public Schools was busily
constructing "The Willis Wagons." The "Willis Wagons" was
the name that was given to the demountable buildings that were
erected in the playgrounds of overcrowded Black schools.

Those demountables were erected to keep the Black students
from "crossing the boundaries" and going over into white
neighborhoods to integrate those schools. That egregious
practice was instituted under the direction of Dr. Willis while he
was the Superintendent of the Chicago Public School System.

Back in the mid '60s and late '60s and even into the 1970s, there were certain schools in the city of Chicago that were considered "white schools." They were in "white school districts" and the white citizens of the city were doing everything humanly possible to keep Black students from being admitted into those schools or crossing over into those districts. That was fifteen to twenty years after the 1954 *Brown v. Board of Education* decision.

Racism, however, had a much longer history in this country and in this city than 1954. Do not forget! This is the city of the famous race riots where the church for "uppity Negroes" was burned down! Pastor Jamerson led the congregation in the fight against that kind of racism.

During this same period of history, 1967 through 1971, when Pastor Jamerson served our congregation, not only was Black Gospel Music hitting the Black college campuses and churches of every denominational stripe. It was also in 1968, that Black students all across the nation started asking for Black Studies Programs. They demanded Africana Studies courses and they argued for massive curricula changes on Black and white campuses across this country. It was also in 1968 that James Brown's famous song, "Say It Loud! I'm Black and I'm Proud!", hit the airwaves.

It was also in 1968, that John Carlos and Tommie Smith raised their fists in the Black Power Salute after having won the Bronze and Gold Medals at the 1968 Olympics!

In 1968, the Black churches of every denomination started claiming their African heritage all across this country. That "Black Revolution" did not skip past Trinity United Church of Christ.

Many members who felt that Trinity was too European in its worship and in its notions of "class" began to leave the church and that added yet another reason why those 400 members dwindled down to eighty-seven adult members!

For the first ten years of its existence, Trinity United Church of Christ had bought into the UCC's notion of "integration" which really meant assimilation and/or acculturation. For most whites in the 1960s, and for far too many Blacks, "integration" meant that African Americans had to become European Americans in worship style, in preaching style, in liturgical style and in mission focus!

The mission focus, incidentally, was a "missionary" focus which meant doing something in mission "for *those* people." This was the same mentality that governed the operation and the curricula of those 500 mission schools set up by the New England Missionaries from the American Missionary Association of the Congregational Church of New England! After 1968, however, that mentality began to change! (It changed at Trinity Church from a mission *for* to a ministry *with*; and it changed from *those* people to *our* members!)

It was in 1971 when the membership had dwindled down to 87 adults that Pastor Jamerson left us and it was in 1971 that the congregation then had to ask itself a difficult question. In putting together their "profile" for the denomination and for their next Pastor, they asked the hard question: *"Are we going to be a Black church in the Black community? Or, are we going to continue being a white church in Black face; because that is all we are!"*

As the congregation grappled with its painful identity question, a part of the problem they had to address was the mindset of its own members! Some of the members of Trinity United Church of Christ actually saw themselves as being of a higher social class than the people who lived in the projects right down the street (Princeton Park and the Governor Lowden Homes). That is the bad news. The good news is this: What was going on across the world in the Field of Missiology was also taking place in microcosmic form at Trinity United Church of Christ!

In the Field of Missiology, Mission Boards of many denominations (in the 1960s) were coming to grips with the fact that they had carried their culture into other countries with the presumed and assumed superiority of European and Euro-American culture. Unfortunately, in their minds, their culture was synonymous with Christianity as was just stated!

In other words, in order for persons to become Christians, the Africans, the Hawaiians, the Chinese, the Indians and all "others" (meaning non-white) had to become European in worship style and in mindset! There was the assumed superiority of European culture which was hurting missions and hurting the church of Jesus Christ more than it was helping it! There was also the assumption that European culture and Christianity were synonymous.

As that shift in the Field of Missiology began to take place and persons engaged in other countries began to realize that those persons and those countries had just as rich a culture, just as rich a history, just as powerful a heritage and just as profound a theology as the Europeans, the approach to missions shifted from "a mission *for* or a mission *to*" to an approach which stressed "ministry *with*!" The same thing happened at Trinity United Church of Christ in 1971, as the congregation grappled with its identity.

That is what Vallmer Jordan shared with me on New Year's Eve 1971, and that is what the statement that he put together articulating the hopes, the dreams and the vision of the congregation encapsulated.

The members of Trinity United Church of Christ began to realize that they had no "mission *to*" the people in the projects and the people who did not make as much money as they did. What the congregation of Trinity needed was a ministry *with* all of God's people across cultural, educational and socioeconomic lines!

It was during Dr. Sheares' serving as Interim Pastor that he coined the term, "**Unashamedly Black and Unapologetically Christian.**" That motto captured the new mood of the conscious members who were changing from Negroes to being Black!

At the end of 1971, Trinity United Church of Christ was not related to the community in which it sat at all, outside of its Sunday Morning Worship Services which were not inviting and its yoga class which was open to the public. There were no programs in ministry that related to the community. There was no Bible study to which the general public was invited. There was still the attitude that only a "certain kind of person" was welcomed at Trinity United Church of Christ.

Unfortunately, the congregation still had the illusion (in 1971) that white persons were going to join a church that had decided to be relevant to the Black community, that white persons were going to join a church that sat in the heart of the Black community, and that white persons in large numbers would come and embrace this new focus of self-affirmation, self-identity and equality of races. That illusion still prevails in many churches in the 21st century!

I will share with you when I get to that part of the *Sankofa* narrative chronology what the attitude was concerning the residents of Princeton Park, the Governor Lowden Homes and "ordinary Black people" in the year 1972. I will also share with you what the feeling was concerning having any kind of ministry that related to the projects or that was attractive to "those nickel and dime Negroes!" (Only the church officer who said that to me did not use the word "Negroes." They said the actual N-word!)

The leadership of the church decided that they were going to be a Black church in the Black community. The Search Committee asked Vallmer Jordan to put in words what their thoughts and feelings were about changing the way they had been from 1961 until 1971.

They asked Val to articulate the direction in which they wanted to go as a Black church in the Black community, related to the Black community, doing ministry in the Black community and welcoming all members of the Black community. Mr. Jordan put that statement together and that statement was shown to every candidate who applied for the Pulpit of Trinity United Church of Christ.

In the fall of 1971, when I had left the employ of the Beth Eden Baptist Church of Morgan Park where I had served as an Assistant Pastor for two years, I received a call from Reverend Dr. Kenneth Smith. Ken wanted to know how many tickets our church needed for the Virginia Union University Concert Choir that was coming into the city for its Annual Choir Tour Concert.

I told Pastor Smith that I no longer was at Beth Eden. I gave him the name and phone number of Mr. Robert Eugene Wooten, Sr., their minister of music, to contact in order that he might be able to better answer that question and help Ken get the tickets sold for the forthcoming Fall concert. At the end of our conversation, Ken asked me, *"Well, since you aren't at Beth Eden anymore, where are you now?"*

I told him I was not at any church and then I playfully asked him if he had any churches open in his denomination. I had already been downtown to the Northern Illinois Conference of the United Methodist Church and I had been to the Conference office of the Disciples of Christ in the state of Illinois. I had filled out applications there and was waiting to hear from them. Ken said to me, *"As a matter of fact, Jerry, the church I served as Founding Pastor is vacant. They are looking for a new Pastor!"*

Ken told me to go downtown and fill out an application for ministry with the Chicago Metropolitan Association of the Illinois Conference of the United Church of Christ. Dr. Smith also gave me the names and numbers of persons who worked in the national church, so that I could contact them and put together my profile to receive a Call from a United Church of Christ congregation. He indicated to me that he would talk with the chairperson of the search committee or with someone on the search committee of Trinity Church, but that I should follow through on my end by doing the same thing with the United Church of Christ that I had done with the United Methodist Church and the Disciples of Christ denomination.

I went downtown and filled out the papers. I wrote New York and gave them my information. I got the forms I needed from them to follow through properly on the process and on December the 30th, I got a call from Vallmer Jordan asking me if he could stop by my house the next night! Val Jordan rang my doorbell at six o'clock in the evening on December 31, 1971, and the rest, as they say, is history!

Let me share a little of that "history," so that you can understand this "Sankofa moment" at an even deeper level. You can find all of the details to that "history" in my autobiography. I am still working on that! In the meantime, let me share these pertinent "Sankofa" facts with you.

Val Jordan was supposed to meet with me for an hour on the night of December 31, 1971. I had a Watch Meeting Service to attend and I planned to be there between eight and nine o'clock in the evening. I was going to St. Mark United Methodist Church to their Watch Meeting Service. God had other plans, however!

Val Jordan and I hit it off to such an extent that our one-hour conversation went well past four hours! He shared with me the vision of the Trinity congregation. He shared with me the painful history of the congregation. He shared with me how the congregation wanted to change the perception that community members had of them. They wanted to be known as a welcoming congregation. They wanted a worship service that was exciting and attracting to African Americans who were now "conscious" African Americans, unashamed of their history, unashamed of their legacy, unashamed of their culture and highly-skilled in every profession imaginable!

Val Jordan shared with me the struggle that many middle-income Blacks were having as they tried to wrestle with what it meant to be Black in the 1970s. They asked existential questions about their being Black Christians in the city where the Nation of Islam had its headquarters and where the Black Hebrew Israelite Nation was heavily populated.

He told me the members of the congregation wanted to do a ministry in the 95th Street community, the Roseland community and the surrounding communities that positively impacted the lives of the residents on the Southside of Chicago. They wanted a worship experience that attracted people of all socioeconomic levels and educational levels, and they wanted a ministry to those persons following the Benediction on Sundays.

They did not want to be just a church with a "throw down worship service" on Sundays like so many other popular Black churches in the city of Chicago. Being popular was not their goal. Being faithful was what they were concerned about. They wanted to be faithful to the Gospel of Jesus Christ. They wanted a ministry that followed in the footsteps of Dr. Martin Luther King, Jr.'s ministry. They wanted a church that confronted head-on the problems of the city of Chicago and the problems of Africans both on the Continent and in the Diaspora. As Val and I talked, I could tell that this was going to be a "marriage made in Heaven!"

He asked me about my journey. He wanted to know where my head was. I shared with him my disenchantment with Black churches that were hypocritical. I shared with him my having left the church during the period that I was in the military. I shared with him my wrestlings with the Uncle Toms in the church and the reluctance of Black clergy to follow the leadership of Dr. Martin Luther King, Jr. during the Civil Rights movement.

I shared with him my involvement in the Civil Rights Movement. I shared with him my experiences in the military. I shared with him my work with Dr. John Lovell in the area of Black Sacred Music and I shared with him my having been at Howard University when the Howard University Gospel Choir's formation became a turning point in the history of that Black university!

Val said that I would be hearing from him within a few days. He left my home and I rushed out of the door trying to get to St. Mark United Methodist Church before all of the seats were gone. By the time I got to church it was quarter to eleven on New Year's Eve!

I got a call from Mr. Jordan during the first week of the New Year. He asked me if I could preach that following Sunday. Mr. Jordan told me that their Interim Pastor, Reverend Reuben Sheares, would be preaching and serving Communion on the first Sunday of the new year and that they had another candidate for the Pulpit slated to preach on the third Sunday, but it would be very helpful if I could come and preach for them on the second Sunday in January.

I preached that Sunday and was invited back to preach one more time during the month of January!

I met with the search committee—the full search committee—between my first and second preaching engagements at Trinity and on the second Sunday in February, the congregation met to hear the recommendation of the search committee. The recommendation was unanimous that I be called as Pastor of Trinity United Church of Christ.

The congregation voted to call me as its third Pastor on the second Sunday in February and I started my work at Trinity on March 1, 1972. I was installed as Pastor on April 9, 1972 and then the fun began!

In order for the church to grow, in order for the church to be perceived differently (as per Vallmer Jordan's conversation and his Mission Statement), the first thing that had to change was the worship service! The worship services as stated above were

not "inviting." Black folk were not attracted to worship at Trinity
United Church of Christ in 1971. They had not been attracted
from 1961 to 1971 because the church's worship style was
Congregational—New England style!

The first changes in the Worship Services, however, were really
not that drastic or radical. The congregation had said it wanted
to change its way of worship, so as to attract members who lived
in the community in which the church sat. The worship service
they had been engaged in for ten years of their existence and for
six years at their present site was not attractive to the Blacks
who lived in the 95th Street community.

The first changes in the Sunday worship service were simply the
addition of an Altar Call, (a Pastoral prayer and a song). The
Altar Call was inserted into the worship service right before the
sermon. The only other change in the Sunday worship service
was the addition of a Hymn of Invitation. The Hymn of Invitation
was inserted into the Order of Worship right after the sermon.
Prior to my taking over the reins of the church as Pastor, Trinity
had no Hymn of Invitation!

Following the model used by many UCC congregations to address
the possibility of getting new members, Trinity simply had a notice
in its Weekly Sunday Bulletin which read: *"If you are interested
in joining this church, please fill out the card found on the back of
the pew in front of you and drop it in the Offering Plate. The
deacons will come and visit you."*

The songs that I chose for the Altar Call and for the Hymn of
Invitation, however, and many times the song that I chose for
the Morning Hymn were songs that were not found in **The
Pilgrim Hymnal**. **The Pilgrim Hymnal** was the hymnal of the

Congregational church. (Do not forget the "Pilgrims" of Massachusetts and the Mayflower Compact!)

The Pilgrim Hymnals that Trinity had, moreover, were old, left over, worn out and beat-up hymnals that had been donated to the young congregation by a white UCC church in 1966 when the members of Trinity moved into their first facility at 532 West 95th Street.

Prior to my coming to Trinity, the Church Council had commissioned a "hymnal committee" to select a new hymnal to replace the worn out *Pilgrim Hymnals*. The chairperson of the hymnal committee suggested to me that since I was selecting songs each week for the worship services that were not found in that *Pilgrim Hymnal*, and I was selecting songs that had to be printed up in the bulletin each week, that perhaps I needed to suggest a hymnal that contained the hymns that the congregation was now singing.

I went to a Christian bookstore and chose a nondenominational hymnal. The book I chose was *Hymns for Praise and Service*. I say, "*That is when the fun began*," because that is when the first congregational fight broke out! Instead of factual statements about the new nondenominational hymnal which I had suggested and the hymnal committee had approved, rumors got out that I had brought a "Baptist hymnal to our church."

The church, Good Shepherd Congregational, incidentally, was using the *National Baptist Hymnal* in its Sunday worship services in 1972; but that was not an issue for them. Only for the members of Trinity who definitely did not want to be considered "Baptist" or anything remotely resembling Pentecostal was that an issue! (Remember the 1966 decision to make sure that no outsiders would think we were Pentecostal.) That is why our Bulletin Board read "Congregational."

The rumor, therefore, that I had brought a "Baptist hymnal" into the church spread like wildfire among the members who had not been to church or to worship since the new hymnals had been purchased. A large crowd came out to hear me on my first Sunday as Pastor and the peripheral members of the congregation dropped by my Installation Service to hear the Wooten Choral Ensemble from Beth Eden Baptist Church.

Mr. Robert Eugene Wooten's Wooten Choral Ensemble sang for my Installation Service. Those "occasional members" (as Tim Wise calls them) were not every Sunday worshippers, however, and they did not see the new hymnals that came into the church in June. (Lest you think negatively of our members, however, please remember that most church members in America do not attend church every Sunday. The average attendance at all the churches in this country is fifty percent of the persons whose names appear on those churches' membership rolls. That is across denominational lines!)

A handful of founding members of the church were stirred up by the "rumor" and they decided to introduce a motion before the congregation at its third Sunday in July (1972) Quarterly Meeting that I be made to pay for the hymnals because they were "Baptist hymnals." That motion and that "movement" went nowhere!

The fight was quickly squelched. The rumor was killed and the first contingent of those members who were disgruntled by my leadership left. They felt that I was leading the church in the wrong direction.

The second "hiccup" on the radar screen of my pastorate and the second installment of what I call "the fun beginning" which resulted in another group of members leaving the church between March of 1972 and November of 1973 also had its roots in the issue of Black Sacred Music!

First, there was the matter of the hymnals and songs that were not normally sung in the Black religious tradition. Then there came the issue of the teenage choir, the Youth Fellowship Choir or what evolved into the Trinity Choral Ensemble!

Worshippers who have entered Trinity United Church of Christ on a Sunday morning over the past twenty-five years are accustomed to hearing a well-honed music department with five choirs. Our Sanctuary Choir, our Women's Chorus, our Men's Chorus, our teenage choir and our youth choir are all taught by excellent musicians in all of the *genres* of music. They are taught to sing anthems, hymns, spirituals, traditional Gospel music, contemporary Gospel music, Gospel Hip-Hop, common meter, short meter and long meter hymns, Caribbean music, West African music and South African music!

Because that is what members have heard in the sanctuary of Trinity United Church of Christ for over twenty-five years, they think that is the way it has always been. This Sankofa moment will help them to understand the way over which we have come. It has not always been that way!

As I have already stated, the music that made up our worship services from 1961 to 1971 was not "inviting." It was European. It was flat-out "classical" (meaning European) sacred music and it was not a part of the Black Religious Experience. Make no mistake! It was a part of the Black Religious Experience that had been given to us by white missionaries.

It was the same part of the Black Religious Experience that Dr. A. Knighten Stanley writes about when he talks about those churches that were started by the missionaries after the Civil War no longer being in existence because they did not take into account African culture, African music and African worship styles.

What follows is the story of how our "Youth Fellowship Choir" came into being. On the Sunday that I became the Pastor of Trinity United Church of Christ, both of my youth sponsors quit on me. It was a Philippians 4 issue (Euodia and Synteche). They were angry with each other for some reason. To this day I do not know what that reason was. Nor, do I know what happened to make them fall out with each other. All I know is that they both quit. That meant that I became the new youth sponsor in addition to being the new Pastor.

I remained the sponsor of the youth until I was able to identify a young couple in the fall of 1972. That young couple was Dr. Julia Speller (who was not a seminary professor at the time) and her husband, Clyde. Clyde went on to become a deacon at our church and Julia went on to become a tenured professor at Chicago Theological Seminary!

Since I was the new youth sponsor, however, I had the teenagers over to my home on July 4, 1972 for a cookout. It was during the cookout that the president of my youth ministry, Mr. Vallmer Wayman Jordan (the son of Vallmer Edward Jordan) said to me, *"Rev., we want a choir for the young people! The kiddies have their elementary school choir, but we want a teenager choir!"*

I told Val to get with the music director of the church, to rehearse the teenagers who wanted to sing in the teenage choir for a few times and to let me know when he thought they were ready to sing on a Sunday. That was on the July 4th weekend. I did not hear anything from the teenagers until the middle of September. That did not concern me, however. It was summertime! They were teenagers!

Besides their having an entirely different agenda which did not make church a high priority on their teenage list of things to do during the summertime when they were out of school, I was the "new kid on the block" in terms of being the Pastor. I had to get on my horse and take off in many different directions at once. I was trying to reorganize the Stewardship Council.

I was trying to understand the process whereby deacons were selected because many of my deacons had never had a Bible class in their lives! I was trying to understand the Church Council which was comprised of twelve deacons, twelve trustees and three members-at-large.

The kids and their music preferences dropped off of my radarscope. When I met with the youth I was dealing with conflict resolution issues, teenage pregnancies and teenage love affairs. I was dealing with trying to get our teenagers interested in the Lord, Jesus Christ and not just interested in having an excuse to see each other socially when they gathered at the Lord's house.

With the fight over the hymnals occurring during the month of July, with the motion being made that I had to pay for those hymnals, the teenage choir issue dropped completely off of my radar scope. On the last Wednesday of September in 1972, however, Val Jordan called me at ten o'clock at night. He was upset.

Val was upset because the music director had the teenagers learning European songs. I asked Val did he tell the choir director what kind of songs he wanted to learn and that they wanted to sing. He said of course he had told her that. I asked what the response was.

Val said that she had not been taught that kind of music. She was a graduate of Talladega College. At Talladega she was taught that Black Gospel music was not sacred music! She was not unique, however.

Most African American musicians who attended Historically Black Colleges and Universities and all Black musicians who attended white universities were taught the same thing. They were trained in "classical music." They were trained in the music of the European composers, the English composers and the American composers who can imitate European styles. They were not taught anything at all about the Black Sacred Music tradition.

Still smarting from my first church fight that July, I told Val (in September) that I could advise him; but I was not going to go out on a limb and get in trouble all over again for him and the young people. I told him that he was raised in the United Church of Christ. (This was really a *déjà vu* situation for me. I had seen the same thing happen at Howard University when the Howard University Gospel Choir was formed.)

I told him that since he was raised in the denomination, however, he needed to take another young person who was raised at Trinity United Church of Christ and he needed to go to the Church Council and make his case. I asked did he have anybody in mind who could teach the kind of music that they wanted to sing and he said, "Yes!" There was a young man who lived at

9656 South Emerald named Jeffrey Paul Radford. Remember, the church parsonage was at 9704 South Emerald, four houses away from Jeffrey's home!

Jeffrey had grown up with the kids in our church. They all knew Jeffrey and he knew all of them. Jeffrey was a sophomore at Governor's State University majoring in Music! He was also learning Gospel music from Mr. Robert Eugene Wooten, working with Mr. Wooten at the Greater Harvest Baptist Church at 51st and State! Jeffrey's father was a jazz musician, so Jeffrey brought the best of all worlds to the table as a musician.

I warned Val that the church might not have any money. When I started at Trinity in 1972 our annual budget was $39,000 a year! Val took with him Reverend Barbara Jean Allen's daughter, Sandi Allen (another young person raised in Trinity Church and active in the Youth Fellowship of our church).

They went before the Council and pled their case. They were given $150.00 for the rest of the year; fifty dollars for October, for November and for December to pay Mr. Radford. They were also promised that the salary would be revisited in the annual budget for 1973.

After rehearsing the young people for one month, Jeffrey had them ready to sing in a public worship service. Val Jordan called me excited on the fourth Wednesday of October and told me that I needed to come hear them because "*We are ready!*" I went to their rehearsal and was surprised.

Mr. Radford had them singing four-part harmony. Most Gospel choirs that were heard in 1972 (and most Gospel groups that are heard today) only sing three-part harmony! They sounded so good that I called the music director and told her that I was designating that following Sunday, the fifth Sunday in October, as Youth Sunday and the senior choir did not have to sing that Sunday. I was going to have the Youth Fellowship Choir sing. They were going to make their debut and we were going to make the fifth Sunday in October, October 29, 1972, Youth Sunday.

As a result of that decision, Youth Sunday became the fifth Sunday of the four months of the year that have five Sundays, for the next several years. Since that October 29, 1972 debut, moreover, we have kept a Youth Sunday during the months that have five Sundays with the only shift being that we have had to change the time of the service as we moved into multiple services to keep the adults coming to the worship service where the youth are in charge.

Once the adults found out that the "children were in charge," they stopped coming. They robbed themselves of the blessing of hearing some of the most powerful messages ever preached at Trinity because they assumed that the messages were not going to be any good because it was the teenagers delivering the message! How wrong they were.

The "hiccup," however, was what happened on October 29, 1972. Prior to that Sunday, our Chancel Choir and our little kiddies choir had simply walked down the aisle to whatever hymn they were singing as their Processional Hymn.

On the fifth Sunday in October, however, the reality of the difference between *saying* that they wanted to be a Black congregation and *experiencing* what that "felt like" to be a Black congregation at worship with Black music, Black rhythms and Black moves (including a choir that could strut better than Florida A & M's marching band) came into stark contrast!

Saying you are a Black congregation, unashamed of your culture, is one thing. *Experiencing* worship where Black culture and Black heritage are honored is another thing altogether!

When our teenagers made their debut in red, black and green dashikis with tambourines and drums on that Sunday, that became the Sunday that I have said for years where *"the fecal matter made contact with the circular rotary blades!"* Our teenagers hit the aisles strutting like the Florida A & M Band or a combination of The Four Tops and the Senior Choir of the First Church of Deliverance.

Most of the complaints I got, however, were from adults who were not complaining about the volume at which the teenagers sang. They were not complaining about the tambourines. They were not complaining about the washboard. They were not complaining about the drums. They were not complaining about the smooth moves of the teenagers. They were complaining about the *name* of the choir. The name of the choir was the "Youth Fellowship Choir" and the adults who came to me complaining wanted the name of that choir changed because they wanted to get into that choir!

About fifteen members of our congregation, however, who were uncomfortable with this Black worship and who were more comfortable with the European worship style joined the initial group that left the church because of the hymnal issue. As a result, twenty-two members of the eighty-seven that I found at the church in March of 1972 left the church within the first eighteen months of my trying to serve this congregation! That is also a part of what I mean when I say "the fun began."

The "Youth Fellowship Choir" sang that fifth Sunday in October and then they sang twice more on fifth Sundays between October of 1972 and June of 1973. In June of 1973, the "Youth Fellowship Choir" had its name changed to the Trinity Choral Ensemble in response to the request of a large number of adult members of the congregation and the "TCE" made their debut with their new name at a concert at Kenwood High School.

Once we changed the name of the choir to the Trinity Choral Ensemble (TCE), we had more adults join the choir than there were teenagers already in the choir! As a matter of fact, we had several sets of parents and children who were singing together in the same choir. That was the first major "turning point" in terms of attracting more members to our Sunday worship experience.

When Mr. Radford was hired (and of course his salary was taken up past that $50.00 a month that he was getting in October of 1972), his job description read that he had to teach anthems, spirituals, traditional gospel music, contemporary gospel music, West African music, South African music, Afro-Cuban music, Afro-Caribbean music, meter singing (long meter, common meter and short meter, which most people know as "Dr. Watts" songs) and every *genre* of Black Sacred Music that he could master and that he could get our choral ensemble to master.

We were blessed to have a South African ethnomusicologist, Dr. Elkin Sithole, to come and teach the Trinity Choral Ensemble pure African music and not music arranged by African Americans that was being erroneously called "African." One of my students at the seminary, Bonganjalo Goba was from South Africa. He introduced me to Dr. Sithole and literally brought him to our church.

"Bongo" (which is what we called him) and Dr. Sithole brought a young South African woman to our church who was in

seminary at Chicago Theological Seminary. Her name was
Reverend Thanda Ngcobo. Thanda's coming into our fellowship
literally changed the direction of the church in many ways. We
will talk more about that later.

There were several problems created with the formation of the
Trinity Choral Ensemble, however. First of all, the crowds on
Sunday began to be overwhelming. We had more people than
we had seats! The popularity of a choir comprised of teenagers
and adults with the versatility of the Trinity Choral Ensemble
was unheard of in United Church of Christ circles. The model
for that choir was the Wooten Choral Ensemble which was based
at the Beth Eden Baptist Church in Morgan Park.

Dr. Robert Eugene Wooten (the founder and director of the
Wooten Choral Ensemble) was my oldest daughter's Godfather!
Mr. Radford studied gospel music under Mr. Wooten as indicated
above. As crowds thronged our Sanctuary on Sunday to hear
the Trinity Choral Ensemble, many of the charter members and
I began to feel good about what was happening. We had to put
chairs down on the Sundays that the TCE sang. I moved the
Trinity Choral Ensemble from singing just on fifth Sundays, to
the point that they were singing every month on second and
fourth Sundays.

Mr. Robert Mayes (a classmate of mine at Howard University
back when the Howard University Gospel Choir was formed)
was the director of music at Christ Universal Temple. He was
Reverend Dr. Johnnie Coleman's right hand person. When the
director of our senior choir resigned, I offered the position to
Mr. Radford. Mr. Radford, however, was not yet twenty years of
age. His mother (who had joined our church) was in the Senior
Choir and he did not feel comfortable trying to be a choir director

for a choir in which his mother sang. He turned me down, so I asked Robert Mayes to come fill that position.

Robert Mayes came and worked with the senior choir of our church and changed the quality of their singing on Sundays remarkably. The name of the Senior Choir was changed to the Chancel Choir while Mr. Mayes was its director.

The next problem we created, however, was that with two different choirs singing on Sunday mornings we then started developing two different congregations! One group of folk would come to hear the Chancel Choir on first and third Sundays. Members of the TCE and their devotees would come on First Sunday because it was Communion Sunday. They would pack the church out on every second and fourth Sunday. Their displeasure with the Chancel Choir, however, caused our third Sunday services to lose a lot of persons whom we had hoped would be in worship every Sunday of the month!

I then had the problem of having an overcrowded Sanctuary on the first Sunday, a half-empty Sanctuary on the third Sunday, and crowds so large on the second and fourth Sundays that in the warm weather we had to have the windows opened with people standing outside, so they could hear the choir!

Now remember! The Trinity Choral Ensemble sang anthems just like the Chancel Choir did. The Trinity Choral Ensemble sang African American Spirituals just like the Chancel Choir did. The Trinity Choral Ensemble sang hymns just like the Chancel Choir did. The Chancel Choir, however, refused to sing the kind of gospel music that the TCE sang and as a result the members of the Ensemble and the members of the congregation would not come on those Sundays when the Chancel Choir was singing.

I began switching the Sundays on which the two choirs would sing so that the members would not know who was singing until they got to church. The members outsmarted and outflanked me. They started calling on Sunday morning to see what songs were listed in the bulletins. They could tell by the titles of the songs which choir was singing. There were two different congregations being formed – one that liked the Chancel Choir and one that liked the TCE!

Creating two congregations was not a good thing. The crowds were nice. The increased amount of money in the weekly offerings on the Sundays when the Ensemble would sing was badly needed, but the reality of having two different congregations is never a healthy thing, in my opinion, for any congregation. We limped along like that with two different congregations, however, for five years.

In 1977, I called a meeting of the presidents of both choirs during the month of October. I asked for the section leaders (soprano, alto, tenor and bass) to meet along with the officers of the choirs and in the home of Reverend Barbara Jean Allen (and Sam Allen). I laid out for them my vision for the new direction in which our Ministry of Music would be headed starting the Sunday before Christmas. I explained to the officers of both choirs that from the Sunday before Christmas (in 1977) and every Sunday thereafter we would have one adult choir— the Sanctuary Choir of Trinity United Church of Christ.

I explained to them that the Sanctuary Choir would sing anthems, hymns, spirituals, gospel music and every other *genre* of Black Sacred Music that there was in 1977. I explained that if any of the choir members in either choir had a problem with any of those *genres* there were many other places that they could serve in our congregation, but our congregation would hear one kind of music, one quality of music and one consistent choir fifty-two Sundays a year.

The Sanctuary Choir (made up of the combined memberships of the Trinity Choral Ensemble and the Chancel Choir) made its debut on the Sunday before Christmas in 1977.

Mr. Radford (who had been with us for five years by now) was extremely nervous about merging the two choirs into one choir. He said to me, "*Rev.! They don't like each other. They are going to get out of this combined choir thing!*"

I explained to Mr. Radford that if we stuck with the vision that God had given me, God would send the voices to make up for those who had gotten out of the combined choir. I told Mr. Radford that God would send thirty-fold, sixty-fold and one hundred-fold persons who loved the Lord and persons who wanted to sing the Lord's praises on a Sunday, using every *genre* in our rich history and legacy that he (Mr. Radford) taught!

The Sanctuary Choir membership climbed to over 200 persons!

W.E.B. DuBois said, in 1903, that there are three ingredients to every Black church: The preaching, the music and the Holy Spirit! W.E.B. DuBois also said that if you take any one of those three elements away you would no longer have a Black church! You would have a social club, a mutual aid society or a mutually congratulatory bourgeois Negro gathering, or you would have a social action group; but you would not have a church carrying out the mission of the Lord, Jesus Christ or trying to be what a church ought to be.

I was doing everything I could to make sure that the preaching element was "on target" as described by DuBois. Mr. Radford was charged with the responsibility of making sure that the music was excellent Black Sacred Music fifty-two Sundays a year! It was Mr. Radford and my shared belief that if the preaching and the music were the very best we had to offer every week in every worship service that the Holy Spirit would show up and do what only the Holy Spirit can do!

Looking back in our "Sankofa moment," however, there were many, many things, also going on which are equally as important as the change in music and worship style was; and to see the way over which we have come, you really need to review the other aspects of our ministry and the way in which the Lord added to our church daily, weekly and monthly in the years following 1972.

Chapter 2
Formative and Transformative

*T*he years 1972 through 1975 are what I call the "formative years." As you look back at what took place in our congregation during those years you can also see why I call them the "transformative years."

Between March of 1972 and the fall of 1972, as the "new kid on the block," I did what we used to say when I was in the military. I got on my horse and I took off in several different directions at once! I set about the task of trying to put flesh on the skeleton that was handed to me in the statement that Val Jordan shared with me, the statement the congregation voted upon in 1971, and the statement which affirmed the congregation's desire to go in a new direction!

I give thanks to God for leaders like Val Jordan, Blaine DeNye, Sam Allen, Barbara Allen and countless others. I really should not try to name those leaders because I will get in serious trouble by leaving somebody out; but I lift up those names in this instance because those persons formed the core leadership of our Church Council. The Church Council was absolutely amazing in terms of helping me put flesh on the skeleton. Mr. DeNye's contributions were absolutely invaluable.

By taking off in several different directions at once, I attended the monthly meetings of our Deacon Ministry, our Trustee Ministry and our other official "Boards" (which is what they were called in 1972) to find out what their thoughts were in terms of where they saw themselves and what their thoughts were in terms of addressing the question, "*How do we as a congregation go in a new direction?*"

When I called a Stewardship Ministry meeting to meet those officers of the church, three people came. The church Constitution said that there were nine persons on that official body. There were only three, however, who were functioning.

At my first meeting of the Board of Christian Education (which had six names listed as officers of the church) only two people came—Reverend Barbara Allen and one other person. The other person soon left when they discovered in the following year that we would be doing Christian Education from the Black perspective. That other person not only left the Board of Christian Education, that person also left the church!

One of the critical issues that we had to face as a Church Council and as officers of the church trying to head in a new direction was the question of identity! I do not mean just changing our identity in terms of the way we were perceived in the community. I mean we had to change our image of ourselves *for* ourselves! We first had to stop looking at the neighbors around the church as "those people." We then had to stop seeing ourselves as having a mission to "those people." We ultimately had to change our focus and make "those people" *our members*!

The conversation about the mission of a church, the purpose of a church and the ministry of a church changes radically when questions are asked like these:

What are the needs of *our* community?
What are the needs of *our* people?
What are the needs of *our members*?

The conversation changes because it is no longer a discussion about the "haves" doing something for the less fortunate (the "have-nots"). The question changes the focus of the congregation from addressing the needs of the people in the neighborhood around the church to addressing the needs of the *members* of that congregation who are in the church and who are a vital part of the church!

In addition to the official meetings and the wrestling with how to carry out the stated desires of the congregation, I began something really radical. I started a weekly Bible class! I had as my goal in starting a weekly Bible class the idea of connecting the study of God's Word to where it is we lived as a Black people in Chicago in 1972.

I had grandiose ideas about connecting the Bible story to our story as Black people, connecting the Bible story to where we as Blacks living in the United States were in 1972, or are today (psychologically, historically, spiritually and socio-economically). I wanted to connect the Bible Study with what it is that Black people had lived through and what it is we were living through contemporaneously in 1972. What I discovered, however, is that adult members of the congregation were almost functional biblically illiterates!

That was not an isolated phenomenon. It still is not an isolated phenomenon in the year 2009! Most adult African Americans are still biblically illiterate! In 1972, I was faced with the reality that most grown-ups had not been anywhere near a Bible since they graduated from high school and went away to college.

Some had purchased Bibles and read them sporadically once they got married and had children, but there was no systematic, ongoing, in-depth Bible Study in the homes of our members and in the homes of the average Black Americans across America (and across denominational lines!).

Black Christians were gullible. Black Christians would fall for anything that they saw on television (whether it was from white televangelists or Black televangelists!) and they would fall for anything that they heard on the radio calling itself religious programming or worship services, because they were functionally illiterate when it came to what God's Word said. That was in 1972. Things really have not changed that much in three decades!

Finding out where our members were when it came to the study of God's Word caused me to scrap my grandiose plans for Bible Study and start with very basic biblical facts. I had deacons who did not know the Word of God. I had trustees who did not know the Word of God. I had deacons who would not come to my Bible Study. There were twelve deacons on the Deacon Board roll in 1972 (8 active) and I only had eight people in Bible class (and most of them were not deacons!).

I had trustees for whom the word "Bible" was almost a cuss word. As a matter of fact, during my first two years as a Pastor, our trustees would not come to church to worship with us. They would come to church to count the offerings on Sundays and then leave after they had counted!

Getting them interested in the Bible was just not something that was on their radar scopes! I had one PhD in my "faithful eight" Bible class who thought that Jesus and Moses were contemporaries. That is a sign of how little she knew about the

Word of God. She had a PhD in Education, but she did not know God's Word.

I called my Bible class "the faithful eight" because that is the name my father gave it. When he found out that I had eight people in Bible Study faithfully each week, he told me to thank God for the "faithful eight!"

Those members who started with me in 1972 in Bible Study hung in there with me for several years. About five or six years later as the numbers of my weekly Bible Study class began to grow, new members started coming to Bible study and they felt lost! The new members started asking me if I had something a little simpler in the way of Bible study. The core of my class had developed to such an extent that they were really into advanced Bible Study five years later and the new members (in 1977) were back at the level of my PhD member who did not know how many years there were between the death of Moses and the birth of Jesus!

I asked my best Bible student if she would lead a beginner's Bible class. We would call it "Bible Basics." That student told me that she could not take on anything extra outside of my Bible class. She was the mother of six. She worked full-time and she just did not have the time to teach a class and take a class.

I asked another student who was equally as good as my best student, if she would lead the Bible class for beginners and she said only if she had access to me or the ability to call me to ask me any of the difficult questions that the students might ask of her if she took on the responsibility of teaching that class. I said she could call me at any time and she proceeded not only to do an excellent job, she proceeded to set up our entire Bible Study Development Program which today is known as the Center for

African Biblical Studies. (She only called me once, incidentally, in the ten years that she served in that position!)

Going back to the formative years, however, I give thanks to God for the members who were serious about engaging God's Word. Many of the ministries at our church started in the early '70s and the mid-'70s and many of the ministries we have today grew directly out of the members wrestling with the *text* (in God's Word) and wrestling with our context as African Americans living in Chicago in the 1970s.

In 1973, I was elected by the denomination to serve on the Board of Directors of one of the Instrumentalities of the National Church. That Instrumentality was the Social Justice Ministry and they oversaw the work of the denomination in all of those areas that dealt with social justice. I was on that Board of Directors when the denomination changed that Board's name officially to the Office for Church in Society. I was elected Secretary of the Board of Directors of the Office for Church in Society.

I brought the notion of a social justice arm in the ministry of the church of Jesus Christ back to the Executive Council of our congregation and it was immediately ratified. We formed a Church in Society Ministry and that ministry was charged with the responsibility of keeping the members aware of all of the social issues that our denomination addressed and that we as Black Christians needed to address.

That ministry held political forums, asked us to sign petitions and caused us to become actively involved in seeking justice in our city, our state, our nation and our world. That ministry transformed a church that had been known for only having one-hour worship services on Sunday and that was it for the rest of the week. That ministry along with our Bible classes and our members' excitement about heading in a new direction transformed our church into a seven-day a week ministry that sought to relate to the community in which we sat in every way!

When addressing the questions: *"What do our members need?"* and *"What do our neighbors need?"*—two pressing needs leaped off the newspaper pages at us and presented us with an "in your face" kind of reality. The first need we saw was quality childcare at an affordable cost. Our members and our neighbors needed childcare. They could not afford what it cost for the privately-owned childcare centers in the community.

The second need we saw was the need for a reading tutorial ministry. Surprisingly enough we found out that the students in the elementary schools sitting closest to us, Kipling School, Wacker School, Medgar Evers, Fort Dearborn, etc., had the lowest reading scores in the city of Chicago.

The *Chicago Sun-Times* and the *Chicago Tribune* published the reading scores by community and zip code in their papers. Our children in our community needed help with reading. That caused us to start our Reading Tutorial Program in 1974. The need for childcare started us investigating how to best service poor, unemployed and underemployed families with quality childcare in 1975.

My being elected to the Commission for Racial Justice in 1975 also caused a radical change in our focus, our understanding of ministry and the role that we played in seeking racial justice for African Americans in the city of Chicago, the state of Illinois, this country and the world! The year 1975 was also the year, incidentally, that we saw the first female ushers at Trinity United Church of Christ.

One of the Founding Members of the church had said publicly that he would be *"dead and in his grave before he saw a woman 'sashaying' up and down the aisles of our church as an usher!"* Today our Usher Ministry has more women serving than men! I wonder how that founding member feels having made such an ugly pronouncement!

The day I started serving as vice chairperson of the Commission for Racial Justice was the day that the Supreme Court refused to entertain a *Writ of Certiorari* in the case of the Wilmington 10. My first meeting with the Commission as its new vice president was Ben Chavis' last meeting with the Commission before going to jail. He entered prison in January of 1975 and was incarcerated until the week of our Dedication Services for our new building at 532 West 95th Street.

Those services were held during the first week in December of 1978 and it was not until then that the Wilmington 10 case got to the 4th Circuit Court of Appeals. The case was immediately thrown out and Reverend Chavis was set free! Our members corresponded with Rev. Chavis every week he was in prison. I kept his name (and address) at the top of our church's prayer list in the weekly bulletin from January of 1975 through December of 1978!

Back in 1975, however, Reverend Thanda Ngcobo's and Reverend Bonganjalo Goba's being in our midst and being in our ministry caused yet another major transformation to take place in our congregation.

Bongo and Thanda brought with them to our congregation inside information and personal experience about what was really going on with Blacks in South Africa. Unfortunately, the corporate-owned media in this country only lets the public know what the corporate media owners want the public to know. You never get the true story in this country. Thanda and Bongo saw to it that we got the true story.

Members of the congregation became sensitized to the Sharpsville Massacre, the Soweto uprising, the death of Hector Pietersen and the evils of Apartheid and the racist Afrikaner government. Members of Trinity started celebrating the *Umoja Karamu* on Thanksgiving Day of 1975 and have celebrated it every year since 1975.

In 1975, Reverend Thanda Ngcobo was the first minister ordained by our congregation into the Gospel of Ministry. At her ordination Dr. Bonganjalo Goba gave Thanda, her charge to ministry in Zulu. It was also during her preparation for Ordination, however, that she told me that she had just finished three years of seminary and had not read one book by anybody Black or one book about anything Black in graduate school! It was that painful truth that she shared with me that caused me to start our Ministers-in-Training (MIT) program in 1975.

Our Ministers-in-Training program has been designed so that no other student from Trinity United Church of Christ who enters seminary will be able to finish seminary without having read a minimum of three to five books each year by African and African American authors throughout the academic year. Where Reverend (now Dr.) Thanda Ngcobo was the first member of our congregation to finish seminary and be ordained, God has blessed me to ordain a total of forty-two women and men to the Christian ministry who are graduates of fully-accredited seminaries in the United States of America.

Trinity Church had nine of its members receive Master of Divinity degrees in May of 2008 (at the end of the last year of my service) from the Samuel DeWitt Proctor School of Theology at Virginia Union University. The MIT program has been one of God's richest blessings in my ministry.

It was also during the "formative and transformative years" that the Christian Education focus at the church was radically changed. During the 1973-74 period, I received an invitation from our denomination to attend a life-changing seminar that was being sponsored by the Joint Educational Development (JED) team. The Joint Educational Development team was comprised of Christian educators from the United Church of Christ, the Evangelical Lutheran Church in America, the United Presbyterian church, the United Methodist church and the American Baptist church.

JED invited pastors and directors of Christian education from all of the participating denominations to a two-day seminar on "Teaching Christian Education from the Black Perspective." The seminar/workshop was being held by the participating denominations because those denominations realized that a significantly large number of their memberships was African American and the Christian education materials in each of those denominations was inaccurate, a-historical and almost outright racist!

Through false images and erroneous artistic representations which ran the gamut all of the way from biblical stories with pictures of white disciples, white biblical characters and a white Jesus, all of the way through and to the illustrations being used in Church School materials and adult education materials which were all "so very white," a subtle racist Christianity was being taught.

The white denominations participating in JED wanted to change that. They wanted to have printed materials primarily for their African American constituents and secondarily for all of their other constituents to learn the truth about Africa, the role of Christendom in the Trans-Atlantic Slave Trade and the "miseducation" of Black, white, brown and Asian Christians that had been taking place since the Asiento!

These "formative and transformative years" at Trinity Church, incidentally, were taking place during the Black Revolution of the 1970s in this country and across the globe! Following the Civil Rights Movement of the 1960s the Black Revolution and the Black Consciousness Movement were in full-tilt during the 1970s. That phenomenon ran all of the way from the Black Consciousness Movement of Steve Biko in South Africa to "The Last Poets" in the United States of America! The Black Consciousness Movement did not miss or skip the Black church in North America or the Christian educators in the participating denominations of JED.

The Christian educators in the JED project wanted all of the members of their various denominations to learn the truth about the origins of Christianity, the invaluable and central role played by Africa and Africans in the Judeo-Christian story, and they wanted their memberships to know about the racism in Christianity that affected its mission work in Africa and the formation and development of the Black church both on the Continent of Africa and in all three Americas (North America, Central America and South America).

Christian educators from those participating denominations put their heads together and came up with a comprehensive program for teaching (in congregations across denominational lines) who Jesus was, who the disciples were, who Abraham was, who

Abraham's wives were, who Moses' wife was, who the Queen of Sheba was, who Harriet Tubman was, who Bishop Henry McNeal Turner was, who David Walker was, who Gabriel Prosser was, who Denmark Vesey was and how God was in the midst of that Black faith story from its beginnings on the Continent of Africa up through the 1970s.

Those are the areas the two-day seminar covered and I was overwhelmed! This is precisely what I had been studying at Howard University under Dr. John Lovell. It was what I had been exposed to at Howard University under the teachings of William Leo Hansberry and Chancellor Williams. It is what I had studied at the feet of Sterling Brown, Arthur Davis and Stanley Alsop.

It is what I had fought for at The University of Chicago Divinity School. It is what Dr. Charles Long had been teaching me in the History of Religions at the Divinity School and it was the same thing now in the field of Christian Education! It was the same thing that the Black students at Howard had said in the field of Music in 1968 and the same thing that my teenagers at Trinity had said in 1972!

Among the many friends that I met at that two-day JED workshop/seminar were Rita Dixon of the Presbyterian church, Jamie Phelps of the Roman Catholic church and a beautiful Black sister from the United Church of Christ named Reverend Yvonne Delk! (Yvonne Delk, incidentally, had provided the funding for Dr. Ed Simms to publish his **Umoja Karamu** and several other African-centered resource materials for Black families and Black congregations several years before the JED Workshop.)

Yvonne had an entire African-centered curriculum from kindergarten through adult education on teaching Christian education from the Black perspective. She put an outline on the print sheets at the seminar and showed us how to incorporate truth in our curricula at every level and stage of development for African American Christians from the kindergarten level through adult education. I took feverish notes. I copied her entire outline!

I came back to our church ecstatic. I was *beyond* excited. I could not believe that the Christian educators in the participating JED denominations had stumbled on to the same truths I had been teaching (studying and learning) for almost a decade. I anxiously awaited the new JED curriculum. I told our department of Christian Education and I told our Church School faculty about the forthcoming JED curriculum.

Some of the teachers were skeptical. After all, this was the same Trinity church whose Executive Council had told Reverend Barbara Allen before I started as pastor that parents did not send their children to Church School at Trinity to learn about Black things or to learn about Black people. They sent their children to Church School to learn about Jesus (who in their minds was white!). The Church Council "censured" Reverend Barbara for coloring the pictures in the Church School materials and making them people of color and not all white.

With that mentality still reigning among some of our Church School teachers, they quietly resigned when I came back from the JED conference excited about the forthcoming curriculum and the change in our educational program. That is also when that other active member of the Board of Christian Education left the church.

My wait for the JED curriculum, however, was in vain. The white denominations who were participating in JED very quietly responded to our questions (the next year) as to when the curriculum would be ready. Their response was that they were sorry. Money and "the profit motive" won out over prophetic publication and the propagation of truth! In other words, they told us, there was no market for that curriculum. Their black members did not want that curriculum and the churches they attended would not buy that curriculum, so it did not make any sense to spend the money to print that African-centered curriculum.

The words of Reuben Sheares were ringing true! When my hymn book fight erupted in July of 1972, I went to Reverend Sheares for advice and counsel. He had been the Interim Pastor at our church and he had more years of experience in serving than I did. He had also coined the phrase "**Unashamedly Black and Unapologetically Christian.**" Reuben told me when I went to talk to him about the hymn book problem: *"Jerry, you have got to understand this! Many Black people joined white denominations to get away from Black people! They joined a white denomination because they did not want to have anything more to do with ordinary Black folks. They did not want to hear any more Gospel - - preached or sung!"*

Reuben was talking about the self-hatred that Na'im Akbar writes about in his book about psychological chains that are still on black minds as a result of chattel slavery. What the participating denominations were saying to us was that because their Black members did not see themselves as Black there was no market to publish the materials that taught Christian education from the Black perspective!

I shared that painful decision with Reverend Barbara Allen. Instead of being as devastated as I was, however, Reverend Allen was determined! Reverend Allen took the notes that I had brought back from Dr. Yvonne Delk's presentation and she put together (from Yvonne's outline) the first curriculum for Trinity United Church of Christ which taught Christian education from the Black perspective. Reverend Allen used Dr. Delk's notes to design a curriculum that covered every age (from kindergarten through adult education).

That was a transformative moment for our congregation. That was also an example of putting some flesh on the skeleton. That was bringing to life the affirmation on paper that the congregation had made in 1971 of our wanting to go in a different direction and be a Black church in the Black community!

As a result of Reverend Allen's Herculean efforts, I later asked her to become our Director of Christian Education and she accepted. She was commissioned by the United Church of Christ as a Commissioned Minister and held that position until she died. About a decade after Reverend Allen put together our first African-centered curriculum, Dr. Colleen Birchett came to our church, came on church staff and further developed what Reverend Allen had laid out from Dr. Delk's outline. Reverend Allen and Dr. Birchett's work also provided the foundation for the Center for African Biblical Studies.

In 1974, during the "formative and transformative" years of my pastorate, our denomination started its "17/76 Campaign." The 17/76 Campaign was the stewardship effort on the part of our denomination, challenging its 6,000-plus congregation to join together to raise 17 million dollars by 1976 for six of the eight Black colleges (still in existence) that are related to the United Church of Christ.

(Because Clark-Atlanta is heavily supported by the United Methodist church and because Howard University sits on federal property in the District of Columbia and gets its budget from the United States Congress, our denomination does not support those two schools with financial resources. We are still supporting, however, the other six Black colleges and universities related to our predecessor denomination, the Congregational Church.)

Our small congregation in 1974 (during the transformative years) pledged $3,000 a year toward the 17/76 Campaign. We easily raised that $3,000 a year by lifting an extra Offering on the third Sunday of each month. We started raising money in 1974 and by the year 1976 we had paid out our $9,000 pledge.

Our Stewardship Council said to me as we made the stewardship recommendations for the 1977 church budget that we ought to keep that third Sunday Offering. It was their feeling that the members had grown accustomed to the third Sunday Offering being an offering for higher education with all of the monies that we lifted going toward the goal of our $9,000 pledge to the Historically Black Colleges and Universities related to the United Church of Christ. We had been lifting that offering for three straight years.

We kept our third Sunday extra offering. We called it our "Scholarship Offering" and we then started using all of the monies raised on the third Sunday during the second offering to award a scholarship to the "top student" who was a member of Trinity United Church of Christ, graduating from high school and going into college the following fall.

One of our teenagers in the Trinity Choral Ensemble, Cheryl Guyton, died in her sleep during her senior year at Academy of

Our Lady High School. We named the Trinity scholarship after Cheryl Guyton and its first recipient was on "Scholarship Sunday" in June of the year following the 17/76 Campaign - - June of 1977. That Cheryl Guyton Scholarship which was awarded to a graduating high school senior who had excellent grades and who was active in his or her church and his or her high school beyond the classroom has grown tremendously.

Scholarship Sunday now not only includes the Cheryl Guyton Memorial Award. Members of Trinity United Church of Christ graduating from elementary school, high school, college, city colleges, universities, graduate schools, seminaries and professional schools are all recognized in a special service each year by our congregation.

The dollar amount of scholarships that are awarded each year on Scholarship Sunday climbed up to over $100,000 a year for the last two years of my pastorate! The scholarships are now awarded to graduating high school seniors, to students in specialized areas of study (nursing, law, etc.,) and to seminarians who all take part in the competitive application process.

The awarding of those scholarships has moved from the purview of the Stewardship Council to a Scholarship and Education Committee that now receives the applications, reviews the applications and awards those scholarships on the basis of their voting process. Cheryl Guyton's mother, Mrs. Barbara Dorham, is an active member of that committee.

Adding to the Guyton award where the monies are raised on the third Sunday through the second offering, families have set aside monies for special scholarships in honor of their deceased loved ones. Sororities have joined in by awarding deserving students monies each year on Scholarship Sunday in honor of deceased members of their sorority. One such sorority award is the Dr. Mary Henderson Wright Award given by the AKA's in honor of my mother's scholastic achievements.

In 1981, the Manford Byrd Scholarship was added to the long and growing list of scholarships awarded each year by Trinity Church. Students who compete for the Manford Byrd Award have to write an essay exemplifying how they adhere to the Black Value System which was put together in honor of the service of Dr. Manford Byrd and put together as a congregational effort to articulate what it meant to be **Unashamedly Black and Unapologetically Christian** in the year 1981.

Students who compete for the seminary scholarships have to write an essay demonstrating how their ministry exemplifies the characteristics of the ministries of clergypersons for whom the scholarships are named; persons like Reverend Samuel Ellis (our first Sick and Shut-in Visitation Minister at Trinity), Dr. Martin Luther King, Jr., and my father, Dr. Jeremiah A. Wright, Sr.

The massive amounts of money and the unforgettable memories that are shared each Scholarship Sunday all grew out of the offerings that were started on the third Sunday in the month, which was the Sunday set aside for higher education and for raising resources for six of the eight Black colleges historically related to the United Church of Christ during the 17/76 Campaign.

The year 1975 was a benchmark year for several reasons. In addition to my becoming a member of the Commission for Racial Justice, in addition to the Ordination of Reverend Thanda Ngcobo, in addition to the institution of **Umoja Karamu** as our Thanksgiving Day service, in addition to our Christian Education from the Black perspective efforts taking off and taking root while raising financial resources for six of the eight Black colleges related to the United Church of Christ, our congregation not only became excited about its Building Fund and raising monies in order to build a new Sanctuary; our congregation not only became energized about raising monies for a new worship center; our congregation also experienced its first major ministry outside of the state of Illinois and its first traumatizing "hit" because of its denominational commitment!

In 1975, the Trinity Choral Ensemble started its unforgettable adventure in traveling with me as I went to different churches. In 1975, the Trinity Choral Ensemble went to Minneapolis, Minnesota, with me to sing before the General Synod of the United Church of Christ! The white members of our denomination loved the Trinity Choral Ensemble. Several of our Black members were "embarrassed" by the moves and the "get down Gospel" being sung by the Trinity Choral Ensemble. Reuben Sheares' words were coming back to haunt me once again.

The Trinity Choral Ensemble went with me to Rockville, Maryland, to sing at the church where I was ordained into the Christian ministry—the Mt. Calvary Baptist Church of Rockville. That east coast tour also included a concert in Washington, D.C., at the church where Reverend Reginald Green served (Reverend Green had been a classmate of mine at Virginia Union University).

The biggest out of town "splash" made by the Trinity Choral Ensemble on their trips accompanying me out of town was their trip to the Grace Baptist Church of Germantown in Philadelphia, PA—the church where I was raised! The woman who used to babysit me when I was a little boy, Peggy Goffney, said to me, *"You know the only reason drums got up in your daddy's church is that you brought them here. Right?"* My father had been taught at Virginia Union University that drums were "pagan," "heathen" and "of the devil."

Those teachings were part and parcel of the Eurocentric curriculum that was at every historically Black college and university established by the missionaries!

As a result of that teaching (or "training"), my father did not allow drums at the Grace Baptist Church of Germantown in Philadelphia, Pennsylvania. When I took the Trinity Choral Ensemble to Philadelphia, however, we not only had drums at the Grace Baptist Church of Germantown for the first time in its history. We also rented a Hammond B-3 organ so that the members of Grace could hear an authentic Gospel music sound. That was in 1975. There was one other tremendous event that took place in 1975, however.

At the General Synod in 1975, our denomination's representatives voted to ordain homosexuals into the Gospel of Ministry. The story of that vote, the "story behind the story" involving a Black constituency at that Synod (and my role as a voting delegate), the story of my conversion from being homophobic to being able to see, to understand, to embrace and to love all of God's people as equals, is a story that I will begin to address in the next chapter.

Room does not permit me to go into that thirty-three-year history in these pages. I will write more about that both in the next chapter and when I publish my autobiography. Suffice it to say right here, however, that that experience, our denomination's vote, my awakening, my conversion and our congregation's coming to grips with issues of sexuality, can all be traced back to

1975 and the "formative and transformative years" through which our congregation was struggling and growing.

The "formative and transformative" years were full of excitement, growth, new learnings, pain and tears! Let me share just a little of the pain (and joy!) with you.

Eighteen months into my pastorate, I asked for an appointment with our Founding Pastor, Reverend Dr. Kenneth B. Smith. I asked for the appointment with him because I felt as if I had let him down. I felt as if I were a failure.

It seemed to me as if everybody was leaving our church. It felt that way to me because the members who were leaving as a result of the hymnals, the Youth Fellowship Choir, the Trinity Choral Ensemble, the change in worship style and leaving because of me, included founding members, members of the search committee that had called me and people whom I had grown to love who looked me right in my face and lied to me about not leaving (while already having left Trinity and joined other congregations like the Congregational Church of Good Shepherd Church or Park Manor Congregational Church!).

I felt as if I were letting Dr. Smith down. I felt that he had recommended me to someone on the search committee at our church. He introduced me to Val Jordan. He was responsible for my being considered by the congregation to be its pastor. His recommendation had caused them to give me a hearing and to subsequently call me and now I was running away all of "his members."

I went to him to apologize and to ask for his advice. I poured out my heart about how the first eighteen months had been during my pastorate. I shared my pain with him and after listening to me for over an hour, he blessed me tremendously! Dr. Smith said to me, *"Jerry, how many members have left?"* I had no idea. I said to him, *"I don't know! It seems like everybody is leaving."* He then suggested to me that we count how many had left, so we would have an accurate figure.

Because he was our Founding Minister, back in those days we sent Reverend Smith a copy of everything that we did. He therefore had our latest Church Roster and he took it out and counted along with me how many members had left. That is when I found out that twenty-two members had left in my first eighteen months as pastor. I did not know it was only twenty-two until that day. When you have a congregation of eighty-seven, it seems like everyone is leaving when you lose one-quarter of your congregation! He then said to me, *"How many have come since you have been there, Jerry?"* I had no idea.

I told him I did not know and he suggested that we call back to the church to ask the church secretary. Dr. Julia "Judy" Speller was the church secretary in the fall of 1973 and we called her. Judy pulled the Annual Report from 1972 and told us that sixty-three members had joined in 1972. Dr. Smith then asked her how many had joined thus far in 1973. It was November of 1973 and seventy members had joined through November. Eighty-three was the total number for that year, but as of November only seventy had joined and been given the Right Hand of Fellowship.

Kenneth Smith thanked her, hung up the phone and then said to me words that I will never forget.

Dr. Smith's advice to me was, *"Jerry, do not neglect the 133 souls that God has sent you agonizing over the twenty-two persons who have left you. Those twenty-two are persons who will never let you be their pastor! You are neglecting doing ministry with the 133 that God has sent agonizing over the twenty-two who have left!"*

I had not seen my pastorate in that light until that day. Dr. Smith and I disagreed about many things. My understanding of worship and his understanding of worship were not the same. My love for Gospel music, for Black worship and for the African elements that were resonant and are still resonant in the lives of Africans in Diaspora is something that was not where Ken Smith was liturgically.

Yet, he supported me in my pastorate though we were dichotomously opposed in terms of worship style, in terms of the nature and role of the ministry (and the pastor) in middle-income congregations. I felt the pastors should be prophetic. He felt they should be priestly. We were very different when it came to ideology and theology, but he helped me. He supported me and he stood behind me in what I was trying to do even though he did not agree with what I was trying to do!

I used to ask him why he was not active in the Black Caucus of the United Church of Christ. Dr. Smith was not active in the Ministers for Racial and Social Justice— the Black Clergy Caucus of the United Church of Christ—and he was not active in United Black Christians (the lay and clergy caucus together).

I could not understand that, but I did understand that what he said to me in November of 1973 changed my life. It changed my focus. It helped me.

It blessed me and it caused me to leave his office renewed, revived and restored! Those were truly the "formative and transformative years" of the "marriage made in Heaven" that I had envisioned on the night of December 31, 1971 when Val Jordan and I talked for four hours.

In addition to the sixty-three members who joined in 1972, the eighty-three members who joined in 1973 and the excitement among the 250 members who were busily trying to raise funds to erect a new worship center while being a part of the Black Consciousness Movement and the exciting worship that was now taking place on 95th Street, our church continued to see a steady influx of new members. Eighty-six new members joined in 1974. In 1975 (our benchmark year), we took in over 125 new members. By the time we broke ground for our new building in 1977, we had over four-hundred active adult members of the church. Our numerical growth continued at a slow and steady pace until 1979 when we went on the radio. Once we went on the radio, our growth took off.

During the "formative and transformative" years, raising money for our building program was only one aspect of the exciting, draining and congregation-changing process of erecting a new worship center for God.

Raising the funds, to have money on hand to be able to enter into conversations with banks for a construction loan, consisted of far more than my standing up on Sunday and asking members to give an extra offering.

The first thing that our denomination recommended when we told them we needed to build was that we should enter into a Capital Stewardship Campaign. Our denomination had paid staff persons who went into local churches and did Capital Stewardship Campaigns with those congregations.

Because our denomination is a predominately white congregation, however, that meant that we would have a white UCC staff person or a similar white professional who would be coming into the 95th Street community on the Southside of Chicago bringing principles, lessons and examples that were as far removed from our experience as Black people as the East is from the West!

Plus those staff persons or those professional fundraisers required monies that we did not have. The leader of a Capital Stewardship Campaign or the resource person for that campaign does not come free. They require a fee! We were doing all we could to raise money to start building a larger sanctuary. We did not have any extra money to pay a resource person. My thinking was that we ought to ask my father to help us.

My father had built a new church in the city of Philadelphia. Subsequent to building that first unit, he had led his congregation in building an educational wing. They had constructed a multimillion dollar facility and paid for it in less than five years. They had done it solely through tithes and offerings.

My father did not believe in selling chicken and chitterling dinners to raise monies for ministry. He did not believe in congregational fundraising. He believed that a church should be supported by the tithes and offerings of its members. That is what he preached, taught and lived for the forty-two years that he served the Grace Baptist Church of Germantown and that is the way he raised me. I not only followed in his footsteps methodologically in terms of stewardship, I went one step further. I called him and asked him if he would lead our Capital Stewardship Campaign as we tried to raise funds to build a new worship center in 1975 and 1976.

My father came into our church for the cost of his airfare. There was no hotel fee because he stayed in my home! He trained our church leaders first and then he made the appeal to the congregation. He and my mother went one step further than just teaching. They set an example. They made the first pledge to our congregation's building fund! (They also paid out that pledge and continued to give financially and substantially to our ministry until the Lord took them home!)

It was because of my father's teachings with the leadership of our church as he conducted the first Capital Stewardship Campaign at our church that several of our church officers began to tithe! I had asked the church officers to tithe. I had preached about tithing. My asking and my preaching, however, had fallen on deaf ears. My father's patient and powerful testimony and teaching transformed many of their ways of thinking about God's money and resulted in their becoming tithers and our being able to raise enough money to hold a conversation with banks about lending us money for the construction of a new worship facility to the Glory of God.

Another aspect of the building process was the formation of and the subsequent work of the building committee. Mr. Blaine DeNye, once again, was an invaluable asset to the ministry of this church. Blaine DeNye was one of the founding members of Trinity United Church of Christ. He and his wife, Doris, had come to Trinity from Park Manor Congregational Church in 1961. Blaine had served as a deacon in our congregation and was elected chairperson of the church council shortly after I began to serve as Pastor.

Mrs. Doris DeNye was a faithful member of our church school staff and an important member of our Christian education team. Doris continued to teach adult Bible study until her work at our church's senior citizen housing complex no longer afforded her the time or the energy to maintain her role in that position.

Blaine DeNye pulled together a team of persons who became the core group of the building committee. He drew on the names of persons with whom he had a relationship before I came to the church. I suggested names of the persons whom I had seen work faithfully for the three years that I had been serving as Pastor of the church and together that team gelled to do the hard work of putting together the plans that we followed in erecting the new sanctuary at 532 West 95th Street.

The first task we had before us was the selection of an architect. Once again the years rob me of an accurate memory of all of the persons who were gathered there and once again running the risk of getting in trouble by leaving out some important names. I can recall, however, Blaine DeNye, Mildred Chapman, Sonny Chapman and others meeting in the living room of Reverend Barbara Allen and Mr. Sam Allen to interview the final three persons whom we were considering as the architect for our new worship facility. Back in the mid-'60s, when our first unit was put up, we had a white architect.

As a Black church that preached supporting our own professionals, we definitely wanted to make a statement by hiring the best Black architect available! The man who stood head and shoulders above the other two finalists for the position was Wendell Campbell.

We unanimously voted to employ Mr. Campbell as the church architect and he served faithfully in that position until his health no longer allowed him to function. Mr. Campbell not only served as the architect for the construction of the 532 West 95th Street building, he also built the Human Resources annex to that building.

Mr. Campbell also was the architect for both of our senior citizen housing complexes—Trinity Acres and Trinity Oaks. Mr. Campbell also oversaw the rehabbing of the 421 West 95th Building and the construction of our present worship center at 400 West 95th Street!

I was blessed to be asked by our member (and Wendell's widow), Mrs. June Campbell to preach the eulogy for the funeral services of Wendell at the First Unitarian Church of Chicago in the year 2008. Wendell was given the victory by God after an extended period of illness in the years 2007 and 2008.

Wendell Campbell made a presentation to me on the day that we dedicated the new facility (after three long and hard years of toiling together) and he made his presentation in the form of a plaque. His "speech" is inscribed on the plaque and he said to me on that Sunday (and on that plaque) that while he was trying to build a visible brick and mortar "church" for an ever-growing and expanding congregation whose numbers kept changing on him, God was using me to build a human and spiritual "church" of consecrated and committed persons whose efforts would outlive the concrete, bricks and mortar that he was in charge of! That plaque still hangs in my office today.

The building committee had as its task not only the selection of an architect. They also had to interview every active ministry of the church to see what their need requirements and space requirements were. That entailed meeting with the music department, the Christian education department, the deacons, the trustees and every other ministry that would use the worship facility on the Lord's Day and during the week.

The building committee compiled all of those meeting notes from all of those various constituencies and put together a narrative which we gave to Mr. Campbell. It is from that narrative that he designed the 532 West 95th Street building and a decade later it was from a similar narrative that he designed the 400 West 95th Street worship center. We were limited in the process by the amount of money that we could raise. He was limited in the process by the size of the site upon which the building he designed would sit. In spite of the limitations, however, God got the glory both times!

After designing the facility, Mr. Campbell then "shopped" his design with several Black general contractors to get their bids. We told him we had to have a Black general contractor. He then made his recommendation to us as to what he felt was the best bid and we then had a dollar figure to put in our proposal and in our asking as we went (with three years audited financial statements) to get funding from the local banks to construct the first worship center we built on my watch. Nobody would lend us a dime!

When our church opened its doors in 1961, we were banking with the Illinois Service Federal Savings and Loan institution. They would not lend us a penny to expand our facilities at the 532 West 95th Street address in 1976. Shortly after we were chartered as a church we opened a bank account with Independence Bank. These were two Black institutions. In the 1960s, our church was committed to keeping our money in Black institutions. Independence Bank would not lend us a penny either in 1976. The Black institutions would not help us at all.

We ran into the same dead end at Seaway Bank and with Highland Bank. The white banks laughed at us before we could get through the door and the Black banks treated us like the lead character in Ralph Ellison's *The Invisible Man*. They just kept us running. They would not tell us what the "real deal" was!

God's providence, however, is always greater than the roadblocks that human beings put up when you are trying to do God's Will. God providentially arranged for my dentist, Dr. Raymond Pierce, to become a key figure in our receiving the necessary dollars to construct the 532 facility. Dr. Pierce introduced me to his banker, Mr. Charles Allen, who was a loan officer at the First National Bank. Mr. Charles Allen is currently a member of the Hartford Memorial Baptist Church in Detroit, Michigan, where the Reverend Dr. Charles G. Adams serves as Pastor.

Dr. Pierce took me to Mr. Allen's home along with my three years audited statements so he could review (unofficially) what we were presenting to banks and perhaps give me some insights about why we were being turned away by all the banks. Charles Allen read our materials that cold January evening in 1977 and then Mr. Allen told me (painfully and graphically) why bankers were turning me away.

He told us what we needed to put in our loan application package as we went to any bank in the future in order to ensure that we could get the loan and to reassure the banker that it was a good loan! What he told us to do, in 1977, turned out to be exactly what was needed. It also turned out to be what became fodder for the vicious media attacks on me twenty-one years later as white racists tried to derail the Presidential candidacy of Barack Obama in 2008!

The congregation voted, in 1977, to sweeten my retirement package with assurances that let the bankers know that I would not go anywhere until the church loans were paid off or paid out! Among those "sweeteners" was the stipulation that whatever parsonage the church built for me would be mine at retirement. *Fox News* and Bill O'Reilly have not let that vote from 1977 go yet! They refuse to "let it go!"

With Charles Allen's suggestions incorporated as a part of our loan package, God's providence kicked in on another front. God providentially arranged it so that I was a voting delegate to the Annual Meeting of the Pension Boards of the United Church of Christ. It was at that meeting that I heard of Ron Grzywinski. It was at that Pension Board meeting that I was introduced to the phenomenal work of Ron Grzywinski and our denomination's role in the purchase and growth of what was then called the South Shore Bank of Chicago. Today it is called ShoreBank!

When I came home from the UCC Pension Board Meeting I took our Charles Allen-augmented Performa and our three years audited financial reports to the South Shore Bank at 71st and Jeffrey and asked for a meeting with Ron Grzywinski. He was not in. I then asked, "*Well who is in charge while Mr. Grzywinski is away?*" I was given the name of Milton Davis and I was allowed to see Milton Davis for five minutes before his next appointment. God's providence was operating at full steam!

Mr. Davis called me the next day and asked me if South Shore Bank could put a sign up on the property if they lent us the money and I told him we would change the name of the church to the "South Shore Bank of Chicago United Church of Christ" if he would lend us the money to build that facility. He laughed. He said he thought it was doable and within a matter of weeks the loan committee of South Shore Bank had voted to loan us the money.

I found out later that our denomination, which only loaned us $10,000 in a "grant mortgage," could have loaned us the entire amount that we were asking banks for as we were trying to construct a new sanctuary. They could have loaned us the entire amount that we needed, but they had no faith in me or in this "new breed" and new brand of Black church worship within the United Church of Christ on the Southside of Chicago. In the words of John Potts, the denomination's Building and Loan Director, they did not think *"we would make it!"* Mr. Potts said that publicly at a meeting of the United Black Christians in Detroit, Michigan, in 1980! United Black Christians is the Black Caucus of the denomination.

With the loan in place, the monies in place, the architectural drawings completed and a contractor signed, we broke ground in those "formative and transformative years" in December of 1977. The new facility was dedicated during the first week of December in 1978. The Dedication Week was a special time, a sacred time and an unforgettable time that will live forever in the history of Trinity United Church of Christ.

The Dedication Services lasted a week. They started on Sunday with my father preaching the Dedication Sermon and they closed that Friday night with Reverend Clarence H. Cobbs preaching the final sermon in a week-long series of services dedicating the new facility.

My father's initial sermon that Sunday afternoon was followed by a banquet during which he and my mother were surprised when the banner celebrating the new facility was ripped off of the wall and beneath it was a plaque dedicating our educational facility to them, Dr. and Mrs. Jeremiah A. and Mary H. Wright. That is how we got the name "Wright Hall" for the facility at 532 West 95th Street. For the first time in my life I saw my mother speechless!

On Monday night, Dr. Charles Cobb, the Executive Director of the Commission for Racial Justice of the United Church of Christ, preached the first sermon of the services being held that week. On that night, he also announced the decision of the 4th Circuit Court of Appeals that had just a few hours before he stood to preach overturned the Wilmington 10 verdict and had released his "son in the ministry," the Reverend Ben Chavis.

On Tuesday night, Reverend McKinley Young brought his choir and congregation for the Services of Dedication. Reverend Young was the Pastor of the Ebenezer African Methodist Episcopal Church in Evanston. He is now a Bishop in the A.M.E. church.

On Wednesday night, Reverend Clay Evans, his choir and the officers and members of the Fellowship Baptist Church came and led us in worship as we dedicated the new facility. On Thursday night, Bishop Louis H. Ford and the St. Paul Church of God in Christ came to lead us in worship during the Services of Dedication. Bishop Ford brought all of his ministers in his jurisdiction with him and publicly demanded that each of them give him $100.00 to help us pay for that new facility! They all complied with the Bishop's directive.

On Friday night, Pastor Clarence H. Cobbs and the First Church of Deliverance Choir came. His sermon culminated a weeklong series of ecumenical services celebrating God's blessing the congregation of Trinity United Church of Christ with a new facility. Two important things were noted that night that impacted the ministry of our church and brought to a climax the end of the "formative and transformative" era.

Those two things were as follows: 1) What Dr. Cobbs said to me during his sermon that night; and 2) the question that was raised with me by the officers of the church that night concerning the absence of a denominational presence during the six-day celebration of the dedication of our new facility!

During Dr. Cobbs' sermon on Friday night, he stopped in the middle of his sermon and turned around to me and said to me, *"Boy, the Lord will give you as far as you can see! If all you see is right here at 95th and Parnell, then that is all the Lord will give you. If you can see beyond here, all of the way to 95th and Stony Island or even further, the Lord will give you that. The Lord will give you as far as you can see!"*

It was Reverend Cobbs' prophetic pronouncement to me in the midst of his sermon that became the basis for our Long Range Planning Ministry that came into being a few weeks after he preached that sermon. (Fred Nelson, Jr., the son of the famed organist for the First Church of Deliverance, Fred Nelson, Sr., who served that church for over forty years, wrote a song based on what Pastor Cobbs said to me that night. The title of the song is, "The Lord Will Give You As Far As You Can See.")

Much more will be said about Pastor Cobbs' prophetic statement and the way in which our church members took that statement, took that challenge and took those concerns to God in the next chapter. For now, what is important is the other matter which pertained to our Dedication Week.

The Chicago Metropolitan Association of the Illinois Conference of the United Church of Christ was not represented at our Dedication Services in any of the six gatherings of the congregation. They sent no representative to congratulate us. They sent no staff person to celebrate along with us. They were silent as one of the two still existing new church starts from the 1960s (There were four new church starts that were tried by the denomination in that decade.) not only continued to grow, but was building a brand new sanctuary! Trinity United Church of Christ was the only Black new church start that the denomination tried in the 1960s. The officers of the church asked me why our denomination had not recognized our tremendous achievement.

I had no answer for their question, but I told them I would ask the Association and the Illinois Conference why there had been no denominational representation. At the time, our Conference Minister, Dr. W. Sterling Cary, became a member of the church. He pointed out that he had been at the Sunday worship services for the dedication of our new facility and that he had been at the service when Dr. Charles Cobb from the Commission for Racial Justice spoke.

He was there, however, as a member and as a friend of Charles Cobb. He was not there "officially" as the Conference Minister. He, too, wondered why the Chicago Metropolitan Association had not acknowledged what God had done for us, through us and with us; and in response to the formal letter that we wrote to the Association and to the Conference, Dr. Cary said he would take the matter up with me and the Association Minister when we gathered for the Conference Council Meeting in February of 1979.

Yes! Among my many denominational posts outside of Trinity I sat on the Conference Council of the Illinois Conference of the United Church of Christ. That was in addition to my being the Vice Chairperson of the Commission for Racial Justice, my being the National Vice Chairperson of the Black Clergy Caucus and my being the local Vice President of the same caucus; my position as Secretary of the Board of Directors of the Office for Church in Society; and my sitting on the Board of Services Committee of the Chicago Metropolitan Association of the Illinois Conference of the United Church of Christ!

Sam Allen and I went to the Conference Council Meeting in February of 1979 and at the end of the meeting Dr. Cary took me and the Association Minister into his office. Sam Allen waited outside Dr. Cary's office. Dr. Cary started the dialogue in his office by asking the Association Minister why no one from the Association had attended our Dedication Services - - all six services!

He pointed out that Trinity Church was not only one of our new church starts in the 1960s and that no new church starts had been attempted by the Illinois Conference of the United Church of Christ since the 1960s with the exception of those "crossover" churches that were a part of the Churches in Transition Program of the Community Renewal Society. He pointed out that Trinity Church had grown to become the largest church in the Chicago Metropolitan Association and in the Illinois Conference; and was rapidly heading toward becoming the largest church in the denomination.

He reiterated points raised in the official letter from the church that the officers of the church were concerned that no representation from Chicago Metropolitan Association had been forthcoming to acknowledge God's tremendous blessing in the construction of our new facility. Then he asked the Association Minister to respond to the letter from the congregation.

The Association Minister said, "*Well, Sterling, Jerry has formed a cult out there on 95th Street; and he has a big ego. Unless his ego is being stroked he is not happy. That is my read on why you got the letter and why I got the letter. That is also why I have not responded to that letter.*"

I sat there and listened to the rest of his ramblings, but I was acutely aware of the fact that he was calling us "a cult" two months after the Jim Jones incident in Guyana. During the same month that we dedicated our new facility, what was all over the news media was the mass suicide that took place in Guyana when Jim Jones' cult members drank Kool-Aid that was laced with poison. I could not believe my ears. Here was our Association Minister calling Trinity United Church of Christ a "cult."

I would be less than honest if I said I did not "lose it!" I waited for him to finish and then when Dr. Cary asked me how I responded, I pointed out to the Association Minister that he had no idea what Trinity United Church of Christ was like in February of 1979. He had only been to our church three times in seven years. He was there when I was installed in 1972.

He was there when Reverend Barbara Allen was commissioned as a Commission Minister in the United Church of Christ and he was there when we broke ground for the new building in 1977. Since he had not been there but three times in seven years, I said to him that all he had to go on in terms of forming his perceptions of our church was the complaints of the "Exodus 22" folk. (Those are the twenty-two people who made their exodus during the first eighteen months of my ministry.)

Many of the twenty-two folk who left our congregation did not leave quietly. They left complaining. They went running to "massa" to tell a white man what they thought was happening to their Negro church. Reverend Smith had told me that as he tried to calm me down about the twenty-two leaving who would never let me be their pastor.

I told the Association minister that he was used to Black churches where the worship was not Black. He was used to bourgeois

Negroes who wanted to be white. He was glad that the 1960s were over and that the era of confrontation had passed (so he thought); but what he did not realize was that a whole new breed of African American Christians had come out of the '60s who were, as Reuben Sheares defined them, "Unashamedly Black and Unapologetically Christian."

When I say "I lost it," however, I mean I *really* lost it! I then jumped up and said I am one of those new Blacks who was shaped by the '60s, a new Black who is not ashamed of his Blackness and I then said to him, "I will whip your butt right here in the Conference Minister's office for daring to insult our congregation in this manner." (I believe my language might have been a little stronger than that.)

Sam Allen heard me "going off" in Dr. Cary's office. He rushed into the office and grabbed me. He bodily (literally) carried me out of the office and told me that the insult had been against him and other members of the congregation, and that they would take care of the matter. He asked me to back down and let the members who had been insulted by that name-calling take over the fight for me.

The Executive Council of the congregation demanded a meeting with the Executive Council of the Chicago Metropolitan Association. The Association sent an investigatory team to talk with members of our church and the members of our church asked me not to be present at the meeting.

Mildred Chapman, Dr. Sokoni Karanja, Dr. Ayana Karanja, Dr. Carol Wooley, Reverend Barbara Allen, Sam Allen, Blaine DeNye and others met with the white members of the Chicago Metropolitan Association who came to investigate "the problem." They were completely blown away with African Americans who had earned PhD's from Northwestern, from Loyola and from Brandeis, who confronted them along with "ordinary Black folk," all of whom were on the same page and were not buying into the class distinctions and societal understandings of E. Franklin Frazier's **Black Bourgeoisie**!

One of the PhD's from Northwestern University said to that committee that she not only loved the worship services at Trinity, she came to get her soul fed at Trinity. Her PhD had nothing to do with her spiritual life, except for the fact that she was hearing sermons that made sense for Black people in the 1970s and hearing sermons that fed her soul at the same time! The committee members sent by the Chicago Metropolitan Association stayed bright red throughout the testimony and the lecture that was given to them by our members. The Association Minister was found guilty of a gross and egregious insult to the congregation of Trinity United Church of Christ.

When the Executive Council of the Chicago Metropolitan Association of the Illinois Conference of the United Church of Christ rendered its verdict on the inappropriate behavior of the Association Minister, the Conference Minister (our member) called me. Dr. Cary pointed out that he had been placed in an awkward position. He was a member of the church that had been offended. He was the first Black Conference Minister in the history of the United Church of Christ. For him to fire a white Association Minister because of an insult to the congregation where he was a member would make it look like a "set-up."

The best he could do would be a reprimand of the Association Minister and issue a directive that the Association Minister apologize to the congregation. He asked me if we wanted the apology during our Sunday worship services or if we wanted the apology in writing.

I told him to have the Association Minister put the apology in writing. Once we got his "official" written apology we read it at all three of our Sunday morning services and then we put it in the glass bulletin board and left it on display for a full year, so that new members could see how the Association Minister publicly apologized for mischaracterizing, misjudging and disrespecting our congregation.

If you will notice in the above paragraph I said, "*Our three Sunday morning services.*" In the "formative and transformative years," our church continued to grow by leaps and bounds. On the first Sunday we walked into our new sanctuary, we had to have chairs put down in each of the aisles! The new sanctuary was designed to seat 900 people. We had four rows of chairs in three aisles that would provide us seats for an additional 100 people.

We had folding chairs in the pulpit to accommodate the growing crowds and that still was not enough. Within a few months after we moved into the new sanctuary, we moved to having two Sunday morning services. Shortly after that, we moved to having three Sunday morning services!

By the end of 1979 and in the opening years of 1980, a group of members (led by Reverend Barbara Allen's brother, James Salome, and Reverend Allen's high school classmate, Joyce Davis) held an offsite fundraiser to get monies to give to the church to enable the church to purchase a "Playboy television screen." That screen was put up in the carpeted section of Wright Hall and an additional 100 chairs were used every Sunday at the first two services to accommodate the growing congregation.

It was not long, however, before members began standing in the aisles of the sanctuary for all three services! People had given up on even trying to find a seat in the sanctuary. They claimed their special spot "on the wall" each Sunday.

They became just as territorial about their spots on the wall as some members are about their seats in the sanctuary!

Two of the officers of our church proposed marriage to their fiancées during one Watch Meeting Service while standing on the wall! When the worshippers went down on their knees at five minutes to twelve, after the prayer had ended, praying out the old year and praying in the New Year, Bert Allen and Anthony McKinney slipped engagement rings on their fiancées' fingers asking them to be their mates for life!

My health (and my growing older) would not permit me to continue the hectic and insane pace of three Sunday morning services. My doctor suggested to me that I needed to push that third service back to the evening to give my body, my throat, my voice and my respiratory organs a rest between the eleven o'clock service and the final service of the day.

We then moved from having services at seven-thirty in the morning, nine o'clock in the morning and eleven-thirty in the morning to having them at seven-thirty in the morning, eleven o'clock in the morning and six o'clock on Sunday evenings. Because 2nd Chronicles **7:14** says, "*If my people who are called by my name will humble themselves and pray…*," we started our first service on Sunday morning, just as we started our midweek Prayer Service on Wednesday evening, at **7:14!**

At 7:14 the first prayer would be prayed on Sunday mornings and on Wednesday evenings. The next fifteen minutes on

Sunday mornings would be devoted to the deacon devotions (back in the 1980s) and then to Praise and Worship when "Praise Teams" became the latest addition to the liturgy in the African American church across denominational lines. It was also in those "formative and transformative" years that our dance ministry was started.

Ayoka Goodman and Jewel McLaurin introduced sacred dance as a part of our *Umoja Karamu* services that started in 1975. They expanded the dance ministry to include sacred dance at more than the *Umoja Karamu* services.

Their vision, their foresight and their powerful interpretations have led our dance ministry to the place where there are now five separate dance ministries ministering every Sunday of the year, with the exception of most Communion Sundays.

No mention of the dance ministry of Trinity United Church of Christ would be complete in this "Sankofa moment" without lifting up the name of Anthony Hollins. Anthony Hollins built on the foundation that was laid by Ayoka Goodman, Jewel McLaurin and Deborah Merchant. Anthony's love for the Lord, Anthony's love for liturgical dance, Anthony's understanding of the African concept of bodily expressions of praise became invaluable in building and strengthening our dance ministry at Trinity Church.

Anthony Hollins argued continuously for the importance of and the centrality of sacred dance as a part of the worship services. Anthony even wanted me to put a Minister of Dance on my pastoral staff! He felt that the ministry of dance was just as vital to worship as the ministry of music! Anthony was subsequently called into the Gospel of Ministry. Anthony acted on his Call by attending and graduating from Chicago Theological Seminary with a Master of Divinity degree!

Anthony worked tirelessly with the Samuel DeWitt Proctor Pastor's Conference, our church's HIV/AIDS ministry and our dance ministries until he was called home unexpectedly during the Christmas season of 2007! He was not called home, however, before he implanted firmly in the minds of the members of our congregation the importance of sacred dance and the necessity for dance in the multiple services that we were having every Sunday at our church.

Anthony even convinced several couples to include sacred dance in their wedding ceremonies. Anthony also brought the sacrality of dance to the Services of Homegoing for several members of the congregation. Dancing for joy in honor of our member's soul having begun an internal dance with God was a powerful statement that was added to the Memorial Services of Worship when different members of the congregation died and their families knew the importance of dance which had been underscored by Anthony Hollins' teaching.

The multiple worship services we were forced to commence because of our growing congregation, moreover, changed the configuration of the music department also. The music department was transformed! When we started multiple services, the Sanctuary Choir sang for all of the services. Having to sing three times on a Sunday morning (and then later having to come back for a Sunday evening service) put a tremendous strain on our choir members.

Our choir members included single parents. Our choir members included married parents. Our choir members included persons who had to make arrangements for their children and in some cases for their parents to have caregivers because they were tied up from seven o'clock in the morning until two and three in the afternoon. With the adding of an evening service that meant that they were tied up all day on Sunday!

It was at that point that I asked Mr. Radford to transition our Men's Chorus, our Women's Chorus and our Teenage Choir which had been reformulated under the name *Imani Ya Watume* and to have those choirs sing not just on Men's Day and during Men's Week, not just on Women's Day and during Women's Week and not just on the four Youth Sundays a year, but to have them sing at one of our multiple services every month of the year!

Prior to the multiple service operation at our church, the Men's Chorus had only sung on Men's Day. Beginning in 1979, we moved from Men's Day to Men's Week and the men would then sing six times for the year. The same was true with our Women's Chorus. It started as a Women's Day Chorus and expanded to a Women's Day/Women's Week Chorus. Our multiple services were demanding a different kind of commitment on the part of choir members.

Mr. Radford then started having the Sanctuary Choir sing at the 11:00 a.m. service every Sunday. They would also sing at the first service on Communion Sundays. He asked the teenagers and the Little Warriors for Christ to sing at the early services every second Sunday.

He then asked the Women's Chorus to sing at the early service on the third Sunday and to sing on Communion Sunday in the evening. When there were five Sundays in a month, the Women's Chorus would also serve at the second service on the last Sunday of that month.

The Men's Chorus sang on fourth Sunday mornings and on third Sunday evenings. Having a split singing (ministry) schedule like that enabled people to participate in the ministry of music without having their entire day tied up while being in the Lord's house and engaging in the ministry of music, to bless the people of God in the House of God Sunday after Sunday.

Also during our "formative and transformative" years, Judy Speller, who had not yet become Dr. Julia Speller started our Youth Church. Judy said that we needed a place for toddlers to be during the worship services. Before we built the 532 expansion in 1978, Judy would hold Youth Church in the basement of the small building where our sanctuary seated 200 persons.

Youth Church was designed for youngsters who were potty-trained, up to the age of eight. That vital ministry continues today with Youth Church being held during both services on Sunday morning and with volunteers supplying the Youth Church for our Sunday evening "Hour of Power" services.

When Pastor Moss started at our church, he and his wife introduced the notion of a nursery, so that children who are not yet at the Youth Church age could have a place to be on Sunday mornings. It was and is a combination "cry room" and nursery with a flat screen television, so that either the parents of infants and toddlers too young for Youth Church (the parents or the caregivers) could watch services while the infants and toddlers had a place to be in the House of God.

In the "formative and transformative years," Judy used her own materials for the children. She designed their worship services, so that they could learn the basic elements of worship while enjoying being children!

Judy also used Reverend Allen's curriculum for teaching Christian education from the Black perspective to make sure that our Youth Church children learned who they were as Christians, who they were as African American Christians and whose they were as children of the Most High God!

Two of the many other important ministries that were started during the "formative and transformative years" were the Federally-Chartered Credit Union of Trinity United Church of Christ and the "Food Co-op" Ministry. Before we had a Long Range Planning Ministry, the Church-in-Society Committee, the Men's Fellowship, the Executive Council and the leadership of the church thought that we should have our own Credit Union.

After investigating which route to take—whether a State-Chartered Credit Union or a Federally-Chartered Credit Union—it was decided that the Federal Credit Union offered advantages that a State Credit Union did not offer. The investigatory work was done. The necessary papers were filed and our Credit Union opened its doors for business in 1977.

As of this writing the Credit Union has in excess of three million dollars in assets. As of this writing our Credit Union has been asked to take over another church's failing Credit Union and put it back in fiscally-sound standing with the federal government. Our Credit Union has successfully done just that! As of this writing we still do not have ten percent of our membership who save in their own church's credit union, however. The lack of participation by the members of the congregation has always been problematic for me.

The principle that my parents taught my sister and me about tithing included the principle of saving! When they would give us our fifty-cents allowance as children they told us that the first nickel belonged to God. That was not even ours, so we should not cast our eyes on it with any designs for it! They then took the second nickel back from us and said that was for our savings account. They explained to us that after we paid God first, we needed to pay ourselves second.

We then had forty cents to spend for the week. We could spend it all in one day. We could spend a dime a day for four days. We could spend a nickel a day for seven days and have another nickel left over at the end of the week, but there was no more money forthcoming for an entire week.

They took our weekly nickels and watched us fill out our tithing envelopes. They took our second "weekly nickels" and opened up passbook savings accounts for us. We got the biggest kick out of seeing our interest entered into those passbooks in red each quarter! It is that principle that every African American child (and adult) needs to follow—especially those who are members of the household of faith.

If we tithe to God first and then tithe our earnings to our savings account each week, we would not be in the position financially that many of us are in today!

Watching our members give in excess of ten million dollars a year in tithes and then watching the Credit Union's receipts grow in the neighborhood of $100,000 a year has been painful for me. If our members saved one-tenth of their earnings in their own church's Credit Union, we would have been averaging a ten million dollar a year increase in assets in our Federally-Chartered Credit Union. That was not the case, however, and that is not the case.

Where many people, therefore, are in amazement and awe at the phenomenal work that the Credit Union has done and congratulate us on being a Black church-owned Credit Union that has in excess of three million dollars in assets, I keep saying to myself, *"That is pitiful!"* I know what is possible, but I see what we are not doing and that hurts. Just trying to encourage church members to open up a savings account in their own church's Credit Union has been an uphill battle. It is the only financial battle that I have found more difficult than teaching the principle of tithing!

Our congregation has had to bury members who had no insurance. (They did not save!) Our congregation has had instance after instance where people could not pay their rent, could not pay their car notes, could not pay their water bills, their light bills or their heat bills. (They did not save!)

When we started our Endowment Fund in 1977, we had an insurance company make available to us a term life insurance policy with no physical examination! We told the members of our congregation, however, that we would not let them open an account making the church a beneficiary of that insurance policy (to build up our endowment) if they had no personal insurance on themselves for their families to take care of the expenses for their funerals when they died. We were overwhelmed at the large number of members who had no insurance on their lives in the formative years! I am still in amazement at the large number of folks who have no insurance on their lives in the 21st century!

In addition to our Federally-Chartered Credit Union, the Men's Fellowship came up with another tremendous idea. That idea was built upon and expanded once we got a Long Range Planning Ministry, but it was in place before we got that ministry. The men of the church would take weekly grocery orders from the members of the church. The men of the church would get up early on the day that the farmers came into the city of Chicago. They would drive down to the markets where the farmers came and they would buy the fresh fruit and produce directly from the farmers, cutting out the middle man (like A&P, Jewel, Dominick's, etc.,) and save the members from fifty to seventy-five percent of what they would have paid had they gone to the grocery stores in their communities!

As the Food Ministry and "Food Coop" concept grew, the grocery list moved beyond fresh fruit and produce to include meats and dairy products. That service was provided weekly until we got a Long Range Planning Ministry and the Long Range Planning Ministry began to look into a full-blown food coop like the Hyde Park Food Coop. More will be said about that effort in the next chapter.

Reverend Barbara Allen instituted during the "formative and transformative years" what is known today as the "Food Share Ministry." On Thanksgiving Day, as we celebrated *Umoja Karamu*, Reverend Allen thought it was absolutely ridiculous for us to celebrate our pilgrimage as Africans in this country, lifting up the way over which God had brought us from the days in Africa before chattel slavery up to and into the 20th and 21st century where we now had Black elected officials, while ignoring the hungry who were right in our midst.

She said that she did not understand how anybody could in good conscience reflect over the way that God had brought us during that *Umoja Karamu* service and then go home to be with family and friends and eat a scrumptious meal while ignoring the hungry who were at our doorsteps!

It was from her vision that we started asking members to bring non-perishable food items to the church during the weeks leading up to Thanksgiving in order that we might put together Thanksgiving baskets to feed the hungry, the needy and the less fortunate. That simple, yet profound, effort back in the mid-'70s has grown to the place where the congregation gives in excess of 2,000 baskets to the less fortunate every Thanksgiving Day.

Jean Davis-Cook and her husband El, raised with us many years later (in the 1990s) the same disparity when it came to celebrating Christmas. We would have our Sunrise Christmas Service and then we would go home to enjoy Christmas Day and a Christmas meal with our families while there were single mothers, abused women and orphaned children who would know no Christmas each year. That is when the Cook Family started organizing busloads of residents of women's shelters to be brought to Trinity Church on Christmas Day and to have all of their children given toys and gifts (clothes and blankets for the cold weather).

Somewhere between Reverend Barbara Allen's Operation Share and Jean and El Davis' Christmas Day benevolence, one of the members raised the question, "*What about the other 363 days of the year?*" Addressing the issues of hunger meant far more than participating in our denomination's Hunger Project. It meant more than being active members of Bread for the World.

It also meant more than having a few dollars available and a few food coupons available to help the hungry who walked in off of the street from time-to-time.

What evolved from that question was our Food Share Ministry, which feeds the hungry 365 days a year through the gifts, the tithes and the offerings of Trinity United Church of Christ.

During the "formative and transformative years" we not only saw our first women ushers. We also ordained our first woman in ministry and our first women deacons! Most African American Christians do not know that there is no such word as "deaconess" in the Bible. That word is not in the New Testament which was written in Greek. The decision to use that word was made by male translators in the 17th century in order to "keep women in their place."

Most African American Christians do not know that there were women deacons in the first century. They do not know that Phoebe is called by the Apostle Paul a deacon who serves the Lord and serves the Lord's church just as he served the Lord and served the Lord's church. Most African American Christians also do not know that there were women apostles in the first century! Junia was an apostle whose name is given who was on the battlefield for the Lord before Paul was converted!

Most African American Christians do not know that there were women pastors in the first century. Particularly was this practice widespread when the church used to meet in houses and not in sanctuaries, synagogues or temples.

Most African American Christians do not know that the Baptist church was ordaining women as deacons back in the 1700s! The idea of a woman deacon, therefore, was as alien to the members of Trinity United Church of Christ in the mid-'70s as was the notion of a woman usher!

Through patient teaching and Bible Study, however, the stereotypes were destroyed, the perceptions were clarified and women became full-fledged ordained deacons walking alongside the male deacons of our congregation during the "formative and transformative years" of the congregation while it struggled to make a living reality the professed desire (in 1971) to go in a different direction.

With the dedication of the new facility at 532 West 95th Street, there came another "seismic shift" in the life of our congregation. The question for many of the members and officers became, *"What do we do now?"* We have this new building up. The new building is already too small. What do we do now?

We had been working for four years trying to get a new sanctuary. We had been sacrificing. We had been giving. Our numbers had been growing. Our ministries had been growing; but what do we do now as a congregation? How do we see ourselves? How does God see us? How does God want to use us? It was then that we moved into an era of ministry that I call "Casting the Vision."

Chapter 3
Write the Vision!

*I*n the second Chapter of the Book of Habakkuk, the prophet says:

> *Then the Lord answered me and said:*
> *Write the Vision;*
>   *make it plain on tablets,*
>   *so that a runner may read it.*
> *For there is still a vision for the appointed time;*
>   *it speaks of the end, and does not lie.*
> *If it seems to tarry, wait for it;*
>   *it will surely come, it will not delay.*

The prophet is told by God to write the vision that God gives him. Throughout the Book of Amos, God asks Amos, "*Amos, what do you see?*" God asks those who are in a covenantal relationship with Him not only to say to Him and explain to Him what it is they see. God also asks them to spell out, to say to God's people, to "make it plain" what God has shown those who are in that relationship.

Reverend Clarence Cobbs interrupted his Sermon of Dedication on the last night of our church's celebration to turn around to me and say, "*The Lord will give you as far as you can **see**, Jeremiah!*" Those words of Scripture and the words of Pastor Cobbs became the controlling images that shaped the next decade of Trinity's life.

One month after our new facility was dedicated I called the building committee together for a spiritual retreat. We met at a hotel in Oak Lawn, Illinois. On Friday night we relaxed, laughed, reflected and remembered the journey that we had been on as a building committee since 1975.

We talked about the selection process in our choosing Wendell Campbell as our architect. We talked about the difference between this contractor (C.F. Moore) and the contractor who had built our first Sanctuary in 1966. We reminisced about the members of the committee who had died since 1975. We shed tears of sadness and we shed tears of joy.

We thanked God for the way over which God had brought us for four years. The Friday night session of the Retreat was a session of relaxation and celebration.

On Saturday morning, I changed the mood of the retreat from relaxation and celebration to rededication. After a thirty-minute Devotion at nine o'clock focusing in on rededication and the Scripture passages where God asks the people of faith to articulate the vision that God gives and then to write it down, I made the following assignment. I asked the members of the building committee to separate for the next two hours.

I reminded them of what Reverend Clarence H. Cobbs had said to me on the last night of our Services of Dedication. I said to them, "*Reverend Cobbs said to me the Lord would give me as far* *as I could **see**. I say to you as you talk with God over the next two hours that Pastor Cobbs was right.*

"The Lord will give us as far as we can see! If all we can see is 95th and Parnell where we have just finished building a new Sanctuary, then that is all God will give us. If we can see much further than 95th and Parnell, God will give us the vision that God shows us!"

I asked them to take the 8 ½ x 11 memo pads that I was giving them, to take their Bibles and to go off silently and separately to different places in the hotel for the next two hours.

There were three sets of husbands and wives on the committee and I had the wives go back to the hotel rooms they had slept in on Friday night while the husbands were asked to find a quiet place in the hotel, a reading room, a corner of the Retreat Room or a lounge, so that they could be away from their wives.

I asked them not to talk to each other as husband and wife and not to talk to anybody on the committee or in the hotel, for that matter, for the next two hours. I asked them to be silent before the Lord and talk only to Him for two hours.

I asked them to take their Scriptures with them and to enter into a two-hour season of prayer, where they asked God for God's vision for their church for the next two decades. I told them to ask God, *"What next?"*

I told them to ask God, *"What do You want for Your church in the next five years? What do You want Your church to be doing ten years from now? What do You want Your church to be doing fifteen years from now… Twenty years from now?"*

I explained to them that there were no right answers or wrong answers. I asked them to write down on their tablets whatever it was they heard or thought they heard and to join me back in the retreat room at eleven-thirty in the morning. The members of the building committee pulled off by themselves and entered into their "conversations with God."

At 11:30 a.m. we gathered back in the retreat room and I put newsprint up all around the room—one piece of newsprint for each member of the Committee. I asked them for the next half-hour just to call out whatever it was they had heard from God that was on their sheets, so that I could write it down on the newsprint.

For thirty minutes the committee read off their lists to me (and to each other) adding editorial comments on what it was they heard God saying as the vision for a particular ministry of their church. There were a total of over forty different things that the members of the committee heard.

What was most awe-inspiring and phenomenal, however, was that twenty-seven of those forty items were heard by everybody on the committee. Each committee member heard God say the same thing twenty-seven times! For twenty-seven times God's vision came through clearly to the people of God and so they wrote the vision down on paper!

During the afternoon of the retreat, we began to prioritize those twenty-seven items that were all the same. We categorized them under the headings of short-term and midrange term items; midrange term and long-term visions. Some of the things they heard and some of the things they saw were things that could happen within a year. Other things would take five years. Still other things would take ten years and some would take twenty years and even longer.

The retreat ended on a high spiritual note, but the work that God had placed before us was just beginning! I came back to the congregation and during the Annual Meeting of the Congregation at the end of January 1979, I shared with the congregation the vision that God had given at that retreat.

I shared with them the vision that had been written down like God told the Prophet Habakkuk to write it down. I shared with them the vision that God had given in response to the question asked of Amos, "*What do you see?*" I reminded the congregation that God would give us as far as we could see.

The congregation overwhelmingly voted to form a Long Range Planning Committee. They wanted those who had "seen the vision" to continue to work together in implementing what it was that God had shown and that is how our Long Range Planning Committee began.

Within a matter of months, the committee was hard at work dividing these tasks up, so that some persons were working on short-range goals. Some persons were working on midrange goals and some persons began the hard, tedious and unrewarding tasks of working on long-range goals!

Within a year the congregation voted that the Long Range Planning Committee become an official Board of the church. The word "committee" was dropped and the body became the Board for Long Range Planning. A By-law amendment was proposed and the duties and tasks of the Board for Long Range Planning were spelled out. We began to concretize the vision that God had given and we began to shape our ministry around what it was that God said God wanted God's church to be doing.

Space does not permit me to talk extensively or exhaustively about the work of the Board for Long Range Planning, but I need to share with you at least three of the tasks that were tackled and the successes and failures that we experienced both as a Board and as a congregation in trying to make the vision a reality. One sub-committee of the Board for Long Range Planning began working on the school. All of the members of the Board for Long Range Planning had heard God say, "*An African-centered Christian school.*"

We began the long and tedious task of putting together all of the components of starting a school that was African-centered and Christian. We did not want a "cookie-cutter" school like the Jerry Falwell schools that were sweeping the country. We did not want a "conservative right wing Christian" school that taught Scripture by rote and turned children into judgmental, narrow, conservative bigots.

We wanted a school that would prepare our students academically to stand shoulder-to-shoulder with students from Whitney Young, students from North Side Prep and students from anywhere in terms of their ability to achieve and score highly on the ACT and SAT exams.

We also wanted a school that taught our children the principles of the Christian faith (stripped away from the racist underpinnings of "Americanity" and the hierarchical lies enforced by the Transatlantic Slave Trade). We wanted our children to know the African origins of their faith and the African heroes and heroines of their faith both on the Continent and in the Diaspora.

We had sitting on the school committee (and sub-committee) persons with proven track records as excellent educators. We had Blaine DeNye who had taken the Manley School from a middle school up to a high school. We had Dr. Dorothy Bryant and we had Dr. Manford Byrd on the sub-committee. We had people who knew education and the "system" of the Chicago Public Schools inside out.

That committee or sub-committee wrestled with issues such as: do we begin as an elementary school and work our way up through the 12th grade, adding one grade a year? Or, do we start as a high school and work down through the middle school years to the primary education years? We already had a successful childcare program in place.

Our childcare program not only had the benefit of having as its Executive Director Mrs. Margie Parent, whose excellent administrative abilities caused our childcare program not only to get high ratings and rankings from the Department of Children and Family Services each year. The Mayor's Office of Childcare even asked Mrs. Parent if she would take over a failing childcare program that was about to be lost to the 67th and Stony Island community. Mrs. Parent took over the Deton Brooks Center and that Center became a part of the Trinity United Church of Christ Childcare Programs.

It was the sub-committee on education's thinking that with an excellent childcare program we needed to start our school at the kindergarten level or the first grade level, so that the children coming out of our childcare program could feed right into that school. The school committee had gotten all the way down to site selection in their planning when the congregation voted to build the 400 West 95th Street worship center. That pushed the plan for a new school to the back burner of the items on the agenda of the Board for Long Range Planning!

One of the aspects of the school planning was revolutionary in its approach to quality education. The members of the sub-committee on education wanted a topnotch school that would turn out topnotch scholars. They did not want any child, however, to be turned away from the school because of his or her zip code.

In other words, they did not want any child to be turned away from admission to the school because his or her parent(s) lived in the projects, was on welfare or could not afford the cost of a high-end magnet school or private school. We wanted a child to be admitted into the school on the basis of his or her ability to *learn,* not on the basis of his or her parent(s) ability to *pay*!

That kind of venture was going to cost money and it would cost money that would not be realized by tuition and tuition alone. In other words, the school needed a revenue stream that was not solely dependent upon the adults whose children were students at the school.

One of the long range plans that had to be put in place was retail and for-profit corporations that would be bring money into the corporation set-up to fund the school, so that we could pay for the school. That threw the education committee into close contact and constant dialogue with the sub-committees of the Board for Long Range Planning that were working on economic development and retail ventures for revenue streams to carry out various ministries that were given as a part of the vision for our congregation.

Two of the retail ventures the Board for Long Range Planning entered into were a food coop and a flower shop. We already had the success story of the modified coop program at work where the men would take the members' grocery lists and go meet the farmers once a week. What we now wanted to do was expand that modified program into a full-scale food coop like the Hyde Park Food Coop.

That sub-committee looked around for a building in which to house our grocery store and they found a grocery store on Cottage Grove Avenue that was owned by the Nation of Islam. The Nation of Islam was trying to sell their building and it was an ideal opportunity for us to capitalize on our dream.

At that time (1979) there was a United States National Consumer Coop Bank. We applied for a grant from the coop bank and we were going to use the monies from that grant to purchase the building and use those monies as "start-up" funds to move our modified weekly shopping with the farmers into a full-scale food coop.

We put a sizable amount of money down on the building as security to hold it for when the monies came through from the National Consumer Coop Bank.

In 1980, President Carter lost the election! In 1980, President Reagan came into office and did away with the country's National Consumer Coop Bank! Our grant application was then "null and void." The Muslims would not give us back our earnest money. The purchase of the supermarket on Cottage Grove fell through and we learned a painful lesson about "failure" in one of our long range plans.

Here is another painful lesson we learned. The economic development committee working on retail ventures reasoned that everybody buys flowers. People buy flowers for birthdays. People buy flowers for graduations. People buy flowers for Mother's Day. People even buy boutonnières for Father's Day!

People buy flowers and plants because they like growing them and caring for them. People buy flowers for funerals. What we needed, therefore, was a place for them to buy flowers. We needed to start a flower shop.

We purchased a building at 421 West 95th Street and renovated the first floor to house our flower shop. Offices and classroom space were on the second floor of the 421 Building. We even constructed storage spaces for our landscaping equipment and we opened up our floral and landscaping business.

What we did not take into account, however, was the hard business facts of (**a**) Black folks driving past a Black-owned flower shop to buy their flowers at white-owned flower shops; and (**b**) large chain stores like Jewel and Dominick's being able to sell their flowers at less than half (in some instances) the cost of what we were selling our products.

Philosophically, it is one thing to say we support our own businesses. Economically, however, people go where the cheapest prices are. For a concrete example of that truth just consider this: our denomination has been fighting and boycotting Wal-Mart and its unfair practices for a decade as of the writing of this book.

Our members, however, still go to Wal-Mart and Sam's Club because the prices are cheaper there. The flower shop and the landscaping business also taught us another lesson about "failure."

"Land banking" was another aspect of an industry and resource building that the Board for Long Range Planning engaged in its early days. It was a successful venture. One of our staff members, the Reverend Donald J. Fairley, was hired to work specifically for the Board for Long Range Planning, and one of his primary jobs was to be present and accounted for at every tax sale that the city of Chicago had.

Reverend Fairley would have the list of the tax properties in his hand and with Board recommendations, and recommendations from business persons in the church, he would go to those tax sales and bid on those lots that were up for sale because the taxes were in arrears.

The church acquired several pieces of property because of that strategy and we started learning what the taste of "success" was like in terms of our Board for Long Range Planning. Some of the properties that were purchased have been used by the church for its own purposes. Other properties have been sold across the years at a tremendous profit, proving that the initial purchase was a good investment for the economic health of the Board for Long Range Planning's plans and projects.

An additional item on the list of the members of the Board for Long Range Planning was quality senior housing. The need for senior housing was obvious. The need for low-income quality housing for our senior citizens was more than obvious. What we wanted as a congregation, however, was not just some concrete blocks and bricks and mortar thrown up as a place to put our elderly in when they were "put out to pasture."

What we wanted was a senior citizen housing facility into which we would proudly move our mothers and our fathers, and one in which we would not mind living ourselves! We wanted housing

that was secure, housing that was beautiful, housing that had all
of the amenities of the high-end condos that were found in the
center of the city, but housing at the same time that did not cost
an arm and a leg.

While the sub-committee on senior housing was busily doing its
work the providence of God kicked in one more time! The
Housing and Urban Development Department of the United
States Government started its HUD 202 Housing Program.
Government funds were made available for the construction of
senior citizen housing and our sub-committee on housing began
busily trying to get funding for one of the proposals that it
submitted to the government for HUD 202 facilities. Every
Notice of Funding Availability that came out, our sub-committee
on housing submitted an application.

Submitting the applications meant that the sponsoring
organization had to do several things. One of the things it had
to do was to obtain a state charter and start a new corporation
where an application was submitted in response to a
governmental Notice of Funding Availability (NOFA).

Another "must" in terms of the grant request was control of the
land on which the proposed senior citizen housing was to be
built. That meant that the sub-committee on housing had to
work with the land control sub-committee that was busily buying
up the taxes of vacant land and it meant trying to find a piece of
property over which we had control that we could use as the
address for the proposed housing when we submitted it to the
federal government.

Another aspect of the proposed senior housing project required
the signature, the "okay" and the blessing of the alderman (or
alderwoman) in whose ward the proposed property sat. That
seemingly simple task turned out to be "more than a notion."

One of the invaluable lessons learned in that process was that many of the aldermen wanted a minimum of $1,000 under the table before they would sign off on the church's proposal to build a senior citizen housing project in their ward.

Whether the proposal was granted or not, the alderman was getting $1,000 up front! That $1,000 was just for his or her signature on the proposal. There was no guarantee that the government would grant the proposal or that the housing would ever be built in that ward! These are the kinds of things that you learn "on the way to being a Pastor" of a Black church in the city of Chicago!

After being rejected several times by the federal government and rejected for proposals that we thought were excellent, Mr. DeNye and members of his sub-committee began an informal investigation. They began looking at the projects in the city of Chicago that did receive funding as opposed to and compared with the proposed projects that we submitted. What we discovered was absolutely mind-blowing!

We found out that the "good ole boys" system was alive, well and hard at work. We found that chicanery was at work. We found out that the $1,000 per aldermen in some wards was only the "tip of the iceberg!" We found out that the federal government through its HUD 202 program was also engaging in a monetary rip-off much bigger than the aldermen's take. We found the federal government in violation of its own policies!

After our fourth proposal was rejected (and it was an excellent proposal) we compared the projects that were awarded 202 monies in the city of Chicago with that NOFA and we found that HUD had violated federal guidelines. Their guidelines said that no project was to be funded if the sponsoring organization had not established a new corporation while submitting a proposal for that current NOFA! Two of the projects that were awarded that year had not started new corporations! There was no charter on record for them in Springfield, the capitol of Illinois.

Another HUD requirement stated that included in the filing of the charter for the newly proposed housing, an application for a 501-C3 exemption also had to be on file with the Internal Revenue Service. Three of the awardees in the city of Chicago had no such application with the IRS on file!

We also found out that one of the projects that had been funded was being sponsored by a church that was in default for its already-existing HUD project. HUD guidelines state clearly that no awards will be given to entities that are in default in any other HUD project. The government had violated its own rules because of its favoritism games while ignoring us in our attempt to build facilities in which we would proudly place our relatives!

We took the Federal Government to court!

We sued HUD and we went into Federal Court with all of the facts and all of the proof on our side. We went before a Reagan-appointed judge, however, and we lost! With all of the facts proving that we were right, with all of the facts proving that the United States Government was at best dishonest and at worse downright evil, with all of the facts showing us that HUD had violated its own guidelines, the Reagan-appointed Federal judge ruled against our claim!

Human fear, however, kicked in with Holy providence and once again we were blessed. On the very next day after our case was lost in Federal court, I got a call from a high school classmate of mine whom I had not seen since 1959! He worked for the

Department of Housing Urban Development in its national office and he called me to ask me what we had done to scare the Chicago HUD office so badly?

I told him that we had taken HUD to court. I told him about the court case and I told him about the judge's decision. He said to me that he was calling me to give me a heads up.

We might have lost the court case, he said, but we had won the battle. We had scared HUD so badly that they had received a directive "from the top" saying that they should fund Trinity United Church of Christ on its next submission no matter how badly written the proposal was or no matter what it lacked in terms of HUD guidelines. They were told to fix the proposal if it needed fixing and to make sure that we got funding before we took our lawsuit to the Appellate Court.

He said that HUD realized we were right and to "buy us off" they (the staff) were given a directive to make sure our very next proposal got funding. Needless to say, on our very next submission we were granted an award and Trinity Acres was built.

The Board for Long Range Planning realized that the success of the Trinity Acres Housing Program would depend on its having excellent management. One of the things we learned about housing and the due diligence done by the housing sub-committee of the Board for Long Range Planning was that the key to success was competent and excellent management.

The Board then took the bold step of asking Mrs. Margie Parent who had been an excellent manager with our childcare programs to leave that program and to become the manager of the Trinity

Acres Housing Program. That decision can also be categorized under the heading of "God's providence."

Mrs. Parent has not only been an excellent manager of that program; Mrs. Parent has not only received commendation after commendation from the federal government and never had any of her reports questioned or her management evaluations less than perfect; Mrs. Parent has also been the manager of our second senior citizen housing complex, the Trinity Oaks!

Because we wrote the vision down, because we made it plain and because we knew what it would take for that vision to become a reality, two excellently appointed senior citizens housing facilities are now up, operating and succeeding because of God's grace.

Just so you will have a better glimpse of the hard work done by the members of this congregation and the putting into practice the principles upon which we stand, you need to know something about the construction of and the operation and maintenance of those two senior citizen housing facilities.

When HUD says "yes" to a proposal, it is truly a "barebones" project as far as architects and contractors are concerned. The profit for them in such projects as set by federal guidelines is truly a minimum. Most contractors and most architects back in the 1980s were running away from HUD projects because there was no real profit to be made in those ventures.

In order to close the gap between what the Federal Government gave for such a project and what our Long Range Planning Ministry envisioned in building housing for our parents and for ourselves, that required creative thinking and a substantial financial commitment on the part of the church. When HUD only provides money for one color of paint in a building that has seven floors, any additional monies for painting each of the halls on the different floors different colors to help seniors remember more easily which floor they are on, the church has to provide the money for those different colors of paint.

In order for the buildings to be secure with electronic monitoring, TV cameras and twenty-four hour security guards, the church has to provide the money for that. HUD makes no such provisions in their 202 Housing budgets.

In order to transport the seniors safely to and from the grocery store, safely to and from the banks, safely to and from the places where they can cash their social security checks and safely to and from the churches of their choices, the church has to bear the cost of the van and insure that the driver retained to transport the elders has a license that the State of Illinois has granted for driving that category of vehicle. The church also has to pay the insurance for the van.

HUD does not pay for those kinds of costs. (The safe passage for the elders is of crucial importance because of the location of the two senior citizen housing facilities. For readers outside the city of Chicago of this work, our two senior citizen facilities are located in the "heart of the ghetto." For Chicagoans those addresses are 39th and Calumet and 63rd and Drexel!)

How to pay for those "frills" and how to pay for quality education in our childcare programs—which again, is over and above what the federal government allows in its Title 20 Program for reimbursement—the Board for Long Range Planning had to do two things and still has these two things on its ongoing operations. First, it has to come up with monies in the church budget to close the gap between what the federal government offers and what Trinity United Church of Christ is providing.

Then it has to come up with retail ideas in terms of creating a revenue stream that will pay for these quality items and take the pressure off of the church's annual budget and the costs that are being covered by the tithes and offerings of the members. The Economic Development Committee of the Long Range Planning Ministry is still wrestling with this ongoing challenge.

Midway through the decade of the eighties, our numerical growth continued at a phenomenal pace. Once we went on the radio station, the number of new members who joined the church each year exceeded 325 a year and climbed as high as 1,000 members per year! Our going on the radio, however, is not as simple as reading that sentence. Determined to live by the principles of our **Black Value System**, we wanted to keep the monies from the tithes and offerings of African American Christians in the African American community by doing business with African American business persons! We did not just want to be "on the radio." We wanted to be on a Black-owned radio station.

We started off our radio broadcast with one of the white-owned stations—a station owned by Percy Crawford's family. The racism in the broadcast industry (and in all of the media) was laid bare early in the 1980s, however, when I received a letter from the Crawford Broadcasting Company telling us that we had to give up the time that we were currently on their station because it was "white time!" Can you believe that?

In the 1980s, a Christian broadcasting station had certain hours of the day that they considered hours that were set aside for white churches. Those were the primetime hours or the hours during which people would normally be at church. They pushed Black churches broadcasting on their stations to early in the morning hours or late in the evening hours and they thought they could do that with us.

The Crawford Broadcasting Corporation did not know that I was a member of the Commission for Racial Justice of the United Church of Christ. They thought we were just your average "garden-variety" Black church on the Southside of Chicago. Through my work with the Commission for Racial Justice I found out how to deal with racist radio stations. Our denomination had challenged the license of a racist station in Mississippi, and had not only put that station out of existence, but had gained control of the license and was now broadcasting an inclusive message in the state of Mississippi!

When I wrote the Crawford Company back and threatened to challenge their license on the basis of the racist policies they were practicing (and I had the letter in their own words as proof in my hand), they sent a representative to us to offer us one full year free if we would not sue them. While we were enjoying that "free year," however, I was busily pursuing getting our church services broadcast over WJPC. WJPC was the broadcasting station owned by the Johnson Publication Company.

Charles Mootry told me that Mr. Johnson was having a big problem with putting me on his station, however, because all he could see was lawsuits coming at the Johnson Corporation because of the things that I preached. I did not preach just about Heaven. I did not preach about prosperity. I preached about racial justice. I preached about social justice. I preached about the things that affected the lives of African Americans in the 1970s and 1980s and Mr. Johnson had heard tapes of my sermons.

He told Mr. Mootry that he already had enough lawsuits because of his airing Jesse Jackson and Operation PUSH on his station. The last thing he needed was some more lawsuits because of my preachments.

God's providence intervened again, however, and Mr. Mootry got Mr. Johnson to consider the fact that he (Mr. Johnson) belonged to a United Church of Christ congregation and that Trinity was a United Church of Christ congregation. He ought to give us a chance to see how things went. Mr. Johnson let us on his station and no lawsuits were ever filed against him or the station because of my sermons.

When we went on a Black-owned station, however, the regular radio listeners of the Black "doo-wop" stations in the late seventies and early eighties could not believe their ears. They could not believe that there was a church in the city of Chicago where there was preaching every Sunday that dealt with the lives of Black people living in an era of Apartheid and Reaganism. Especially could they not believe that they were hearing those kinds of messages coming from a church that had a choir like the Sanctuary Choir.

As they called the church they would say to us that they could hear those kinds of messages on Operation PUSH and they could hear those kinds of messages at the Mosque at 72nd and Stony Island. They were not used to hearing substantive messages and soul music coming from a Black church!

New members flocked to join us, but they caused a seating problem, a worship service problem and a problem for our Board for Long Range Planning and the vision that God had given us. With the increased number of members we had to change from three services on Sunday to three services *and* a Saturday night service! With members already standing around the walls on

Sunday and with the overflow "Playboy screen" crowd already having to adjust to not being in the sanctuary on Sundays, it was not long before the members stood up and voted to build a new sanctuary!

When the vote was taken to build a new sanctuary, the Board for Long Range Planning began looking for a site on which to build a sanctuary that the congregation had voted.

Trying to build a new church, trying to raise funds to go back to a bank for a second time to ask for a loan for building a new worship center and trying to do the work on the other "prioritized" list of the Board for Long Range Planning items was not possible. The long range items had to be pushed to the back burner and the focus and energy had to be given to all that it takes to find a site to build, to raise the funds to build (and to borrow), and to get from the growing membership and the growing ministries of the church what the needs would be in such a new site.

The first time we built, the cost of the land and the construction of the building was $90,000. When I was called as Pastor and we had to build out on the rest of the 95th and Parnell Avenue property, the cost for that construction was $1.5 million dollars. By the mid-'80s we were looking at what we thought would be an $8 million dollar project. It turned out to be $16 million dollars! That kind of venture put most of our "vision" items on the back burner until the 400 West 95th Street building was up and paid for!

Once the mortgage was paid for, incidentally, the members of the Board for Long Range Planning who were charged with the responsibility of implementing the new strategic plan (which I will get to in a moment) immediately pulled the African-centered

Christian school off of the backburner and were charged with the responsibility of getting that school up, open and operating as quickly as possible.

A part of making the vision become a reality and wrestling with prioritizing a vision given to the original members of the Long Range Planning Committee was informed by and in many ways shaped by the **Black Value System** that the congregation put together in 1981—two years after the Bylaw change which brought the Board for Long Range Planning into existence.

In 1981, Manford Byrd—one of our charter members ran head-on into the buzz saw of racism Chicago-style and plantation politics. Those twin demons kept him from being named as the Superintendent of Schools in the city of Chicago. The city of Chicago had never had a Black superintendent before 1981. The city of Chicago had been burdened by racist superintendents (and racist Boards!) as was evidenced by the "Willis Wagons" which was the issue being fought by the Black community when I moved to the city of Chicago in 1969.

By 1981, we had some Black persons sitting on the Board of Education of the Chicago Public Schools and we thought in the Black community that the obvious choice for the superintendent, Dr. Manford Byrd, would be named with no problem to that position. The mayor of the city of Chicago, however, still controlled the decisions of the Board of Education and the mayor did not want Manford Byrd in that position.

Political pressure convinced the Board that to have a strong, African American male at the helm of the Chicago Public Schools was not a good thing. What the mayor needed and what the Board needed was someone who would go along with the program. Manford's name was not the name at the top of the short list.

Manford Byrd was from Alabama. Manford Byrd was from a poor black family whose mother had raised him to believe in himself, to believe in God, to believe in the Black community and to pursue excellence. Manford Byrd had worked his way up through the Chicago Public School ranks. Manford Byrd had an earned PhD from a white institution, yet he never gave up his Black identity. Manford was not the kind of role model that plantation politics was looking for, so Manford was being ignored. The Black citizens of the city of Chicago rose up in protest!

When the name of the person suggested to be the new superintendent was announced, it turned out to be a Black woman who lived in another city. For her to get the imprimatur of both the mayor and the Board was of deep concern to the Black citizens of the city of Chicago—especially those who had children in the Chicago Public School System.

A delegation of Black women including Reverend Willie Barrow flew to the city where the woman was living and urged her not to be a part of the racist games being played in Chicago. They urged her not to buy into the plantation politics in which she was being used as a pawn. They urged her not to do this to a Black man, but to turn down the offer and to let the Black man who had earned it take his place as the new School Superintendent.

The woman would not hear the pleas of the strong, Black women who went up to reason with her. She came into the city as the Superintendent of Schools and Manford Byrd was relegated to the position of "Deputy Superintendent."

In subsequent years (much later on), Dr. Byrd was appointed the Superintendent of Schools of the City of Chicago, but in 1981 he was messed over. In response to his being messed over and because he was a charter member of our congregation, the members of the congregation met to draft several statements.

First they drafted a letter to the Chicago Public School System, to its new president and to the Board of Education lodging their formal protest with the decision that was made disrespecting Dr. Manford Byrd. Then they put together a statement to articulate what it was they felt about having a strong Black man who had gone against the odds and who had succeeded; but who was still a "Negro" in the eyes of white racists. (Of course they did not say Negro, but the word did start with an "N.")

Then after wrestling with what it meant to be Black and to be Christian, a sub-committee of the Executive Council of the church pulled together twelve principles of what it meant to be "Unashamedly Black and Unapologetically Christian." They called the results of their study the **Black Value System** and they articulated those values as follows:

1. **Commitment to God**. "The God of our weary years" will give us the strength to give up prayerful passivism and become Black Christian Activists, soldiers for Black freedom and the dignity of all humankind.

2. **Commitment to the Black Community**. The highest level of achievement for any Black person must be a contribution of strength and continuity of the Black community.

3. **Commitment to the Black Family.** The Black family circle must generate strength, stability and love, despite the uncertainty of externals, because these characteristics are required if the developing person is to withstand warping by our racist competitive society. Those Blacks who are blessed with membership in a strong family unit must reach out and expand that blessing to the less fortunate.

4. **Dedication to the Pursuit of Education.** We must forswear anti-intellectualism. Continued survival demands that each Black person be developed to the utmost of his/her mental potential despite the inadequacies of the formal education process. "Real education" fosters understanding of ourselves as well as every aspect of our environment. Also, it develops within us the ability to fashion concepts and tools for better utilization of our resources, and more effective solutions to our problems. Since the majority of Blacks have been denied such learning, Black education must include elements that produce high school graduates with marketable skills, a trade or qualifications for apprenticeships, or proper preparation for college. Basic education for all Blacks should include Mathematics, Science, Logic, General Semantics, Participative Politics, Economics and Finance, and the Care and Nurture of Black minds.

5. **Dedication to the Pursuit of Excellence.** To the extent that we individually reach for, even strain for excellence, we increase, geometrically, the value and resourcefulness of the Black community. We must recognize the relativity of one's best; this year's best can be bettered next year. Such is the language of

growth and development. We must seek to excel in every endeavor.

6. **Adherence to the Black Work Ethic.** "It is becoming harder to find qualified people to work in Chicago." Whether this is true or not, it represents one of the many reasons given by businesses and industries for deserting the Chicago area. We must realize that a location with good facilities, adequate transportation and a reputation for producing skilled workers will attract industry. We are in competition with other cities, states and nations for jobs. High productivity must be a goal of the Black workforce.

7. **Commitment to Self-Discipline and Self-Respect.** To accomplish anything worthwhile requires self-discipline. We must be a community of self-disciplined persons if we are to actualize and utilize our own human resources, instead of perpetually submitting to exploitation by others. Self-discipline, coupled with a respect for self, will enable each of us to be an instrument of Black progress and a model for Black youth.

8. **Disavowal of the Pursuit of "Middleclassness."** Classic methodology on control of captives teaches that captors must be able to identify the "talented tenth" of those subjugated, especially those who show promise of providing the kind of leadership that might threaten the captor's control.

Those so identified are separated from the rest of the people by:

- Killing them off directly, and/or fostering a social system that encourages them to kill off one another.

- Placing them in concentration camps, and/or structuring an economic environment that induces captive youth to fill the jails and prisons.

- Seducing them into a socioeconomic class system which, while training them to earn more dollars, hypnotizes them into believing they are better than others and teaches them to think in terms of "we" and "they" instead of "us."

- So, while it is permissible to chase "middle income" with all our might, we must avoid the third separation method - the psychological entrapment of Black "middle classness." If we avoid this snare, we will also diminish our "voluntary" contributions to methods A and B. And more importantly, Black people no longer will be deprived of their birthright: the leadership, resourcefulness and example of their own talented persons.

9. **Pledge to Make the Fruits of All Developing and Acquired Skills Available to the Black Community.**

10. **Pledge to Allocate Regularly, a Portion of Personal Resources for Strengthening and Supporting Black Institutions.**

11. **Pledge Allegiance to All Black Leadership Who Espouse and Embrace the Black Value System.**

12. **Personal Commitment to Embracement of the Black Value System.** **To measure the worth and validity of all activity in terms of positive contributions to the general welfare of the Black Community and the Advancement of Black People towards freedom.**

I did not meet with the laypeople of our church at all during this process. I had no input into the formulation of those twelve principles. These were affirmations of faith and the pride that came from the hearts and minds of the members of the congregation of Trinity United Church of Christ.

Our congregation voted to adopt these principles and our congregation voted to let these principles be the guiding principles whereby we approached ministry, did ministry, governed our lives and governed our decisions.

It was these principles that fed into the vision of the Board for Long Range Planning and the votes that were taken for prioritizing the goals of the congregation as they implemented that vision.

Abiding by the principles of the **Black Value System**, carrying out the implementation of the priorities voted by the congregation to implement the long range (short range and medium range) goals of our church and being faithful to what God called us to do resulted in the massive amount of ministry and the exciting successful results that were seen during this decade of realizing the vision or turning the vision into reality.

When Sean Hannity discovered our church's **Black Value System** and the racist media picked up what they thought was the scent for a kill, a local journalist called the church to attack the **Black**

Value System, to deconstruct the **Black Value System** and to pick apart the **Black Value System**. We put that journalist in touch with Val Jordan because Val had been one of the committee members in 1981 who helped to construct the **Black Value System**. When Val Jordan embarrassed the journalist so badly, showing that journalist how inadequate her "miseducation" was, the journalist dropped the story and would not print one word of Mr. Jordan's response. The **Black Value System** is and was a powerful set of principles drawn up by a people whose faith was and is in a God who can do anything but fail!

During the "vision years" my involvement with our denomination and its international ministries, my involvement with TransAfrica and my being a member of the Board of Directors of the Black Theology Project affected our church and its ministry in many different ways.

My travels to Nicaragua, to Costa Rico and to the Island of Cuba opened my eyes to the reality of Africans living in Central American and Africans living in the Caribbean, and the complete "gap" in knowledge about Africans in Diaspora who lived in the other two Americas while pastoring a church which had in its membership Africans from the Continent, Africans from Central America, Africans from the Caribbean and Africans from South America! (My first trip to Brazil was also made in the early 1980s.)

I talked with members of the church who were from Jamaica, who were from the Bahamas and who were from Belize and as a result of my dialogue with them we started the Caribbean Ministry. It was my desire to have members of the church who were born and raised in the United States learn more about the people, the history, the legacy, the culture, the music and the traditions of Africans who were raised in a different part of the West African Diaspora. That ministry now includes persons who are from the Caribbean and persons who are interested in the different cultures that are found in the Caribbean.

The Africa Ministry was started in the same manner. I had an extensive background in understanding African peoples. I had been studying African music and African history for years. My studies in African history started when I was a boy. My studies in African music became the focus of my graduate school studies.

My background in understanding Africa and African peoples did not start with my academic endeavors. It started when I was in elementary school and I was introduced to two Liberian girls whose father and mother had adopted them and brought them to the United States of America. Going to school in the 4th, 5th and 6th grades with Liberians, talking to them about their country, their culture, their history and their experiences opened my eyes to a world that I never knew existed.

Their father was a minister (and a close friend of my father's) and hearing their father and mother talk about Africa as persons who had lived there began to whet my appetite in a way that has yet to be quenched sixty years later!

Our church's involvement in the Lott-Carey Convention was my second experience of learning more about African people, the different African cultures, African languages and African music. The church in which I grew up was an active member of the Lott-Carey Convention. My parents and my grandparents were active members of the Lott-Carey Convention. I would attend the Annual Meetings of the Lott-Carey Convention. I got to meet the missionaries who worked in Liberia because of the Lott-Carey Convention. We not only had them at our church to speak. We also had them in our home.

I looked forward to those home visits to talk with persons who lived and worked in the country I thought I would never get to see. Some of the missionaries were African American and some were Liberian! The stories they shared with me, the insights they gave to me and the wisdom that I learned from the people of Liberia was stretching me and calling me to an understanding of missions that I never dreamed I would have as a teenager.

When I got to Virginia Union University, my involvement with Africans and my study of African cultures expanded by quantum leaps. We not only had Liberian students in our school and in our dormitories. We also had Nigerians. I got to meet and make lifelong friendships with several Nigerian students, and my conversations with Dr. Samuel DeWitt Proctor about Africa, about Liberia and about Nigeria opened up an entirely new world of understanding for me. Dr. Proctor intentionally brought dozens of Nigerians to Virginia Union University during his tenure as president. There were Liberian students there, but the number of Nigerians was incredible.

Dr. Proctor also moved his family to Nigeria to work for six years as the head of the Peace Corps in Nigeria under the Presidency of John F. Kennedy and Lyndon Baines Johnson. Learning more about African countries and cultures from Dr. Proctor's experiences provided a foundation for me that was built upon by the experiences of Baba Asa Hilliard. Dr. Hilliard also lived on the Continent. His time in Liberia helped to strengthen the faith that his Pentecostal background had given him!

My mother and Randall Robinson's mother were best friends. They were in each other's weddings. Randall Robinson moved to Africa and lived in Africa long before he became the CEO of TransAfrica. While he was living there, he was the neighbor of Dr. and Mrs. Sokoni and Ayana Karanja! Randall Robinson's brother, Max Robinson, was a classmate of mine at Virginia Union University and the shared stories about the homeland that I got from Dr. Proctor, Max Robinson, my mother and father, Sokoni and Ayana, and my African friends augmented the wealth of knowledge that I had gotten from my father's library while growing up in Philadelphia. My father was a student of Carter G. Woodson and his bibliographical resources on the Continent and the people of several different cultures, countries and backgrounds caused me to understand how I was an African born in America that cut from the same cultural cloth as Jesus and the people who made up our faith story in our Bible!

Because of my familiarity with the Lott-Carey Convention, with Lott-Carey's story and the awesome work that was done by Wendell Summerville and the Lott-Carey Convention, I convinced the head of the Lott-Carey Convention in the mid-1970s (and I convinced our Stewardship Ministry) to allow Trinity United Church of Christ to become part of the Lott-Carey Convention.

The Lott-Carey Convention boasted proudly that ninety-five cents of every one dollar given in missions to that Convention went straight to Africa, India and Haiti! Most other reports from foreign missions boards and foreign missions ministries report that forty to fifty percent of each dollar is spent on administrative costs. Not so with Lott-Carey! Ninety-five cents out of every dollar went straight to mission!

My familiarity with Haitians started with my exposure to the Lott-Carey Convention as a child. That familiarity deepened and grew during my college years and my early years as a pastor. Finding out the truth about Haiti and why it is the United States has punished Haiti ever since Africans threw off the yoke of slavery and defeated two major European powers have helped me form a kinship with our African brothers and sisters in Haiti, and have given me a passion for righting the wrongs of history and righting the wrongs of our government when it comes to Haitian people and the country of Haiti.

In addition, our church's involvement with Haiti (before we had the Caribbean Ministry) was not just through the Lott-Carey Convention and the reports from those who worked in that field of mission. It was also because of our association and work with Wheeler Avenue Baptist Church in Houston (where Dr. Marcus Cosby serves as pastor today). Reverend William A. Lawson who was the Pastor of the Wheeler Avenue Baptist Church in Texas back in the 1970s and '80s shared with me the work that his congregation was doing in Haiti. We sent one of our members, Deacon Hugh Brandon, to Haiti to look at the work of Wheeler Avenue and to make recommendations to our Stewardship Ministry in terms of supporting that important Haitian work.

The involvement of our government in fomenting civil unrest because of the desire of a Black people to be free of white rule and to end control of their lives and destinies by major, white U.S. corporations caused the civil unrest that forced us to stop our work with the mission church and school started by Wheeler Avenue. We have continued our mission work through the Lott-Carey Convention and our involvement in the Lott-Carey Convention.

Parenthetically, but of crucial importance, you need to know that our involvement with the Lott-Carey Convention started with our joining the Convention. It increased as members of our Stewardship Ministry took a trip annually to the Lott-Carey Convention.

My mother's involvement with the Women's Division of the Lott-Carey Foreign Mission Convention pulled in several women from our Stewardship Ministry. Ida Baker (Finney) became one of my mother's disciples in the Lott-Carey Convention. For over twenty years, Ida has worked faithfully with the Lott-Carey Convention and as a result Ida is now the president of the Women's Division of the Lott-Carey Foreign Mission Convention!

As I watched Ida assume that position of leadership I saw the positive results of my love for Africa, my love for African people, my love for the work of the church in Africa and Haiti paying off in a most tangible manner! Shortly into my tenure as Pastor of Trinity United Church of Christ, however, my involvement with the Continent, the cultures, the languages and the music of Africans took off in yet another direction. It had nothing to do with my academic studies as a student of the History of Religions at The University of Chicago Divinity School. It had to do with people who were joining our church! We had people from Senegal, Cote d'Ivoire and South Africa who were joining our church. We had Ghanaians who were joining our church and we had Liberians who were joining our church.

As mentioned above, my close association with South Africans shaped our ministry in some tremendous ways.

We had South African members who deepened my knowledge about African cultures, African people, African languages and African music; yet we also had African American members who knew absolutely nothing about Africa. I wanted our Africa Ministry to do what our Caribbean Ministry was doing. I wanted an Africa Ministry that would help African Americans "connect the dots" and begin to see how important the Continent of Africa and its people were in shaping African American history, African

American culture, African American religious beliefs and the African American reality.

I wanted African Americans who had been taught that Africa was something negative, Africa was backwards, African cultures were "ignorant" and all of the other things that miseducation taught us to know that those were lies propagated by a Eurocentric miseducation system that was based on the principles of white supremacy. The Continent of Africa and its people had shaped us and caused us to be who we are; and I wanted our members to know that. The Caribbean Ministry and the Africa Ministry were two practical ways of helping our members to know that.

All of these ministries were birthed during what I call "the vision period" of our congregation's history under my pastorate.

During this "vision period" of the church our Singles Ministry started and began to flourish. Our Drug and Alcohol Recovery Ministry was started. Our Prison Ministry was started and members of the congregation began putting more "flesh on the bones" of the 1971 statement, Dr. Sheares affirmation and the **Black Value System!**

Our Drug and Alcohol Recovery Ministry was started with several different components to the ministry. There was Alcoholics Anonymous, Narcotics Anonymous, Al-Anon and Alateen. In addition to those "traditional" recovery and support programs, however, there was also the brand-new "Free-N-One" Ministry structured in the same manner as the traditional 12-Step recovery programs. Free-N-One, however, was created specifically for Christians who were not afraid to name the name of Jesus.

In the traditional substance abuse programs the word "God" and the name of Jesus are not normally pronounced. With sensitivity toward persons in those programs who are not Christian and who do not claim the name of Jesus, the term "Higher Power" is used. For Christians who have been set free from their addictions, however, by the power of the name of Jesus, the Scripture verse, *"If the Son shall make you free, you shall be free indeed"* became the operational verse, the foundational verse and the focus of that particular branch of the substance abuse recovery program.

The "Free-N-One" program was started on the West Coast. It was started in Los Angeles. It was started at the Ward A.M.E. Church when Reverend Dr. Frank Madison Reid III was the Pastor. It was started by Elder Ron Simmons and Reverend Ron Wright. Ron Wright today is the Pastor of the New Visions Church of Jesus Christ. Elder Ron Simmons is now an Elder in the Church of God in Christ faith and a member of West Angeles COGIC.

The two Rons came from the West Coast to Trinity and set-up the first "Free-N-One" Chapter in the city of Chicago. Its founding co-chairpersons at Trinity were Don Moody who went on to become a deacon at Trinity United Church of Christ and Herb Carey who not only became a deacon, but who also went to seminary, was ordained and is now pastoring in Renton, Washington! Thousands of people who are members and not members of our congregation have been blessed by the powerful ministry of our Drug and Alcohol Recovery efforts.

Our Prison Ministry was a ministry that was started with a desire to do more than just go into the prisons and "have church." Worship is important. Praise and Worship is a *sine qua non* for believers whether they are believers who worship on Sundays in our congregation or believers who are incarcerated. The Prison Ministry did not want to do *away* with worship inside the prisons. The Prison Ministry wanted to do *more* than just worship inside the prisons.

Our Prison Ministry began working with the incarcerated to teach GED classes. Our Prison Ministry has lobbied for legislative reform in order that marketable skills may once again be taught to persons who are incarcerated. The prison industry is presently structured to guarantee recidivism!

Forty years ago a prisoner could not only earn a GED while incarcerated, a prisoner could earn an Associate's Degree, a Bachelor's Degree and certification by several different trades while still incarcerated. The state legislators (to insure recidivism) cut out virtually all forms of education for persons who are incarcerated. After all, the vast majority of the incarcerated, not only in this state, but throughout the nation, are African American men and Hispanic men!

When I retired from Trinity, there were fifty-four different professions that a felon or an ex-con could not enter into in the state of Illinois because of his prison record. An ex-con could not even get a barber's license when I retired! Our Prison Ministry has worked across the years in getting those draconic laws changed.

Our Prison Ministry has also worked with the Safer Institute and the PACE Program. Working with persons who are incarcerated and also working with their families while they are incarcerated was a focus of our Prison Ministry. Getting ex-offenders safely placed after they are out of the prisons is also just as important as the ministry provided for them and their families while they are incarcerated. That was the underlying philosophy for our Prison Ministry at its inception and it remains the same today.

"Moms and Me" is yet another aspect of the Prison Ministry. In the "Moms and Me" program, our prison ministers take the children of women who are incarcerated down to Dwight at least once a quarter, so that the children can spend an entire day with their mothers.

Our Prison Ministry (through the efforts of the Reverend Paul Ford) began working along with the Covenant United Church of Christ (located in South Holland, Illinois) Prison Ministry to minister to those who are incarcerated in the federal penitentiary up in Oxford, Wisconsin! All of those efforts grow out of the Lord, Jesus' words in the 25th chapter of Matthew, "*When I was in prison...*"

The Drug and Alcohol Recovery Ministry and the Prison Ministry are two perfect examples of what it means to be a Black church in the Black community, addressing the needs of the community and serving the people who sit in its pews week-after-week.

In addition to the growing number of Bible classes that were taught both day and night each week during the year, I instituted spiritual retreats as a way of deepening the faith of our members and creating a space and a time during which our members could come to grips with what it meant to be a Black church in the Black community. There were retreats for each of the ministries as mentioned above. In addition to those retreats, however, we began having churchwide study courses and we instituted, through our Church-In-Society Ministry, political forums, and through our Health Ministry we instituted health forums and health fairs.

Growing out of the churchwide study courses, we began our annual lecture series, and preaching series. Starting in 1979 (the same year of the Long Range Planning Retreat), we held Sunday afternoon seminars where we had come to the pulpit of Trinity (to lecture, to teach and to engage in dialogue with) such luminaries as: Ivan Van Sertima, Wade Nobles, Michael Eric Dyson, Dwight Hopkins, Henry and Ella Mitchell, Na'im Akbar, Asa Hilliard, Clarice Martin, Randy Bailey, Renita Weems, Jerome Ross, Obery Hendricks, John W. Kinney, Miles Jones and Carlos Moore.

The various disciplines that those scholars represent and the life-changing insights that they brought to our members helped to clarify the focus of an African-centered church that was rooted in the Gospel of Jesus Christ and understood that it did not have to give up its Africanity because of its Christianity.

It was also during the years of "writing the vision" that our HIV/AIDS Ministry was started. Our HIV/AIDS Ministry has a training program for members who volunteer to work in this ministry. That training program consists of sessions led by an epidemiologist, a representative from the Center for Disease Control, someone from the Chicago Board of Health, a chaplain who works with HIV/AIDS patients, a family member of someone who is HIV-positive or who has full-blown AIDS, a person who is positive and a person who has full-blown AIDS.

The training program is to teach those who volunteer to work in this ministry the sensitivities necessary for ministering effectively with persons who have an incurable disease. It is also designed to help those volunteers work with the families of one who is dying and/or one who has a disease for which there is no cure.

A great deal of the training program is to insure that the persons who volunteer to work in this ministry do not have any grandiose notions about being able to "heal" persons who have AIDS. It is also to weed out persons who are homophobic. The largest number of HIV/AIDS patients that we have been working with since the 1970s are same-gender loving persons.

To have someone working in this ministry who does not see all of God's children as accepted by God, loved by God and just as valuable as heterosexual believers is to invite disaster. The last thing in the world someone dying of AIDS needs is a homophobic or judgmental "AIDS minister" who is convinced that what the infected person has is "God's curse on the homosexuals" and that God is sending them straight to hell because of their sexual orientation!

The starting of that ministry during this period of "visioning" is directly related to what I said earlier about my 1975 experience at the General Synod of the United Church of Christ that was held in Minneapolis, Minnesota. I mentioned in an earlier chapter how that Synod was a life-changing experience for me when it came to the vote that was taken by our denomination. Let me explain what I mean.

At the General Synod of the United Church of Christ, only voting delegates are allowed on the floor of the Synod. All non-voting members of the United Church of Christ, visitors, press, etc., are kept off of the floor where the voting delegates and the voting delegations are seated. I was a delegate to the 1975 General Synod.

A note was passed around on the floor of the Synod where the voting delegates sat asking that all Black delegates meet in the room of Dr. Charles Cobb (the Executive Director of the

Commission for Racial Justice) when the Synod broke for lunch.
There were approximately twenty Black delegates who voted at
that Synod. When we broke for lunch, however, I could not go
straight to Dr. Cobb's room. I was stopped almost every ten feet
by people wanting to talk, people wanting to lobby their positions,
people wanting to speak, people wanting to fellowship, etc., etc.
I kept explaining that I had a meeting to get to and I ultimately
got to Dr. Cobb's room, but I was about ten minutes late.

The meeting had not really started. People were just sitting
around, lounging around and chatting. When I walked in the
room, Dr. Cobb said, *"Now that Brother Wright is here we can
officially begin this meeting. Do we have your permission Brother
Wright?"*

He was joking with me, but I was too busy stepping over people
who were crowded into his room. Twenty delegates in a hotel
room is kind of a "tight fit." I made my way over to the far
corner of the room and found a seat on top of the radiator. Dr.
Cobb then said to us that he had invited us to his room because
he wanted us to hear from the president of the Gay Caucus.

Being a homophobic person who was not even aware of how
deep his homophobia was in 1975, I simply wanted to step back
over all of those people I had just walked over to get to my perch
on the radiator and get out of that room! I did not want to hear
a thing that the man had to say.

God's providence, however, kicked in once again. The president
of the Gay Caucus blew my mind when he talked to the Black
delegates. He said that he had not come to meet with the Black
delegates in order for us to affirm homosexuality. He said he did
not even know why they called his caucus the "Gay" caucus.

He said to us that Gays were not gay. They were some of the most miserable people on the face of the Earth (he said). Maybe they took the word "gay" and were trying to turn it on its head just as African Americans had taken the word "Black" and turned a negative into a positive.

He said he simply came before us during that lunch break to ask us not to vote against the Ordination of homosexuals. That Resolution was coming before the General Synod that afternoon, and he wanted us to vote "yes" to accepting homosexuals both as members of the church and as ministers of the Gospel.

He then went on to say that he was not a "practicing homosexual." He was married. He had a wife and children and the Gays knew that when they elected him as their chairperson. He said he could not change his gender or his sexual orientation. All he could change was his behavior; and he had not changed that on his own!

Only the Cross of Jesus Christ had given him the power to live as he now lived and he said to us that he wanted us not to turn away from the Cross of Jesus Christ those persons who were same-gender loving. Many of them were born with a same-sex orientation. He had been one of those people. He was, in fact, one of those people. He said the Cross of Jesus Christ did not change who he was. It just changed how he behaved!

He said, "*We as a Christian church welcome to the Cross of Christ murderers, adulterers, thieves, liars and pedophiles! We keep away from the Cross, however, those people who need the power of the Cross the most and I am asking you not to do that.*"

I was stunned. I was speechless. As I said earlier, I could not talk about what I experienced or what I felt for at least four years. After the Long Range Planning Ministry retreat and the powerful spiritual awakening that the church was going through, I dared to preach during the Lenten Season in 1979 a sermon entitled "Caution! Program Subject to Change."

The text was taken from the passage of Scripture where the Roman Centurion who was programmed to look down his nose at Palestinians, programmed to see himself as superior to people of color, programmed to see himself as a part of the colonizing European Imperial nation and those who were the colonized were "non-people"; and programmed to carry out his duties as a Roman soldier who was charged with the responsibility of crucifying convicted criminals... that man's program was changed!

That is the attitude and the mindset with which he went to Calvary that Friday morning. When God got through with him, however, because of His proximity to that Cross, he cried out, "Surely! This was the Son of God." The main focus of the sermon was that when you get close to that Cross of Jesus Christ, "your program" is subject to change.

I then shared with the congregation publicly the transformation (the change) that had taken place inside of me privately four years prior in 1975 at the General Synod and the change that was taking place inside of me daily as I learned more and more about same-gender loving people and what the Word of God really said (as opposed to what I had been taught it said!).

I shared in that sermon the testimony of the president of the Gay Caucus whose program changed because he got close to the Cross of Jesus Christ and I urged the members of our church not to push away, run away, shove away or keep away homosexuals because they needed the Cross of Jesus Christ just as we who are heterosexual need it.

That sermon opened up the floodgates in our congregation. It not only resulted in our HIV/AIDS Ministry being started, it brought Gay members of the church and family members of gay persons who belonged to the church "out of the woodwork" to talk to me.

Mothers of gay men wanted to know from me why God had created their children to be gay. They knew from the time their children began to walk that they were "different." No old man had turned them out. They had not been molested or raped by a pedophile. They had been gay from birth and the mothers who came to talk with me did not understand why God would allow them to carry a baby in their womb for nine months and then send that baby to hell because of the way he or she was born!

Lesbian members and mothers of lesbians began to talk with me. They were wrestling with deep issues and their previous churches had not addressed those issues. They were excited to be a part of a church that did not bash homosexuals and that opened up the possibility of conversation, dialogue and understanding for persons who were Black, who were Christian, who loved the Lord, who were culturally conscious and who were same-gender loving in their sexual orientation.

Our HIV/AIDS Ministry needed volunteers who understood that the Body of Christ was not and is not just made up of heterosexuals. It is made up of all people, many of whom have sexual orientations that are not the same as the person trying to perform ministry to persons infected with the virus and families affected by the virus. Our HIV/AIDS Ministry was started with that premise and continues to minister today to hundreds of persons who need the love of Christ and not the "judgmental" attitude of those who call themselves followers of Christ.

Our church at the end of the '70s, and during the first half of the 1980s was on the verge of "blowing up" in ways we had no way of foreseeing; and for that I thank God and the providence of God. Truly God's grace and mercy were at work during this season of *writing the vision.*

Chapter 4
Ministry Outside of the Box!

*A*s I stated earlier in this work (and as I have testified publicly across the nation and across the years), many of the ministries of our congregation originated with and were started by (and continue to be carried out by) the members of the congregation. They did not start with the pastor! Much of the exciting work of the church that goes on outside of the eyesight of the general public on a Sunday during Worship is work that was inspired by God and given to the people of God, by the Spirit of God. Across the many years that I served as the Pastor of this wonderful people of God, the members of Trinity have started countless ministries that helped make us who we became and who we are.

An entire book could be written and stand on its own about the ministries of Trinity United Church of Christ. I run the risk of getting in trouble with some of our dedicated members who work week-in and week-out in their ministries by just naming a few ministries, but there are some ministries that I have always considered "outside of the box." I want to lift up a few of those ministries to give you a glimpse of the way over which God has brought us from 1961 through 2009.

When the average person thinks of a church and the work of that church, the average person thinks of the Sunday Morning Services, the choir, the ushers, the deacons and those who host the social hour after the worship services. For the person who has grown up in or around a church, moreover, that concept of "church" would expand to cover the Church School, the Sunday school, the youth programs and the "outreach" ministry. That "outreach" ministry would normally include a feeding program for the hungry, a clothes closet for the homeless and some benevolence monies given to the work of the church of Jesus Christ in "foreign countries."

Those are the lines drawn around the "box" when it comes to the concept of church in the minds of most people. At Trinity United Church of Christ, however, dozens of our ministries have been "outside of the box" and for those ministries, I say, "*To God be the Glory for the things God has done!*"

Isuthu/Intojane

Our Rites of Passage programs and mentoring programs for young boys and young girls have been in existence since 1979. In 1979, our programs for mentoring youth were called "Building Black Men" and "Building Black Women." The ministries were started in an attempt to address the needs of parents and children in the African American community where the families were headed by single parents.

Recognizing that single parents needed help, and that the children in single-parent homes needed role models, those two ministries were started in an attempt to provide the support and the role models that the youngsters needed. It was in the eighties that many of our ministries changed their names to African names and new ministries were started using African names to "self-define" the people working in that ministry and the purpose of that ministry.

Both *Isuthu* and *Intojane* are South African words that describe the process of becoming a grown man and a grown woman in Zulu and Xhosa cultures. There were many lessons that we learned across the years in trying to carry out this ministry. The ministry (*Isuthu*) was started and founded upon the principle of providing healthy and positive options for young boys to see in terms of what they could do with their lives, what God could do in their lives and what was possible in life!

One of our most active members until the day he died, Appellate Court Judge R. Eugene Pincham, used to say, "*You can't be what you can't see!*" By that he meant that a young boy could never be a Black judge, be a Black lawyer, be a Black preacher, be a Black architect, be a Black electrical engineer, be a Black air traffic controller, be a Black ophthalmologist, be a Black urologist or be anything positive if he had never seen that kind of Black man up close and personal in his life or seen that option for his life on his radarscope of possibilities.

Judge Pincham used to point out from painful experience that many Black boys never got to see a judge until they were standing in front of a judge in handcuffs.

Our Isuthu Program addressed and still addresses that need. Our Isuthu Program helps young Black boys to see Black judges up close and personal in their Rites of Passage/Mentoring Program.

One of the lessons we learned when it came to Isuthu is that many men are not cut out to be the kinds of personal "life coach" mentors that young boys between the ages of eight and eighteen need. Many men just do not have the time. Many of the men in our church just do not have the patience. Some of the men who volunteer just do not have the ability to be pulled on and drained in the way that young boys will pull on you and drain you when they do not have a daddy in their homes!

Many men signed up for the program with good intentions, but when they found out what it really entailed they started falling off. Nothing was more devastating to a boy than to think that he had a male mentor, a big brother and an African American Christian brother to whom he could look up, only to discover that the brother flaked out and/or dropped out of the mentoring program!

At first we thought of training the men who were volunteering to serve in that ministry. The training helped and the training still helps. The training does not, however, give a man the kind of patience and willingness to serve "for the long haul" that is required in this program. To keep the men from feeling as if they had failed and to keep the boys with a one-on-one mentoring model and a man in their lives, we shifted the way the program was structured.

For the guys who could handle the in-depth and intense mentoring, we only assigned them one or two boys per year. We then had two other tiers of service in Isuthu whereby the men could participate in the mentoring program while not burning themselves out, not taking time away from their own families and/or not disappointing a youngster.

The second tier of male sponsorship in the Isuthu Program is for the men who are those professionals who only have to come to an Isuthu meeting once a year and spend two to three hours on a particular Saturday talking to the youngsters about what it is they do in life, how it is they got to that point in life, what kind of training is necessary, what kind of skills are required and what passions underlie their purpose for being in that profession.

A cardiovascular surgeon may not be able to be with the young boys twenty-six Saturdays out of the year; but he can give one Saturday afternoon a year to talk about his work and help a young boy *see* what he can be if he applies himself. The same is true for many of the professional men who cannot be present with the boys every week or every other week.

The last tier of sponsorship on the part of Black men who work in the Isuthu Program is to serve as chaperones for baseball games, football games, sports outings and the one week of camping that the Isuthu Program takes the boys on each summer. Some men are able to take a week off as vacation to go along on a camping and fishing trip with the young boys and that puts them in the boys' lives in a very special manner.

Those three tiers of adult male sponsorship give the young men in this program an up-close and personal view of what it means to be a committed, African American, Christian male. That program does not receive the kind of accolades that the Sanctuary choir does because the men working in the program are working "behind the scenes." The program does not get to be in the spotlight, but its effectiveness is invaluable!

Intojane is structured in a similar manner. The young girls in the program learn what it really means to be a Black Christian woman living in the 21st century by being in contact with women who volunteer their time.

The women who volunteer to work as sponsors in Intojane, in Imani Ya Watume, in Young Women's Christian Walk and the

Teenage Sexuality Program all demonstrate by their lives that
what the videos show our young ladies is not the only option
that they have for their lives; and that an African American
Christian female is very different from what the sexy, racy and
bordering-on-pornography hip-hop DVD's put before their eyes!

Project Jeremiah

Once Isuthu and Intojane were up and running in the mid-'80s,
another reality hit the members of the church and the Spirit of
God moved upon the hearts of some of our members to address
that reality and to meet yet another need. The reality was and is
that the majority of African American children do not go to
church! Their parents do not go to church! The questions then
became: How do you reach those young Black boys whose
mothers not only do not go to church, but whose mothers were
not raised in church? How do you reach girls from that
population?

How can a Black boy who does not go to church see what a
Black Christian man looks like if he is never at the church? How
can he be what he *can't* see?

The men of our church were given the inspiration to start a
ministry that addresses that need. Since the boys do not come
to church, the men took the church to them! They named their
program "Project Jeremiah" and what those dedicated men do is
go into the public schools one day a week for every week of the
academic year and they stay there in the elementary school all
day long. They do not take tracts into school. They do not go
into the public schools "preaching Jesus" with their lips.

They do not lay out the "plan of salvation" nor have the
youngsters confess or say a "sinner's prayer." What those men

do is show up at school on the playground one half-hour to forty-five minutes before the first bell rings at nine o'clock in the morning. They then go into the classrooms and sit in the classrooms all day long. They study every subject right along with the students.

They help the youngsters with their Social Studies, their Math, their English, their History, their Music and their Science projects!

They patrol the halls when classes are changing and they stay out on the playground until the last child has left the school grounds. Their weekly presence helps the youngsters to know that there is a Black man who cares about them. They get to see strong Black men who are intelligent and strong Black men who are making an investment in their lives; and those men are not trying to hit on their mamas or get next to the women who gave them birth.

Those men are only helping show them another way of being in the world. Those men are showing them that gangbanging is not the only option.

Those men offer an invaluable gift with the gift of their time and their presence every week. They are in the public schools for the forty weeks that the school is in session every year! They preach Jesus with their lives! That is ministry "outside of the box!"

Tape Ministry

Before our Tape Ministry became sophisticated, before the advent of iPods, iPhones, MP3s and the high-tech recording equipment our church now has and utilizes to "reach the masses," our old

Tape Ministry used to function in a very basic way, yet they also functioned in a most effective way.

Starting from a hand-held cassette recorder that was in the lap of the Stewardship Council members as they recorded the services each Sunday, our Tape Ministry grew and developed into a system that recorded the services on cassette tapes through the public address system of the church. Those tapes were not just for sale at the end of the service; however, those tapes had another purpose! Those tapes were taken by people who volunteered to work with and in the Tape Ministry into the sick rooms and into the homes of people who could not get to Worship Service.

Tape Ministers like Reverend Charlene Porter would carry tapes of the Sunday Services into the hospital wards each week. They would sit with the sick and shut-in and play the entire service for them, ministering to them with a ministry of presence and sharing with them the weekly Worship Services of our congregation.

Tape Ministers like Roebuck "Pops" Staples would pick up the tapes of a service each Sunday after service and take those tapes into the homes, the sickrooms and the senior citizen homes of those people who were "homebound" or who could not get out to worship in a church on a Sunday. Pops Staples never did what he did for publicity's sake or to let the world see that he was a member of Trinity Church. He served quietly and "behind the scenes" to make sure that those who could not get to worship in the sanctuary had a chance to worship in their homes as he took tapes of the Sunday Worship Services to them fifty-two weeks a year!

Domestic Violence Ministry

In the year 2008, Prophetess Juanita Bynum and her husband made the issue of domestic violence an issue that publicly made the church aware of what the church already knew privately for hundreds of years! In the year 2009, Rihanna and Chris Brown, joined by BeBe Winans, took the "Christian domestic violence" issue a notch higher. They opened the eyes of the general public to what the eyes of church members already knew and kept silent about! Domestic violence has been a national problem ever since this country was founded.

This country was founded on the principles of chauvinism and sexism. This country was founded on the principle of violence and the same "cowboy mentality" that made many Americans think we had the right to take another people's country, to take over their land, to rape their women and to have a John Wayne attitude that says, "Do it my way or get off of my planet by sundown" spilled over into our male-female relationships and our marriages.

That sick mentality did not stop at the church door. That sick mentality did not go away because somebody accepted Christ as their personal Savior. That sick mentality was dragged right into the Body of Christ from its inception.

Domestic violence has been a major problem in the church ever since there has been a church. Domestic violence has not skipped the Black church either. Domestic violence is just a sin that is not talked about in the Black church!

Dedicated members of our church, women who were survivors of domestic violence and ministers of the Gospel, like Reverend Sharon Ellis Williams-Davis, did more than just talk about domestic violence privately and pray about it fervently. They formed a Domestic Violence Ministry to make men and women aware of the pandemic and to teach them how to deal with that reality. That ministry offers resources, help, counseling referrals and recovery regimens to help survivors of domestic violence come out of those experiences healthy, whole, healed and headed in a new direction!

That ministry is also one of the ministries of our congregation that is "outside of the box."

Mental Health Ministry

Back in the 1970s one of our health professionals, Mrs. Modestine Fain, said to me that there were members of the church in the Allied Health professions who wanted to be active in their church using the skills and expertise that they had as professionals in the field of health. They did not want to be a traditional "Nurses Board," however. They did not want to wear white in service and run up into the pulpit with handkerchiefs and water for the preacher or for guest ministers.

They wanted to take what it was they learned in school and what it was they did for a living and use that to be a blessing in the lives of the members of the congregation. They did not want to limit the service possibilities to just the Field of Nursing. They wanted to open it up to everybody in the health professions. I told them to run with the idea and they did.

Modestine Fain, Mildred Chapman and several other health professionals gathered together doctors, surgeons, laboratory technicians, nurses, physical therapists, paramedics and as many other professionals in the Allied Health fields as they could gather.

They named themselves the "Health Advisory Board" and they
began a health ministry in the congregation that has been nothing
short of phenomenal!

From having medical personnel stationed throughout the
Sanctuary in every service on every Sunday of the year (and
during services held during the week) to be literally "on-call" in
case of a medical emergency up to and including health fairs,
health seminars and providing vital information for members of
the congregation, the Health Advisory Board has been a ministry
that is "outside of the box."

They changed their name to an African name also. They changed
their name to Immabasi, but the work they did and continue to
do stays the same. Providing free inoculations for school-age
children, providing free mammograms, providing free prostate
testing, providing free dental screening and blood pressure testing
for the membership and the community around the church, on
a regular basis, throughout the years since the 1970s has been
one of Immabasi's ongoing functions.

The start-up of several different support ministries such as the
Cancer Support Ministry (Can-Cer-Vive), the Lupus Support
Ministry, the MS Support Ministry and the Physically-Impaired
Ministry which has evolved into its own ministry named
Kujichagulia has been yet another blessing brought to us by the
Immabasi Ministry which is way "outside of the box!"

Working in concert with the HIV/AIDS Ministry to provide free
AIDS testing and working with the Teenage Sexuality Ministry
to provide crucial information to our teens and their parents
about sexually-transmitted diseases and the tie-in between
sexuality and spirituality has been yet another blessing we have
received through the Health Advisory Ministry and Immabasi.

The formation of our Hospice Ministry which will be discussed in a separate section and the formation of our Mental Health Ministry have been two of the most awesome and visible results of the labors and love put forth by members of Immabasi.

During our annual church foci on specific medical challenges affecting the African American community (hypertension, breast cancer, prostate cancer, etc.), members of Immabasi pointed out to me that there needed to be a separate ministry for mental health. Very little was said about mental health in the context of a church. Very little was being done about mental health in the context of our church except for our Counseling Ministry and our Pastoral Staff which did individual and family counseling.

The Mental Health Ministry was started and began serving (and continues to serve) dozens of families in the church whose family members face mental health challenges. Because of the information provided in the bulletin during Mental Health Month and the "help numbers" listed in the bulletin during Mental Health Month, the Mental Health Ministry has been responsible for persons and their families dealing successfully with schizophrenia, with bipolar disorders, with clinical depression and with countless other mental health challenges. That is yet another ministry that performs excellently "outside of the box."

TUCHC/Amani

Back during the '80s when one of our members, Deacon Prandal White, was stricken with an incurable disease, there were several members of the Deacon Board who rallied around him. Several other members who were not deacons cared for Prandal and expressed their love for Prandal as he wrestled with issues of life and death.

It was in the early '90s that Prandal was diagnosed as being "terminal." He had no family in the church and he was literally dying alone. His approach toward death's door reminded me of what another one of our members, Herman Newman, had said to me way back when we started our HIV/AIDS Ministry. Herman's words still haunt me to this day. He said to me, *"Reverend! Nobody should have to die alone like this!"*

Three of our members, Freddye Smith, Deacon Francis Priester and Deacon Rosalyn Priester made sure that Prandall did not die alone. They not only cared for him up to the day of his death. They not only cared for him and his funeral arrangements after his death. They made sure that their efforts would be immortalized in a ministry that has come to be known today as our Hospice Ministry. They worked with me and with several healthcare providers in the city of Chicago trying to setup and establish a church-based hospice care ministry.

Francis, Freddye, Rosalyn and I sat at the table with Advocate Healthcare for over a year trying to use the resources of Advocate as the financial backing for the hospice program.

After a year of negotiations the management of Advocate decided that it was not economically feasible for them to pursue the idea any further. (There goes that dollar thing again!) There was no financial payoff for Advocate. This is what they told us to our face. Advocate walked away from the table and we began talking with other hospice companies in the city of Chicago trying to partner with those who had the finances as we provided the love, the care and the Christian-based focus for persons who were faced with incurable diseases.

Through the Herculean efforts of Rosalyn and Francis Priester we were able to get a state license as the only church-based, not-for-profit hospice care program in the state of Illinois.

Hospice caregivers were trained. Hospice ministry started being provided. VITAS had one of its field workers as a member of our congregation and when he learned of what we were doing in hospice care, he took a report to VITAS and VITAS came to us and asked us to partner with them in providing the services that we could not provide by ourselves.

Hospice care was very costly and we had no income from our not-for-profit hospice corporation licensed by the state. VITAS showed us how there could be a profit and we gave up our state license to enter into a relationship with VITAS to become the Trinity/VITAS Hospice Care Corporation.

Because a separate corporation was required for the legal matters involving VITAS and Trinity, the Amani Healthcare Corporation was started. That program was still in its infant stages when the white-owned corporate media decided that Jeremiah Wright was unpatriotic. Jeremiah Wright was too incendiary. Jeremiah Wright was too controversial and Jeremiah Wright was not a name with which a respectable company like VITAS wanted to be linked with, so VITAS terminated the relationship.

Hospice care, however, continued and continues to be given because we are a group of Christians who care about palliative care. We are a congregation of believers who cared about end-of-life matters. We are in the ministry serving those who were dying. We are not in the ministry because of Jeremiah Wright, because of Barack Obama, because of who went to Trinity Church, who belonged to the church or what important names were associated with the church. We did what we were doing and are still doing because of Jesus who is Lord and who is the Head of the Church!

The hours spent in the homes and by the bedsides of those who are dying is a ministry that gets no public media play because the general public does not see what the hospice ministers do on a day-to-day basis. Trinity Church is not well known in the public eye because of its Hospice Ministry.

Trinity's Sanctuary Choir, its preaching pastors, its Revivals and its powerful Services of Worship are what made the headlines before "Obamamania" caused unscrupulous media persons to cause Trinity to make the headlines for other reasons. The Trinity United Community Health Center/Amani Ministry, however, was functioning long before "Obamamania" and continues to function today to provide an umbrella for the wide variety of healthcare ministries that are engaged in by the members of this congregation.

The purchase of our Damen Building, the Village Center, from Advocate Healthcare, the purchase of an HIV/AIDS home for persons who are in their final days of life, the HIV/AIDS Ministry which was taken under that corporation's umbrella, the Can-Cer-Vive Ministry and all health-related ministries are all carried out under the loving focus of that ministry which still hears Jesus say, "*When I was sick, you visited me!*"

Trinity Higher Education Corporation

In the 1980s several committed educators who were members of the congregation combined their efforts with parents who had complained to them about their children being steered away from Historically Black Colleges and Universities! Those who worked in the field of Education and those parents of children who were products of the Chicago Public Schools found out that in far too many instances Black children were being steered in the wrong direction by high school guidance counselors!

Rather than get on soapboxes and talk about the racism that was programming Black children for positions that high school counselors felt that those children ought to be in because they were Black and not offering to them the professional and skilled positions that they were advising their white students to pursue, our members decided to start a High School Counseling Ministry.

The High School Counseling Ministry is a ministry that helps African American high school students understand how the sky really is the limit!

The High School Counseling Ministers taught our students that every profession that is open to a human being is available to a human being whose skin is black and whose hair is nappy! All the students had to do was apply themselves.

One of the persons who worked with our High School Counseling Ministry in the 1980s was a young man named Mr. Eric Williams. Eric had a vast amount of experience and expertise in the area of Guidance Counseling and Eric helped that ministry put itself on the map in the life of our congregation in a very powerful way.

Eric left us to go to Knox College. He became an officer in the Financial Aid Department at Knox College. He also became the surrogate father, big brother and faculty sponsor to the Black students at Knox College!

After working at Knox for several years, Eric spoke to me about his desire to be giving his efforts to students in the Black community instead of giving his all at a white college. He was helping many Black students, yes. He was helping an occasional white student, yes. He was doing it in a climate, however, of constantly having to prove himself and justify his existence. Racism was still alive and well in the 1980s!

At the same time that Eric was talking with me about his burning desire to share his expertise in the Black community, Mr. Blaine DeNye was sharing with the Long Range Planning Ministry our need for a "new Silas Purnell" to replace the *real* Silas Purnell the day Silas stepped off of the scene as an invaluable resource for black high school students! Silas Purnell was nowhere near death when Mr. DeNye said that. Silas had just reached gargantuan proportions in the Black community.

Mr. Purnell was responsible for getting thousands of students into college. Mr. Purnell single-handedly put more students from the inner city of Chicago and the projects in Chicago into major white universities throughout this country (many with scholarships!) than any two or three combined agencies trying to do what Silas Purnell did all by himself! Mr. DeNye pointed out to us that once Silas left the scene, however, the Black community would be in a real hurting position. We had no one to replace him.

I asked Eric (who was Providentially placed by God at that specific moment in our history) if he would like to come home and work for Trinity Church. His work would really be doing what he had been doing as a volunteer with our High School Counseling Ministry—only more. Eric said yes, and another ministry "outside of the box" was birthed.

Eric came home and came aboard our staff as our College Placement Officer. I literally said to him that I wanted him to go sit at the feet of Silas Purnell and learn everything that Silas did from the ground up. I wanted him to be so close to Silas that Silas would trust him to give him all of his contacts at all of the colleges, all of their phone numbers and all of the ways in which we could continue to help students get into school once Silas retired. Eric Williams did more than I asked him to do!

Eric became so effective in his position as our College Placement Officer that he carried that job and that position into so many arenas that we had to form a separate corporation for the church! We had to form the Trinity Higher Education Corporation.

Maxwell House Coffee used to have College Fairs for the Historically Black Colleges and Universities. (When I started at Trinity Church, many high school counselors were badmouthing the HBCU's and with our students being hundreds of miles away from those schools, all they had to go on was what their high school counselors were saying about those schools!) Maxwell House Coffee, however, soon ran into the "cost-effective" dilemma that businesses always seem to run into when it comes to serving the Black community.

The Historical Black Colleges and Universities Fair was the first and sometimes the only exposure many Black Chicago high school students had to that rich history and legacy. The college fairs, however, were no longer "cost-effective" for the Maxwell House corporation, so Maxwell House stopped sponsoring them. Eric Williams picked up where Maxwell House Coffee left off! Eric and the Trinity Higher Education Corporation started having Annual HBCU College Fairs. They were serving as many as 1,000 students a year when Eric left the Trinity Higher Education Corporation to go to work for the Chicago Public School System.

In addition to the Historically Black Colleges and Universities Fairs, Eric also began to have Spring College Tours to expose students to the Historically Black Colleges and Universities.

Those tours would offer three to four different routes, so schools as far apart as Prairie View in Texas (outside of Houston, Texas) and Quinn College in Dallas, Texas could be seen by students who attended that tour while other students could see Wilberforce, Lemoyne-Owen (in Memphis), Grambling, Southern and Dillard in New Orleans and other schools in the mid-South.

Yet another tour route would take students to see schools on the East coast like Lincoln University, Howard University, Virginia Union University and Hampton University (with Virginia State, Norfolk State and maybe Elizabeth City and Livingston College) being seen by persons on that tour. The fourth tour would cover the schools in North Carolina and South Carolina that were Historically Black Colleges and Universities.

Eric also expanded the Annual College Tours to cover non-Black schools in the neighboring states next to Illinois and throughout the state of Illinois. The tours grew to such an extent that we had to offer one tour for children in the public school system and another tour for children whose Spring Break had them out of school during a different week than the children from the public school system and the week that they were out of school for Spring Break.

Before leaving us to go to the Chicago Public School System, Eric had expanded the work of the Trinity Higher Education Corporation to include the TRIO Program and other government-funded programs that helped low-income and African American students from the 9th grade through the 12th grade to prepare for college, to increase their Grade Point Averages and to get a "head-start" at the high school and college level that would enable them to be admitted to any school in the nation!

That ministry is not a ministry of the church that is seen on a Sunday in the Sanctuary. It is a ministry that is carried on seven days a week, however, and a ministry that has resulted in hundreds of students being able to go to and finish college because of the dedicated work of those who believed in them when society said that they would never make it! This was truly a ministry "outside of the box."

Our ministry "outside of the box" has a long and exciting history. Many names that are well-known because of their celebrity have grown up in the church while others have been attracted to our church and only been members of the church tangentially; while yet others who have no celebrity have been active, functioning, hardworking members of our church for many, many years. They get no recognition in the public's eye, but they are dear to the heart of God because they carry out the work of God for the people of God; and they carry that work out "outside of the box" of what is normally thought of as ministry that takes place in a Black church sitting in a poor neighborhood on the Southside of Chicago.

Our church has had "big name" members of every possible stripe imaginable. We have had entertainers who are active members of the church. "Common" grew up in our church. He was a member of the Cub Scout Troop here when he was a youngster. Back then his name was Lonnie Lynn. He changed it to Rashid Lynn, but he still is a member of the church. He would freestyle my sermon, before the end of the service, every time he came home to worship with us and my daughter, Jeri, or I would see him in worship service.

Pops Staples, Mavis Staples and Yvonne Staples were active members of the church. Pops Staples, as I mentioned, was one of the most faithful members of our Tape Ministry.

Dr. Manford Byrd was a Founding Member of our church. He ended up being the Superintendent of Schools for the City of Chicago.

We have had elected officials who were members of the church from Aldermen through State Representatives, through State Senators, through a United States Senator, up to and including a President of the United States of America.

The phenomenal ministry of the church, however, is carried out by the ordinary, everyday, "drylongso" people. They make the church happen. They combine their efforts as lawyers and teachers, as homemakers and construction workers, as unemployed persons and Appellate Court judges, as office personnel and electrical engineers. They understand that their professions have absolutely nothing to do with their profession of faith!

For years our church officially followed an "outside of the box" theology in that we called ourselves the "Alphabet Soup Church." We had every alphabet imaginable in our congregation. We had A.B.'s, B.S.'s, M.A.'s, M.S.'s, S.T.M.'s, M.Th.'s, J.D.'s, M.D.'s, PhD's and A.D.C.'s. (ADC for the readers outside the city of Chicago means "Aid to Dependent Children." Those are persons who are members of our church who are on welfare.)

We taught our members this truth openly and we tried to model it out daily: The letters *behind* your name have absolutely nothing to do with the church. The letters behind your name are how you make a living. The church has to do with how you make a life! That approach to ministry was definitely "outside of the box" during an era when Negroes wanted to be middle class, when bourgeois Negroes were very conscious about classism and pretentiously conscious about those with whom they were associated.

The Black Value System which the congregation adopted in 1981 purposely did away with the so-called notion of "classes." We wanted all of our members to know that they were all first-class citizens in the eyes of God and that kind of ministry was definitely "outside of the box" in terms of how churches are normally perceived and how Black churches especially are perceived.

Marvin McMickle's book, **Preaching to the Middle Class,** talks about that strange phenomenon where African Americans see themselves as middle class and see themselves as being "a cut above" the ordinary people. Nothing could be more lethal in the life of a church than that kind of sick mentality.

When I used to teach New Member Class I would illustrate this important principle by sharing this analogy with our new members. The church is the family of God. The church is an extended family. The African American church especially is built on the African principle of family, community and the African concept of *ubuntu*. Class distinctions and socioeconomic distinctions mean absolutely nothing in a family that is genuine, authentic and seeking to live out the Word of God and the Will of God. The same is true for the family of God.

I would share with our new members the fact that my mother's side of the family was saturated with higher education. All of her siblings had earned doctorates with the exception of my Aunt Pearl. My Aunt Pearl, however, had a Master's degree from a musical conservatory. She was an accomplished musician who wrote music.

My father's side of the family, however, was just the opposite. He was the only person in his family to finish college. His father, my Grandpa Jim, had a third grade education. He was a tobacco farmer in Caroline County, Virginia. When our family gathered, however, I could come into the room with four earned degrees and be considered in the eyes of the world, "Dr. Wright!"

I was the one who had spent all of those years earning a Bachelor's degree from Howard University, a Master's degree from Howard University, a Master of Arts degree in the History of Religions from The University of Chicago and a Doctor of Ministry degree from United Theological Seminary. I was the one who had studied Spanish and Latin, German and French, Hebrew and Arabic. I was the one who had taught seminary and was I credentialed to teach at any accredited seminary anywhere in the United States of America.

When my Grandpa Jim called me and said, "*Boy?*," however, I jumped up from wherever I was sitting and went to him saying, "*Yes, Sir? Did you need me for anything?*" Why?

The why was simple. That was my grandpa. We were family. My four degrees and all of that study meant absolutely nothing when it came to Grandpa Jim. It meant absolutely nothing when it came to me and how I saw myself in the eyes of a man whom I respected fiercely and to whom I looked up to in awe and admiration. He had sent my daddy away to college with all of the money he had in the world - - twenty-five cents! When my Grandpa Jim called, I answered.

When Grandpa Jim called me he was my grandfather. He was a respected elder and I gave him the respect he was due. That is how our family functioned and that is how the family of God was to function.

We used to tell new members that anybody who thought that their degrees made them better than some other member of the church had found the wrong church. They needed to go find a social club that majored in class distinctions, class divisions and "bourgeois-ology." That is not who we were and that is not who we would ever be!

We had the Commissioner of Health who was a member of our church. We had elected officials who were members of our church. We had professional entertainers who were members of our church; but we also had members who did hair in their basement, members who did hair in their kitchens, using their stoves for the hot comb because they could not afford to rent a chair in a beauty shop. We had members who did tuckpointing. We had members who worked for minimum wage.

We had members who were unemployed and all of those members were just as important as the Circuit Court judges, the Appellate Court judges, the surgeons and the professors of college and graduate school who sat beside them every Sunday praising God; and who walked beside them and worked beside them each day of the week in the various ministries in which they chose to serve. That was our biggest "outside of the box" achievement as an African American church at the end of the 20th century and we pointed to that reality with great pride and thanksgiving to God.

Several other corporations grew out of the ministry of a congregation that operated "outside of the box." Our housing corporations were in place to oversee the Trinity Acres and

Trinity Oaks housing facilities. Our childcare corporation was in place to oversee the childcare operations at 532 West 95th Street and at 69th and Stony Island. Our Federally-Charted Credit Union was a separate corporation that was in place as an institution in which Blacks could save and from which Blacks could borrow while paying themselves the interest!

Our Higher Education Corporation was in place for giving African American students a chance at secondary education that they might not otherwise have ever gotten. Our Healthcare Corporation was in place to provide for the needs of the members in the community from the toddler age to their senior years.

The for-profit corporations which the Long Range Planning Ministry had indicated we needed were in place to try to generate funds to pay for those ministries that would never be self-supporting.

A Community Development Corporation was started and an Economic Development Corporation was started. Those corporations were put in place to operate "outside of the box" and to generate funds to support the ongoing ministries and the ever-growing ministries of a congregation that was trying to be faithful to its call to be a Black church in the Black community and to continue to be "**Unashamedly Black and Unapologetically Christian.**"

Trumpet Newsmagazine

Yet, another corporation, *Trumpet Newsmagazine*, had to be formed when our *Trumpet* magazine went from being a monthly church publication to being a national religious publication. When I started at Trinity United Church of Christ we had a monthly church newsletter. It was the Trinity Newsletter. Mr.

Rupert Graham, Sr., published that newsletter and it consisted primarily of activities and different opportunities for Worship Service that were going to be held at the church and were offered for the benefit of the Trinity members. Mr. Graham would feature different members from time-to-time in the newsletter. He would share a portion of that person's biography and give our readers some aspects concerning that person's life that were not normally known.

Ten years into my pastorate, Reverend Barbara Allen surprised me on my 10th anniversary with the publication of the first edition of *The Trinity Trumpet*. It was a church newspaper that expanded the newsletter concept and carried articles in its pages for our members concerning not only what was going on at Trinity, but items concerning what was going on in the city, in the nation and throughout the world that affected Africans, Africans in Diaspora in general and African American Christians in particular.

Reverend Allen utilized the news items published by the Commission for Racial Justice, published by the Office of Church-In-Society, published by the President's Office of the United Church of Christ and published in Black publications to keep our membership informed each month about the crucial matters that affected the membership of our church and their extended families.

At the turn of the century and coming into the 21st century, my daughter, Jeri, took *The Trinity Trumpet* a notch higher. She took our church newspaper from its local focus to a national publication with a national and international focus.

With the kinds of articles that I was writing, however, and the social critique that I was leveling against a government that was hell-bent on empire, the racism that still existed in the church, in the country and in the world, and articles that would upset a lot of racists and conservative readers who might pick up our magazine in far-flung, far-away places, our attorneys advised us that we needed to separate the entire media department , which included *Trumpet Newsmagazine,* away from the church.

We did not need any lawsuits against *Trumpet* that would affect the church or that would pierce the corporate veil of the church. The word "Trinity" was dropped from the title and *Trumpet Newsmagazine* began to be published as an independent magazine and setup as its own corporation.

The *Trumpet Newsmagazine* enjoyed national acclaim. My daughter, Jeri, its publisher and editor-in-chief, was honored by Xernona Clayton and the Trumpet Awards for her outstanding work in journalism and *Trumpet* had a readership that stretched from Seattle to San Diego and from Massachusetts to Miami. *Trumpet Newsmagazine* started giving annual awards to persons that the Board of Directors of *Trumpet* felt were deserving of being singled-out for their contributions in their various fields.

Awards were given to persons as varied and as diverse as Reverend Jesse Louis Jackson, Reverend Al Sharpton and Minister Louis Farrakhan. Awards went to Father Michael Pfleger and to Nancy Wilson, Mavis Staples, Kirk Whalum and Frankie Beverly. I was even given an award as was our Pastor's father, the Reverend Otis Moss, Jr.

When the racist media tried to use me and anything associated with me to derail the candidacy of President Barack Obama, they seized upon *Trumpet Newsmagazine* and an article that was written by Rhoda McKinney Jones as one of their "weapons of mass destruction." Mrs. Jones complimented and commended Minister Farrakhan for his awesome work. The media did not bother to point out to the nation that Mrs. Jones wrote the article. They took Mrs. Jones' words and put them in my mouth and said that I had called Minister Farrakhan whatever it was Mrs. Jones had said about him. (I honestly do not remember at this point!)

With that sound byte and *Trumpet*'s name being affiliated with Father Michael Pfleger and Minister Louis Farrakhan, the sharks came after us big-time. *Trumpet* already was suffering financially from a lack of supporters. We could not get all of the members of the congregation to subscribe to *Trumpet Newsmagazine*, while the majority of the growing subscription base was outside of the church, across the country and across international waters. I was reminded of one of the popular sayings that we used to hear back in the 1960s. It said, *"If you want to hide something from Black folk, put it in print!"* We as Black people in general are not a reading people!

Not only could not our national subscriptions continue to support the publication of *Trumpet*, our own membership would not take out enough subscriptions to support the publication of *Trumpet Newsmagazine*. The advertisement market which we sought to help in the publication of *Trumpet* was very narrow because of our social justice focus and our stance on certain issues.

Our fight, for instance, with an institution like Wal-Mart would not allow us to take advertising monies from Wal-Mart or from corporations that discriminated against women, corporations that discriminated against Blacks and Browns, corporations that supported sweatshops in Third World countries and corporations which stood in direct opposition to the Gospel of Jesus Christ.

That cut down the range of places where we could get advertising monies to such a great extent that we were financially not able

to keep publishing *Trumpet.* The media attacks opening up a
can of racist worms who then came after *Trumpet Newsmagazine*
caused us to have to stop publication and dissolve that
corporation.

The idea of a church sponsoring the publication, however, that
talked about far more than bake sales, pastors' anniversaries,
"feel good" self-help columns and "spiritual matters" was mind-
blowing. It was definitely "outside of the box." The idea for
Trumpet, however, had come from one of my mentors at The
University of Chicago Divinity School.

Dr. Martin Marty was my primary professor in Church History
in 1969 and 1970. Dr. Martin Marty is the American Church
History scholar under whom Dr. Julia Speller received her PhD.
Dr. Martin Marty said to me (and to all of us in his class) back in
1969 that church publications were really very much like some
sort of Holy joke!

By that he meant you could walk into any church on any given
Sunday and pick up a church publication - - either its bulletin or
its newsletter - - and think you had stepped from the real world
into a fantasy world.

He challenged us in 1969 to look at the different church bulletins
where we worshipped. *"See if they talked about anything of
substance,"* he said. He asked us to compare church bulletins
with the newspapers to see if they talked about the Apartheid in
South Africa, to see if they talked about the race problem in
America, to see if they talked about what Christians were
supposed to do as persons of faith when it came to the issues
affecting the poor, the Blacks, the Browns and those whom Jesus
called *"the least of these."*

Inevitably, he pointed out, the real world in which Jesus lived (and in which we lived) was left in the Narthex of the church each week and a make-pretend world was entered into as worshippers only dealt with Girl Scout Cookie sales, Women's Clubs, Teas, the color of the usher or choir uniforms or the latest fundraising drive, etc., etc.; and nothing that shaped the world into which those worshippers would be heading at one o'clock when the Benediction was given.

With that kind of challenge from Dr. Marty, I was determined that our church bulletin and our church newsletter would move beyond the "fantasy world" to the factual world. I tried to make sure each week that my Pastor's Word in the weekly bulletin directed the attention of our worshippers to a matter of importance in the world in which we had to live following the Benediction. Reverend Barbara Allen asked me to write a monthly column in *The Trinity Trumpet* and I tried to make sure that my column in that publication did the same thing each month that my "Pastor's Words" were doing each week in the church bulletin.

My daughter, Jeri, took that approach to religious journalism to a higher degree. She wanted to make sure that *Trumpet Newsmagazine* was a magazine that dealt with social justice issues in each issue of the magazine! That kind of "outside of the box" thinking produced some powerful writing. It also produced many enemies throughout the nation!

Our ministry in the 1990s also continued with our "outside of the box" thinking. Our Men's Week, our Women's Week, our Youth Revivals and our Church Revivals could never be classified as "normal," or "typical" in terms of what one would expect to find in an African American congregation.

I grew up in a church where we had an Annual Men's Day and Women's Day. I grew up in a church where we had an Annual Youth Day. That Youth Day was always on "Children's Day" (the second Sunday in June). When I came to Trinity we had a Men's Day and a Women's Day. My first year here I changed our annual "Youth Day" to four Youth Days or four Youth Sundays a year. Even when our Youth Choir started singing every month we kept the four Youth Sundays each year, so that our youth could lead the entire Worship Service on that Sunday.

Beginning in the early 1980s, however, we moved from Men's Day and Women's Day to Men's Week and Women's Week. We would not only have a Guest Speaker for Men's Day and Women's Day. We would have a concert by the Men's Chorus on the Sunday that started Men's Week and we would have a concert by the Women's Chorus on the Sunday that started Women's Week.

Our guest ministers for the week would preach the entire week! That was "outside of the box" for a typical Black church. It was definitely "outside of the box" for a United Church of Christ congregation.

When my wife, Ramah, was wrestling with her Call to Ministry, she and Reverend Barbara Heard took our Women's Week to yet another level! Ramah was a deacon in the church and Reverend Barbara Heard was one of the Associate Ministers of the church. The two of them took their focus on Women's Ministry into uncharted waters and began to have Annual Women's Conferences for our church. The Conferences were so powerful that they began to attract women from all over the country and some women from out of the country (the Caribbean, West Africa and South Africa).

Reverend Ramah and Reverend Barbara Heard would start the Women's Conference on the Friday night leading into Women's Week. The Conference would run Friday night and all day Saturday. There would be workshops. There would be seminars. There would be Worship. There would be small groups wrestling with crucial issues that affected African American Christian women and the results of the Annual Women's Conference were absolutely incredible! That kind of thinking and that kind of ministry was truly "out of the box."

Our men quickly followed suit!

Under the leadership of Reverend John Jackson (our Minister to Men) our men began to have Annual Men's Conferences. They would follow the same format established by the women and they would add their own "twist" to the activities for men that proved literally lifesaving! They added things like physical check-ups for the men who attended the Conference and free prostate testing.

Because Dr. Terry Mason was a member of our congregation, he provided the medical personnel necessary to do the prostate screening at our Men's Conferences and prostate cancer was detected in no less than fifteen men as a result of those annual Conferences. Eight of those men required surgery and are living today (had their lives saved!) because of that ministry which was "outside of the box."

Our Men's Ministry and the Men's Conference were programmatically set up just like the Women's Conference. The Men's Conference would be on the weekend leading into Men's Week; and the Conference would be followed by a weeklong series of services with nightly preaching as the work of the men of the church was celebrated.

Our Married Couples Ministry and our Singles Ministry utilized the same "outside of the box" kind of thinking to host Annual Singles Conferences and Annual Married Couples Conferences. If you will remember, I pointed out that during our transformative stage we had Churchwide Retreats. That was when the entire church would go away for a Friday and Saturday to take part in the spiritual retreat. Those retreats used to culminate with Sunrise Service Baptisms in Lake Michigan on the Sunday that the retreat ended!

Once our membership grew beyond the capacity for any one facility to hold us, however, we stopped having Churchwide Retreats. The Women's Conferences, the Men's Conferences, the Singles Ministry Conferences and the Married Couples Ministry Conferences replaced those Churchwide Retreats. Our Married Couples Conference had over 500 persons gather the first year that they had a Conference. Mary Crayton and her husband, Clarence Crayton, put that Conference together and set the model and paradigm for subsequent Conferences to be held each year. Married couples would start off the weekend with Worship and then have a Friday evening of relaxation.

On Saturday (all day) we would have sessions dealing with Married Couples issues. Some of the small group sessions would be for the couples to attend as husband and wife. Others would be sessions "For Men Only" and sessions "For Women Only." There were some sessions in which hard questions were asked of a panel and the questions were "X-rated" many times because there were sexual issues that Christian couples were wrestling with that they could not talk about in any other context other than in the safe "cocoon" of a community of caring Christian couples, led by committed Christian clergypersons. The same was true with the singles!

Our Singles Ministry was started in the 1970s. The Singles Conferences, however, did not start until the 1990s. Those Conferences were truly "outside of the box." Issues were discussed at a church Conference that one would never have entertained as having been discussed twenty years ago.

In the last year of my pastorate I was able (though it was like pulling teeth and many came kicking and screaming against the idea) to bring the singles together, the married couples together, the men together and the women together once again to have one last Churchwide Conference which was the same as our Churchwide Retreats. Of course, the married couples wanted to have their night all by themselves with no singles present; and the singles wanted to reciprocate. I guess some things never change no matter how much love you have for the Lord and no matter how hard you try to break old patterns and "tradition."

At that final Churchwide Conference while I was Pastor, I was able to bring in a friend of mine and her husband, Angela Bassett and Courtney Vance.

Our *Trumpet Newsmagazine* had just feted Angela and Courtney at the home of Danny Bakewell in Los Angeles. Danny Bakewell is the owner and publisher of the *Los Angeles Sentinel.* We presented Angela and Courtney as they read passages and excerpts from their co-authored book and as they did a book signing. They very graciously accepted Jeri's invitation to come and do the same thing for our Churchwide Conference. They came to the Conference. They read from their book. They signed copies of their book and they worshipped with us. Having Angela and Courtney at a spiritual gathering is ministry that is definitely "outside of the box."

My close association with jazz musicians and popular musicians blessed our church in countless other ways on far too many Sundays (and other opportunities for Worship) too many, in fact, for me to count! Kirk Whalum would bring his entire group to our Sunday Morning Worship Services and would play in both Morning Worship Services. Wynton Marsalis would bring his entire group to Worship with us and to play for us during Worship. Stanley Turrentine used to bring his saxophone to church to play for us whenever he was in the city.

One Sunday, Stanley was in church and I asked him where his axe was. He shrugged his shoulders and said he had just come to Worship; he did not come to play that Sunday. Boy did he get surprised! At that very service (on Easter Sunday morning) Wynton Marsalis and his quintet walked into the services thirty minutes after we opened the service. They came into the pulpit to play "Just a Closer Walk With Thee" New Orleans jazz style. Stanley Turrentine had a fit. He had no sax to play along with them and I told him, "*See? I told you so! Don't ever come without your axe, Stanley!*"

John B. Williams, the bassist for Nancy Wilson, came in to surprise me for my 25th anniversary. He practiced secretly the week leading into my anniversary Sunday. He practiced along with Pops Staples and the Staple Singers to sing and perform with our Sanctuary Choir in a Service of Tribute for twenty-five years of service that I had offered to our congregation. For my 35th anniversary, Frankie Beverly and Maze came in to do an hour and a half performance at my Anniversary Banquet. This was definitely ministry "outside of the box."

It is those moments of ministry, however, that set our church apart as a "different church. Those kinds of ministry did not follow the typical and "traditional" church things as we tried to minister to the whole person and be a church that was a Black church in the middle of the Black community and serving the Lord of the church simultaneously. As I look back over the years and see what God has done for our church as it has ministered "outside of the box," I have to say once again, *"Nothing but a God!"*

Even our Church Revivals were not "typical." I had heard Reverend Dr. James Forbes in 1980 preach one of the most powerful sermons I have ever heard in my life. The sermon was entitled, "The Black Church: Extension of the Incarnation; 'This and That'!" That sermon, incidentally, became the introductory sermon for all of our Bible classes while I was the Pastor. Members (and non-members) who took our Bible classes needed to know that the Word of God and the ministry of our church was not an "either/or proposition." It was both-and. Jim's sermon drives that point home powerfully!

Dr. Charles Adams had been one of my mentors for at least twenty years before I actually got him to come to our church and preach in our church. From the time that Dr. Adams started preaching in our church in 1975, he was with us annually until the year I retired.

God gave me the idea to put Dr. Forbes and Dr. Adams together for a Revival and together they preached nightly for ten years at our church, setting records in terms of attendance and in terms of souls saved for the Lord.

I did not get that "outside of the box" format for a Revival off the top of my head, however. I had been one of three Revivalists each night at the church where Kirk Whalum's father served, the Olivet Baptist Church in Memphis. Kenneth Whalum (or K. T. Whalum) would use three preachers each night. I took his idea and adapted it bringing Forbes and Adams together to make the Annual Trinity Church Revival an event to which people would come from all over the nation!

Even our Revivals were "outside of the box."

The men and women of the Gospel who walked beside me and who served our congregation for the thirty-six years that I was there are an invaluable part of our history, our legacy, our story and our "outside of the box" ministry. It is to their gifts that I now turn your attention.

Chapter 5
Look Where God Has Brought Us!

Building a Team of Ministry

For over two decades we sang every First Sunday as we took new members into the congregation,

Look where God has brought us.
Look how far we've come!
We're not what we ought to be.
We're not what we used to be.

Thank you, Lord. Thank you, Lord...
For what you've done!

That song was one of Reverend Barbara J. Allen's favorite songs. Every First Sunday night she would lead that song with joy, with excitement and with great enthusiasm. As we look back in our Sankofa moment to examine the way over which God has brought us, there is no way that the story of Trinity United Church of Christ can be told without Reverend Barbara Allen's name being squarely in the center of that story.

Reverend Barbara was a Founding Member of Trinity United Church of Christ. Reverend Barbara was my Executive Minister for twenty-five years. She was a strong, Black woman of God, a giant in ministry, a compassionate pastor and a topnotch administrator. I make no bones about telling the world that I could not have done what I did as the Pastor of Trinity Church and we would not be where we are as Trinity United Church of Christ had it not been for Reverend Barbara Allen!

Reverend Allen was not the first staff member to join my team of ministry, however. She was perhaps the most important team member for over thirty years, but she was not the first. When I started at Trinity, I was the only fulltime employee.

I had two part-time Directors of Music, a part-time organist, a part-time custodian and within the first six months of my being there (as indicated above) I had a fifth part-time staff member join the team in the person of Mr. Jeffrey Radford. He was the musician for our Teenage Choir, the Youth Fellowship Choir and the Trinity Choral Ensemble (later the Sanctuary Choir).

In the second year of my pastorate, the church had grown to the point that we had enough money to pay another full-time staff person. Dr. Julia Speller was typing the bulletin at home in March of 1972. She was not Dr. Speller back in those days. To us, she was "Judy."

Each week I would take Judy the Altar Call, the Morning Scripture, the Hymn of Praise for the day, the Invitation, my sermon topic and the Scripture passage on which my sermon would focus. "Judy" would type up the stencil for the bulletin. I would pick the stencil up and bring it back to the church and either Judy or I would run it off on the old hand-turned mimeograph machine!

During the second year of my pastorate the trustees allowed me to hire Judy full-time and she became my full-time secretary, no longer working at home, but working at the Church Office. We worked in the same office space which was about ten feet by twelve feet!

Jeff Radford was to become the third full-time staff member of our congregation. That did not happen "all at once." As his responsibilities grew with the choirs growing and the number of choirs growing, he moved from being a part-time employee who worked only with the youth to being the Director of Music with responsibility for the Sanctuary Choir, the Men's Chorus, the Women's Chorus, the Teenage Choir and the Little Warriors for Christ.

In 1975, I asked Reverend Barbara Allen if she would come on my staff and be a part of my team. Reverend Allen was still a full-time employee with Illinois Bell Telephone Company. Reverend Allen said yes and she was consecrated as a Commissioned Minister in the United Church of Christ. She became our Director of Christian Education. My team was now up to three dedicated, loyal and consecrated full-time staff members.

When Reverend Barbara retired from the phone company she came on board as a full-time staff person at the church and she moved from being our Director of Christian Education to being my Assistant Pastor! Reverend Melbalenia D. Evans became the Director of Christian Education and the team of full-time staff was now four persons!

Reverend Barbara began to assemble an office support team who understood the vision of the church, the direction of our ministry, the focus of our service and the purpose for our being a congregation committed to the community in which we sat and Reverend Barbara put together a team that caused our church to function like a well-oiled machine twenty-four hours a day and seven days a week!

I asked the Reverend Barry E. Brandon to be an Associate Pastor on my team in 1979 and he very graciously said yes. He served with us until he was called to be the Pastor of the Beecher Memorial United Church of Christ in New Orleans, Louisiana.

When Dr. Speller left us to go work with Young Life it was because we were not able to pay her what she needed to take care of her growing family. By then, Judy had two children and a third one was on the way! Replacing Judy in the position of Office Administrator were Donita Powell Anderson at first and then Charlene Porter who succeeded Donita Powell Anderson.

When the Reverend Ben Chavis was no longer with the Commission for Racial Justice, as he moved to the position of Executive Director for the National Association for the Advancement of Colored People, he took Donita Anderson away from us and took her to Baltimore where the NAACP headquarters were.

She became his Executive Secretary and her position at Trinity was filled subsequently by Laura Ward, my daughter, Jeri Wright, and then my daughter, Janet.

Janet worked faithfully with me for fifteen years. Her first love, however, was Early Childhood Education. She not only had a double major from Hampton University in Early Childhood Education and the Emotionally Disturbed Child. She also was working on her Master's degree in Early Childhood Education Administration. Janet picked Ivey Matute to be her successor and Janet moved on to be the Executive Director of our Early Childhood Education Program.

Reverend Barbara's office management and fiscal management team included across the years Mary Jane Marshall, Louise Holmes, Yvonne Smith, Kim Dixson, Marlene Minifee, Barbara Patmon, Danita Green and a group of dedicated men and women who worked along with Reverend Barbara to make sure that our vision stayed intact, that our team of ministry stayed focused and that we continued to strive for excellence in every area of ministry.

When I ordained Reverend Donald Fairly into the Gospel of Ministry, I installed him and Reverend Wayne Robinson as Associate Pastors during the same service and I then had two additional clergypersons on our team of ministry, trying to do God's Will and trying to be faithful to the people whom we served.

Toya Perry came aboard as our Chief Financial Officer and Reverend Samuel Ellis became our first Sick and Shut-in Visitation Minister. After Reverend Ellis' sudden and unexpected death, Reverend Paul H. Sadler became our Sick and Shut-in Visitation Minister while he looked for a church to call him as Pastor. Within two years, Reverend Sadler was called to be the Pastor of the Central Congregational Church of New Orleans. He served there until he left to go to the National Church and work for the Board for Homeland Ministries.

Reverend James Dawkins succeeded Reverend Sadler as our Sick and Shut-in Visitation Minister and he served in that capacity until he retired. With Reverend Robinson overseeing our Youth Church, our youth ministries and assisting Reverend Evans in Christian Education, and with Reverend Fairly overseeing the work of the Long Range Planning Ministry, our team worked together to the Glory of God and to the benefit of the people of God.

Reverend Barbara continued to build our staff team methodically, meticulously and with much prayer, careful planning and thoughtful selection. Dr. Colleen Birchett came aboard the staff as our curriculum writer. With her doctorate in curriculum development from the University of Michigan, she started to work on an African-centered church school curriculum that would be used by our church and African American congregations across the country.

Reverend Wanda Jefferson Washington was added to the staff. Her preaching skills and her administrative experience brought us an invaluable resource as we continued to be faithful. Reverend Barbara Heard was called to ministry and while she studied at Garrett Evangelical Seminary she came on our staff and she started building the women's ministry and the ministry to women that has affected the lives of thousands.

Reverend Michael Sykes followed Reverend James Dawkins as our Minister to Sick and Shut-in and our Minister of Visitation. The countless lives that he blessed with his love, his care and his faithfulness are lives that came to know the presence of Christ and the power of prayer in unprecedented ways. Just before I retired, Reverend Sykes was called to serve the First Protestant Church of Park Forest and Deacon Linda Mootry-Dodd (also a seminary graduate) replaced Reverend Sykes in that position.

After finishing seminary at the Samuel DeWitt Proctor School of Theology at Virginia Union University, Reverend Reginald W. Williams and Reverend Stacey Lynn Edwards-Dunn joined our staff as two committed, capable clergypersons whose passion for ministry, passion for the Gospel, passion for the people of God and faithfulness to Christ became legendary.

Reverend Williams headed up our Social Justice Ministry before being called to serve the First Baptist Church of University Park. Rev Edwards-Dunn serves as our Executive Minister.

Reverend Williams carried on the legacy of a social justice ministry that had taken part in the Free South Africa Movement, the Wilmington Ten struggle, the fight against the "Willis Wagons," the anti-Apartheid/Divestment Campaign and the ongoing task of keeping the church of Jesus Christ active in social justice ministries each day of the week and each week of the year.

Reverend Williams called together a group of churches across denominational lines in the Chicago metropolitan area to work together "in the struggle for justice and peace."

Together those churches waged a campaign against Wal-Mart and its unfair practices to its employees - - especially its women employees. That group of churches also took on the unfair labor practices against several major corporations (including our own denomination's Advocate Healthcare System!).

Reverend Reginald Williams and Reverend Michael Pfleger worked together with a host of Chicago churches to try to stop the closing of Bethany Hospital and to address the ongoing crucial issue of healthcare for the poor in the city of Chicago.

Additional members of our pastoral team of ministry included Reverend Ozzie Earl Smith, Mrs. Barbara Smith and Reverend Michael Jacobs. Reverend Ozzie Earl Smith, Jr., came on to our church staff while he was in seminary at McCormick Theological

Seminary. While studying for his Master of Divinity degree, Pastor Smith and his life's mate, Barbara, impacted our Music Department in an incredible manner. (I call Rev. Ozzie "Pastor Smith" because he is now the Pastor of the Covenant United Church of Christ in South Holland, Illinois.) Pastor Smith brought a level of sensitivity in the area of Pastoral Care and Counseling that has blessed our church tremendously.

Barbara Smith had been the Minister of Music at the Olivet Baptist Church in Memphis, Tennessee. When her husband started seminary here in Chicago and they sold their home in Memphis, the Smiths moved into our city, moved into our church and moved into our hearts!

Barbara Smith became an invaluable addition to Mr. Jeff Radford's musical staff. Reverend Ozzie's undergraduate degree was in Music and he had taken over the duties of the Minister of Music at Olivet Church when Barbara was pregnant with their children! He therefore, brought to the church staff not only his powerful preaching and compassionate counseling skills. He also brought a wealth of expertise and experience to the music staff of Trinity United Church of Christ.

Reverend Michael Jacobs grew up in our church! Reverend Michael Jacobs was a teenager in the Trinity Choral Ensemble. Reverend Michael Jacobs was a soloist in the Trinity Choral Ensemble. Then, after his marriage to Carol, Michael's wrestlings with God in many ways mirrored the wrestlings that Jacob had with God by the River Jabbok. God had a Call and claim upon Reverend Jacobs' life and Reverend Jacobs yielded to that Call, threw himself into the heart of our Youth Ministry and became our Minister to Youth and Children.

While he was in seminary, Reverend Jacobs worked along with Reverend Julia Speller. He picked up the mantle of Reverend Wayne Washington's Youth Church Ministry. Reverend Jacobs expanded Youth Church and the concepts and precepts taught in Youth church while working with all of the youth ministries in our congregation that pertained to children and teenagers. Reverend Jacobs and Carole Jacobs are looked upon by members of our youth choirs as their other mother and father!

Reverend Stacey Edwards picked up the mantle of Reverend Carolyn Young who had started our Singles Ministry back in the 1970s. Reverend Stacey took the Singles Ministry into uncharted waters with her First Fridays Worship Services, her Feasting at the Throne weekly Friday services in the Loop, her Singles Conferences and her single communities (the never-marrieds, the divorced singles, the widowed and the same-gender loving singles).

Reverend John Jackson joined the staff and picked up the reins of our Men's Ministry and our ministry to men. Reverend John worked faithfully as a team member until he was called to serve the Trinity United Church of Christ in Gary, Indiana. Reverend Wanda was called to serve the Grace United Church of Christ in Milwaukee, Wisconsin.

Reverend Regina Reed replaced Reverend Wanda Washington and served faithfully with our senior citizens and our women in the church whose numbers were rapidly becoming overwhelming! Reverend Ramah Wright joined the staff while she was a seminarian at Garrett Evangelical; and as I have already indicated, she and Reverend Heard worked together to bless thousands of women with their commitment to Christ and their seriousness about their ministry.

Reverend Ramah not only blessed my life as my partner in marriage and ministry, and my partner in life and in love; Reverend Ramah also blessed my work at Trinity Church in ways that really require a separate book. Her being a part of the pastoral team at Trinity was God's icing on the cake in terms of my trying to serve the Trinity family with integrity and love.

Reverend Tiffany Trent was added to our clergy staff right before my retirement. Her gifts in the Creative Arts Ministry brought a "fresh shot in the arm" to our Church School and our Drama Ministry and the congregation was blessed by her youthfulness and her fresh approach to serving the "least of these" and the little ones.

Reverend Susan Williams Smith breezed into our church in the early 1980s and became a part of our Pastoral Staff in an exciting and endearing way. I met Susan when she was a second year student at the Yale Divinity School. Our denomination had at the time an intern program for seminarians whereby the seminarian would work with a church for one or two summers when school was not in session. If the internship was successful then the student would be guaranteed a position on that church's staff after graduation from seminary if he or she could not get a Call to a congregation somewhere in the denomination.

Reverend Sue asked me pointblank on the night that I met her while I was in the home of the Dean of the Chapel at Yale University, "Can I be an intern at Trinity Church?" Her innocent honesty, her courage and her being unafraid to ask me outright what she wanted caught me off-guard. I said yes to her request and our congregation was blessed beyond compare because of my saying yes.

Sue came and worked for us for two summers and then following her graduation from Yale she served the St. John Congregational United Church of Christ in Springfield, Massachusetts for a short season. She was an Assistant to the Pastor on the staff there, but when the Pastor left, Reverend Sue had no job. She reminded me of what the UCC covenant said concerning the internship. She reminded me boldly just like she had asked about coming to work as an intern that evening as we ate together at Yale Divinity School.

Of course I said, "Yes," once again and Sue came on our staff with an enthusiasm, youthfulness, a commitment to Christ, a passion for the work of the church and an unprecedented willingness to become Reverend Barbara Allen's daughter.

Reverend Barbara (Allen) took Reverend Sue under her wing and they bonded theologically almost as if they were biologically related. Reverend Sue built the foundation for our Women's Ministry that Reverend Heard and Reverend Ramah took over. Reverend Sue started the Sisterhood Ministry.

Unlike the Singles Ministry that was for women who were single (and men who were single), and unlike the Women's Fellowship and the Women's Guild, unlike the women who were a part of the Married Couples Ministry, Sisterhood was for all of the "sisters." Sisterhood had single women, married women, divorced women, young women, old women—all of the women of the church in its ranks.

Reverend Sue changed the name of our Teenage Choir to *Imani Ya Watume* and worked with them as Mr. Radford brought aboard his staff, Reverend Steve Bland as the musician for that choir. Reverend Sue served faithfully until she was called to be the Pastor of the Advent United Church of Christ in Columbus, Ohio.

Reverend Barbara Allen had a daughter in Reverend Susan Smith. She had a son in Mr. Jeffrey Radford. She taught Jeffrey how to build his staff in the same way that she was building the church staff. Mr. Radford faithfully added to his staff across the thirty years that he served with us: Mrs. Lola Robinson, Reverend Steve Bland, Mr. Don Huddleston, Mr. Ron Anderson, Mr. Bryan Johnson, Mrs. Dorothy Coleman, Mr. MacBeth Harris, Mr. Hyman Johnson, Mr. Darnell Singleton, Mr. Tim Brewer and Mrs. Roxanne Stevenson.

Mr. Radford added Mr. Will Austin and Mr. Glenn Lowe. He added two more guitar players, Mr. Tyrone Jackson and Mr. Wayne Barrett and he had volunteers like Reverend Larry Whitman who worked along with him faithfully as he tried to put together and keep together the musical staff that would provide the same quality of music for the congregation of Trinity United Church of Christ no matter which service they chose to attend!

When Mr. Radford became ill, I asked Mr. Robert E. Wooten, Jr. to leave his home in Montclair, New Jersey, to leave his work in New Jersey, to leave his music profession and the career that he had built in the New York area and to come home to work alongside Mr. Radford with the intention of taking over for Mr. Radford when Mr. Radford became too ill to continue to be our Minister of Music.

"Bobby" Wooten prayerfully accepted my request and came home to continue building the team of musicians who would provide excellent service for the people of God as they gathered in the house of God each week for the worship and praise of God. Mr.

Wooten added his sister, Carol Wooten, to his musical staff and our Music Department continues the tradition of excellence that Mr. Radford started and for which Mr. Radford laid the foundation.

Many people have looked at our choirs, listened to our choirs and been blessed by our choirs and thought that the conductors of our choirs were paid staff musicians and trained musicians like Mr. Radford, Roxanne Stevenson, Mr. Wooten, Mr. Johnson, Mr. Harris and Mr. Anderson are.

They did not know that Jeffrey Radford trained talented volunteers to become choir directors and choir conductors. They did not know that Bobby Wooten selected the gifted persons who were trained in other fields and who had no vocal training in music like he and Mr. Radford were academically trained.

People thought for years that Donald Young was a musician like Jeffrey Radford. Donald Young was not a musician. Donald was a young man who had grown up in our church. He came to Trinity at the age of twelve. Mr. Radford trained him, sent him along with conductors like Ivy Jackson to the Gospel Music Workshop of America and taught them Choral Conducting, phrasing, correct breathing and countless other "tricks of the trade" in terms of getting the best out of the people who voluntarily offered themselves for service in the Ministry of Music of our congregation.

The numbers of conductors for the five choirs has grown across the years. Natasha Robinson is one of those conductors. Natasha learned a lot from Mr. Radford, from Donald Young, from Bobby Wooten and from our trained musicians; but Natasha Robinson also learned a lot from her mother, Mrs. Lola Robinson, who had served as the musician for our Women's Chorus for almost two decades.

All of our staff at Trinity United Church of Christ from the clergy to the custodians worked under the watchful eye and the loving heart of Reverend Barbara Jean Allen. There are no words that can adequately capture Reverend Allen's important role in the history of this church! Reverend Allen worked fifteen to twenty hours a day many weeks of the year. Reverend Allen stayed at the church long after church hours to make sure that every "i" was dotted and every "t" was crossed.

Reverend Allen oversaw the financial, the musical, the physical and the spiritual branches of the ministry, and in the words of Dr. Sterling Cary our Conference Minister Emeritus, Reverend Allen was literally *"the Pastor of Trinity United Church of Christ. She ran the largest church in the denomination and the denomination would not honor her service by ordaining her!"*

Reverend Allen never got the denomination's imprimatur. They never gave her the official recognition she deserved, but God had His hands on Reverend Barbara! God gave her all she needed. God provided for her and she worked with her key managers to put together a staff team whose concept was rooted and founded on the Word of God in terms of serving the people of God and our church became what it became because of her faithfulness!

With Reverend Barbara Allen at my side I was blessed while being the Pastor of Trinity United Church of Christ to ordain more men and women to the Gospel than any other church in the history of the United Church of Christ in such a short period of time. For the reader of this book who does not understand the United Church of Christ and its clergy, you must remember that no person can be ordained in the United Church of Christ who has not finished seminary!

The seminary graduates I was blessed to ordain under my watch are as follows:

Reverend Dr. Thanda Ngcobo (November 30, 1975)
Reverend Dr. Frank Thomas (February 22, 1983)
Reverend Donald Fairly (April 10, 1983)
Reverend Carolyn A. Young (August 26, 1984)
Reverend Barbara J. Essex (December 8, 1985)
Reverend Susan Williams Smith (September 21, 1986)
Reverend Janice Hodge (May 24, 1987)
Reverend Zenobia Brooks (May 29, 1988)
Reverend Dr. Sharon Ellis Williams-Davis (July 31, 1988)
Reverend Kathryn V. Davis (January 8, 1989)
Reverend William Butler (April 19, 1989)
Reverend Marsha McNary-Thomas (May 31, 1989)
Reverend Dora S. White-Merritt (July 14, 1991)
Reverend James Dawkins (December 29, 1991)
Reverend Leona Cochran (December 22, 1992)

I was also blessed to oversee the training of, the seminary education of and the ordination of:

Reverend Herbert J. Carey (February 7, 1993)
Reverend Wanda Jefferson Washington (July 10, 1993)
Reverend Melbalenia D. Evans (March 27, 1994)
Reverend Ozzie Earl Smith, Jr. (May 1, 1994)
Reverend Donovan Young (July 17, 1994)
Reverend Donna Freeman (February 19, 1995)
Reverend Charlene Wordlaw-Porter (May 5, 1996)
Reverend Ronald Bonner (July 20, 1996)
Reverend Diane Bradie-Timberlake (November 3, 1996)

Reverend Patricia Ann Reiger (November 11, 1999)
Reverend Pamela Fox (July 1, 2000)
Reverend Ann B. Patton (March 31, 2001)
Reverend Dr. Vanessa Lovelace (May 5, 2001)
Reverend Barbara Heard (December 1, 2001)
Reverend Douglass W. Dixon (April 27, 2002)
Reverend John E. Jackson, Sr. (November 16, 2002)
Reverend Janet P. Broome-Moore (January 25, 2003)
Reverend Rhoda J. Barnes (March 16, 2003)
Reverend Aletta Jumper (December 6, 2003)
Reverend Beverly A. Scott (February 7, 2004)
Reverend Michael G. Sykes (March 27, 2004)
Reverend Alice Harper Jones (February 19, 2005)
Reverend Edith Greenlee (July 16, 2005)
Reverend Ruth T. Harrison (June 3, 2006)
Reverend Dr. Delores Johnson (July 21, 2007)
Reverend Reginald W. Williams (January 4, 2008)
Reverend Damita Penny Willis (November 11, 2008)

Rev. James Dawkins, Rev. Wanda Washington, Rev. Melbalenia Evans, Rev. Charlene Porter, Rev. Pamela Fox, Rev. Ann Patton, Rev. Barbara Heard, Rev. Michael Jacobs, Rev. John Jackson, Rev. Cedric McCay, Rev. Michael Sykes, Rev. Reginald Williams, Rev. Stacey Edwards-Dunn, Rev. Rochelle Michael, Rev. Ramah Wright and several other ministers of the Gospel not only finished seminary while I was pastor, but also came on staff to carry out the ministry God had given me.

Clergy who studied under me and who were ordained in the Southeast Conference of the United Church of Christ include: Reverend Susan Mitchell and Reverend Derrick Rice.

When I see what God has done through the men and women of the Gospel whom I have been privileged to mentor, I sing

Reverend Barbara's favorite song, "Look Where God Has Brought Us!" When I see what God has done through Reverend Barbara Allen and through Mr. Jeffrey Radford—my right arm and my left arm for over thirty years in this congregation, I sing, "*Look how far we've come!*"

When I look at my own life and see the places where I have fallen short and when I have been all that God would have had me to be, I sing, "*We're not what we ought to be.*"

When I look back over the years, however, and see the footfalls of God all across my path, blessing my ministry in spite of me, blessing our church in spite of my shortcomings, taking the frail and fractured efforts of flawed human beings to get in us and to work through us in spite of us, I sing, "*We're not what we used to be! Thank you, Lord. Thank you, Lord, for what you've done!*"

When I look back over the years that God gave me at Trinity, I am also forced to say, "*Nothing but a God!*" When I went to our church I was the only full-time staff person. When I retired from our church there were one hundred staff people (full-time and part-time) working along with me in this awesome ministry.

The staff at the daycare centers (at both sites), the staff working for our senior citizen housing projects (both Trinity Acres and Trinity Oaks), the staff working for our Higher Education Corporation and our *Amani*/Hospice Care Corporation are all committed servants of Christ whom God has sent to help Trinity realize its vision and live out its mission. I not only say, "*Nothing but a God!*" I also say, "*To God be the Glory for the things God has done!*"

As I said in the opening lines of this chapter, "there is no way that the story" of Trinity United Church of Christ can be told without Reverend Barbara J. Allen's name being squarely in the center of that story. There is also no way that the story of Trinity United Church of Christ can be told without the name of Dr. Iva E. Carruthers being lifted up as a central part of our story.

In the early days of my pastorate, when I was still a student at the Divinity School of The University of Chicago, one of my classmates and close friends, Reverend McKinley Young, blessed my pastorate in several different ways. Reverend Young is now a Bishop in the African Methodist Episcopal Church, but in the early '70s, he was not only a fellow student at the Divinity School; he was also an Itinerant Elder in the African Methodist Episcopal Church. He served at first as the Assistant Pastor at the Coppin Chapel A.M.E. on the Southside of Chicago. He served as an Assistant Pastor under Bishop S.S. Morris.

Pastor Young then moved to the Westside of Chicago and was appointed as the Pastor of the St. Paul African Methodist Episcopal Church. He was subsequently moved by the Bishop to become the Pastor of the Ebenezer African Methodist Episcopal Church in Evanston, Illinois.

While Bishop Young was serving in those capacities he would take me every week to the Tuesday meeting of the A.M.E. ministers in the Chicago Conference of the African Methodist Episcopal Church. I would not stay for their business meetings. I would just go for the devotional period. Hearing those men and women sing the old songs of Zion and pray the old-time prayers truly blessed my life and became a "once a week oasis" in the barren land of academia and Theological Education over in Hyde Park at the University of Chicago.

Bishop Young also blessed my life by giving me copies of the tapes that he had of a man whom I had long admired ever since my college days back in the 1960s. Before coming to Chicago, Bishop Young had served an A.M.E. church in the Boston metropolitan area while he was a student at Andover Newton Theological Center.

Serving alongside him in ministry in the city of Boston was Dr. Charles Gilchrist Adams ("the Harvard Hooper") and Bishop Young had dozens of Charles Adams' tapes. Charles Adams was the nephew of Reverend Gordon Blaine Hancock.

The Reverend Dr. Gordon Blaine Hancock was a graduate of Harvard University in the early 1900s. Dr. Hancock pastored the Moore Street Baptist Church in Richmond, Virginia. He also taught Sociology at Virginia Union University. Dr. Hancock taught both of my parents.

While I was a student at Virginia Union University (for three years), I would walk from the campus of Virginia Union University up Lombardy Street, around the corner to attend Worship Services at the Moore Street Baptist Church. It was about a four block walk from my dormitory to Moore Street Church. My Aunt Pearl, my mother's only sister, was the organist at Moore Street Baptist Church. She not only served throughout the entire tenure of Dr. Hancock's pastorate. Aunt Pearl also served as the organist at Moore Street for fifty years!

One of the biggest "treats" of my undergraduate life at Moore Street Church was the periodic visits of Dr. Charles Gilchrist Adams whom Dr. Hancock would bring in and allow to preach. I had never heard preaching like Charles Gilchrist Adams' preaching.

Fifteen years later, I was a student at the Divinity School and my good friend and classmate, Bishop Young, had thirty or forty tapes of Dr. Adams' sermons from when Dr. Adams served the Concord Baptist Church in Boston. They were colleagues. They were co-workers in the same vineyard of Boston and they were friends.

Bishop Young would bring Charles Adams into the city of Chicago to preach for him, but much more importantly, Bishop Young gave me his Charles Adams tapes (or copies of those tapes) and I was able to hear Charles Adams daily at home during my six years as a student at The University of Chicago Divinity School. That was yet another "oasis" in a vast, dry desert of intellectual coldness in which I found myself suffocating at the Divinity School. Bishop Young blessed my life once again.

Perhaps the most important blessing that Bishop Young brought into my life, however, was a woman by the name of Dr. Iva Elaine Carruthers. Bishop Young shared with me how Dr. Carruthers was setting up his afterschool program at Ebenezer A.M.E. Church in Evanston. If my memory serves me correctly, it was called the Bishop Henry McNeal Turner Afterschool Program. Dr. Carruthers, Bishop Young told me, was a fourth generation A.M.E. scholar. She had a PhD from Northwestern in Sociology. She was African-centered and she was bringing an afterschool program to the youth in Evanston that was unheard of.

The afterschool program that Dr. Carruthers was putting together for Bishop Young was a program that taught young Black children their history, their heritage, their legacy and their own "story." What Dr. Carruthers was doing in Evanston was what I had grown up seeing in the city of Philadelphia as my classmates would attend synagogue school after attending the Philadelphia Public Schools each day. It was in the schools at their synagogues (their church) where they learned their own story.

I had to have Dr. Carruthers come do for us what she had done for the Ebenezer African Methodist Episcopal Church in Evanston! Because it has been over thirty years, the details get fuzzy for me, but somewhere between Bishop Young's introduction and Dr. Sokoni Karanja's introduction to me of Dr. Carruthers, my life was changed forever. My ministry was changed in a most powerful way and the story of Trinity United Church of Christ became deepened and strengthened by the gifts that Dr. Carruthers brought into my life, into our ministry and into your congregation.

Like Reverend Barbara Jean Allen, the gifts that Dr. Carruthers brought to our ministry are too many to try to list in one chapter about the history of our church. A separate book could be written on the contribution of these two women all by itself! I will try to lift up one or two of those gifts, however, in order for you to have "a Sankofa moment" and know more accurately the way over which we have come.

I shared my heart with Dr. Carruthers concerning my long-term desire for an afterschool program that was African-centered and Christian-centered. I shared my enthusiasm with her and what Bishop Young had told me about her work at Ebenezer and Dr. Carruthers set about the task of trying to do the same thing for us at Trinity that she had done for the church in Evanston. Dr. Carruthers began working with Julia Speller to try to set up an afterschool program at Trinity. Ours was called the Sojourner Truth Cultural Institute.

We quickly discovered that Chicago had demographic dynamics, however, that Evanston did not have, where the children in Evanston could participate in an afterschool program without having to cross "turf" boundary lines and go into different gang territories and also without having to cover vast geographical areas by way of public transportation, that was not true for the students in the city of Chicago. It was especially not true for the growing membership of Trinity United Church of Christ. Our members were spread out too far across the Chicagoland area to have a successful afterschool program for their children.

With some of our members living in the suburbs, some of our members living up North, some of our members living on the Westside and some of our members living within walking distance of the church, the gang "turf" lines became a barrier that we could not overcome; so our afterschool program, our Sojourner Truth Cultural Institute, did not flourish like the Bishop Henry McNeal Turner Afterschool Program in Evanston.

My meeting with Dr. Carruthers and sharing with Dr. Carruthers, however, carried my life and my studies into some new directions that went far beyond an afterschool program. Dr. Carruthers' relationship with Dr. Bettye Parker Smith and Dr. Ayana Karanja introduced me to a world of scholarship on the personal level that I had only known about academically!

Dr. Carruthers and Bettye Parker Smith were "daughters" of John Henrik Clark. Dr. Carruthers was a student of Cheikh Anta Diop and she was a colleague of Dr. Carlos Moore. Dr. Carruthers was a personal friend of Dr. Asa Hilliard's and Dr. Wade Nobles. It was in Dr. Carruthers' living room that the first use of the words "afrocentric" and "afrocentricity" were first used.

Those terms were bandied about as adequate terms to try to accurately describe an African-centered approach to education and Africana studies.

Dr. Carruthers introduced me to her ex-husband, Dr. Jacob Carruthers, and a collegial relationship that once again blessed our congregation's life in some exciting ways. Dr. Iva Carruthers brought Wade Nobles to our church. When Asa Hilliard would come to our church each year, it was like a "homecoming" reunion for Dr. Sokoni Karanja, Dr. Ayana Karanja and Dr. Iva Carruthers. Dr. Iva Carruthers brought Dr. Bobby Wright into my life. Bobby Wright is the brilliant Black psychologist whose book, **The Psychopathic Racial Personality** is a must-read for all African Americans.

It was Dr. Jacob Carruthers, however, whose works, **Intellectual Warfare** and **The Irritated Genie** blessed the members of our congregation and the students of our church who were in seminary studying to become ordained clergy in the church of Jesus Christ. Dr. Jake Carruthers came out to our church to talk with our members after they had worked through his exciting work on the Haitian Revolution and its implication for African Americans living in the late 20th century.

Dr. Iva Carruthers pointed out to me, incidentally, that at one point I had the wives and the ex-wives of some of the most powerful Black minds in the 20th century that were African-centered and consciously trying to lead our people out of intellectual bondage. When she said I "had" them, she meant that among the membership of Trinity United Church of Christ were the following sisters: Dr. Easter Wright (the wife of Dr. Bobby Wright), Dr. Muriel Thompson (the wife of Dr. Anderson Thompson), Mrs. Maurice McNeil (the ex-wife of E. Duke McNeil), Dr. Iva Carruthers (the ex-wife of Dr. Jacob Carruthers) and Dr. Ayana Karanja (the wife of Dr. Sokoni Karanja)!

Iva told me that one of their colleagues, Dr. Maulana Karenga called for a special "Summit Meeting" during one of the annual sessions at the Olive Harvey College African American Studies weekends to find out what Jeremiah Wright was doing at Trinity

United Church of Christ to have all of those powerful sisters in one place. As indicated elsewhere in this volume, Dr. Bettye Parker Smith (co-editor of *Sturdy Black Bridges*) co-wrote along with Dr. Ayana Karanja the resource materials that we use for one of our churchwide study courses!

Dr. Iva Carruthers not only became my intellectual sounding board and my spiritual sister as it pertained to African-centered Christian thought. Dr. Carruthers also began to play an invaluable role with our Education Committee and our Long Range Planning Ministry as we struggled to keep that dream alive, to keep that plan alive and to bring into being an African-centered Christian school.

The school got pushed to the backburner because of our building programs and our need to construct a new worship center, but Dr. Carruthers never backed up. She never gave up on making the school happen and she kept the focus on pulling together the school that the congregation had said it wanted and had made such great strides in planning to bring into being.

Iva Carruthers became a "soul sister" with Reverend Barbara Jean Allen. Iva Carruthers and Ayana Karanja walked with Reverend Barbara Allen as she continued to oversee our African-centered Christian Education Program.

Iva and Ayana worked with Judy Speller and Colleen Birchett as they developed African-centered Christian Education materials for our church and Christian congregations outside of our city. Iva collaborated with Haki Madhubuti and Dr. Asa Hilliard in pulling together the curriculum for our African-centered Christian school and Iva Carruthers became a co-lecturer with me at Friendship West Baptist Church in Dallas, Texas (along with Dr. Asa Hilliard) and a co-lecturer with me on our study tours to West Africa, East Africa, South Africa and Brazil.

When my father-in-law was put in hospice in December of 2003, I had to cancel my South Africa trip literally on the day before we were to leave for South Africa. I called Dr. Carruthers and explained the situation. She very graciously stepped in and did all of my lectures for our church's South Africa trip that year!

In the closing years of my pastorate, however, it was Dr. Carruthers' visionary leadership that impacted the life of Trinity United Church of Christ in ways that will live on forever. Her assembling a team to augment the sub-Committee on Education as a part of the Long Range Planning Ministry brought about the school that we had talked about as a Long Range Planning Ministry and as a congregation since 1979.

Dr. Carruthers also played a key (an invaluable) role in putting together my retirement package and in bringing aboard my successor, the Reverend Otis Moss III!

Somewhere between setting up the computer school for our Africa Ministry in Saltpond, Ghana and presiding over the dedication of that school along with Dr. Andy Davis and the Saltpond Redevelopment Institute; somewhere between introducing me to Carlos Moore and to Samuel Akainyah—a brilliant Black-Cuban scholar and an incredibly-gifted Ghanaian artist—Dr. Iva Carruthers who already had her PhD from Northwestern in Sociology went back to school and got a Master of Arts in Theological Studies! Feeling a call on her life that went beyond sociology and anthropology, Dr. Carruthers said "*Yes*" to the Lord and went to Garrett Evangelical Theological Seminary to obtain a degree in Theological Education.

She never felt a Call to preach. Like Julia Speller who went all of the way from being a high school graduate on my watch through receiving her Bachelor of Arts from Chicago State University, her Master of Religious Education from Garrett Evangelical Seminary and her PhD in Church History (under Dr. Martin Marty) at The University of Chicago Divinity School, Judy never felt a "Call to preach." Both of these women acknowledged the life of the mind and the life of a theological educator as legitimate calls to ministry and one of the thirteen professions in full-time ministry; and they pursued their graduate degrees in Theological Education with no thought of Ordination and no thought of ever preaching in a pulpit.

Dr. Carruthers' degree did get the attention of the Urban Ministries Corporation, however, and she served as the CEO of the Urban Ministries Foundation before accepting the Call to become the CEO of the Samuel DeWitt Proctor Conference, Inc.

Dr. Carruthers academic astuteness is recognized internationally. She has been invited to and has participated in academic dialogue with scholars of African descent from all over the globe. Her work as a Pan-Africa scholar has been recognized by UNESCO and by the All African Council of Churches. Her work on the Durban Conference on Racism sponsored by the United Nations and her putting together the anti-racist curriculum that is used ecumenically all over this world are but glimpses of the breadth and scope of this woman of God's scholarship.

It is her commitment to Christ, however, and her commitment to Trinity United Church of Christ that has made our congregation's story a story that will never be forgotten.

New Worship Experiences/New Lessons Learned/New "Souls for the Lord"

Going back to 1975 and our instituting the *Umoja Karamu* Service on Thanksgiving Day, the new worship experiences that I brought to the congregation of Trinity United Church of Christ were innovative, meaningful and quite effective in terms of "reaching the masses."

In the hymn "Lift Him Up," the hymn writer says that the way to *"reach the masses... [those] of every birth, for an answer Jesus gave the key!"* How to lift the Savior up in ways that reached persons who were un-churched and persons who were alien to the "church vocabulary" became an ongoing goal of mine early in my ministry. Long before I was called to serve as the Pastor of Trinity United Church of Christ, I was trying to lift the Savior up through innovative ministries such as the Drug and Alcohol Recovery Ministry of which I was a part (and one of the founders) at the Beth Eden Baptist Church in Morgan Park.

As a youth minister at the Mount Calvary Baptist Church in Rockville, my "rap sessions" with the teenagers was an attempt to translate the ancient story of Jesus into contemporary terms with which and to which the teenagers could relate. I continued that model of ministry in my pastorate.

The *Umoja Karamu* Service reached hundreds of African Americans who had given up on the church. Connecting the story of our faith from the days before slavery to the Jesus of Calvary who set the captives free was a powerful tool of ministry and "many souls were added to the Lord" because of that annual Thanksgiving Day service.

Shortly after instituting the *Umoja Karamu* Service, we began to celebrate *Kwanzaa* as a congregation. Over the past twenty-five years the way the congregation engages in the celebration of *Kwanzaa* has changed radically from what it once was; but at the outset the ministries of the church would join together each night of *Kwanzaa* to present each of the seven principles of *Kwanzaa*.

Kwanzaa is celebrated each year in the African American community from December the 26th through January the 1st. There is no contradiction between *Kwanzaa* and Christmas. Christmas is a Holy celebration. Kwanzaa is a cultural celebration.

Across the years Trinity Church caught a lot of "flak" from Negro churches because of our celebration of the cultural holiday *Kwanzaa*; yet those same "Negro churches" celebrate Memorial Day, the 4th of July and Labor Day. Those holidays are also cultural holidays.

The same churches that would look funny at us because of our celebrating our cultural heritage made sure that they took off every President's Day. They even observed Pulaski Day (African Americans!) and they praised God when we were given the cultural holiday to celebrate the birth of Dr. Martin Luther King, Jr.

Refusing to be a people who were told by the dominant culture who our heroes are and what days we should celebrate, we not only celebrated King's Birthday before it became an "official" holiday, we also observed the birthday of Malcolm X (El Hajj Malik El Shabazz). We also celebrated *Kwanzaa* for six of the seven nights. On the last night we celebrated the last two principles, *Kuumba* and *Imani*, together. We did not celebrate

Kwanzaa on New Year's Day when I was pastor. Our Watch Meeting Services culminated both the celebration of *Kwanzaa* and the end of an old year.

Watch Meeting Services were not observed by the Trinity congregation in 1972. I started that practice on December 31st of my first year as the Senior Pastor. For readers of this work who are outside of the African American religious tradition, Watch Meeting Services are held on December the 31st every year in African American churches all across this nation and all across denominational lines. Watch Meeting Services started on December 31, 1862.

Abraham Lincoln wrote and issued the Emancipation Proclamation on September the 22nd in 1862. In that Proclamation—which did not end slavery, but preserved slavery in the Northern states and set the Africans free who were in the Southern slaveholding states—President Lincoln proclaimed that as of January 1, 1863 slavery would be ended in those Southern states.

Because of his Proclamation, Africans gathered all over the country in their houses of worship on New Year's Eve to "watch" the clock (thus the term "Watch Meeting"). At twelve o'clock midnight jubilee occurred!

At twelve o'clock midnight the captives were set free. At twelve o'clock midnight the celebrations began. At twelve o'clock midnight pistols, rifles and shotguns were fired into the air in celebration of the Emancipation of Africans. Since that New Year's Eve in 1862 up until this year Black churches have celebrated the goodness of God and the power of God by gathering to worship in the house of God on New Year's Eve.

Trinity Church had been started by a white denomination and had followed a white liturgy up until the congregation decided in 1971 that it wanted to be a "Black church in the Black community." One way of doing that was to join in with the other Black churches across the nation who celebrated an African American holiday. That is when we started to celebrate our Watch Meeting Services.

When Dr. Martin Luther King, Jr.'s birthday became an official national holiday, we started having a Dr. Martin Luther King, Jr. Service in our Sanctuary on the Monday following the third Sunday in January. We had done that before it became a "legal" holiday and we continued the practice once the government caught up with us in honoring our fallen Drum Major for Justice and Peace.

As the newness of that 3rd Monday in January being an official holiday day wore off, however, and as subsequent generations found it more important to go shopping, to stay home, to sleep in and to "chill" on the mid-January holiday, it became counterproductive to continue to try to have services on the King Holiday, so we stopped that special service.

Christians all over the world of every denomination, of every culture, of every country and of every color observed the forty-day period of Lent by starting their observances on Ash Wednesday. The majority of Christians in the world celebrate Ash Wednesday. The largest numbers of African Christians in the New World are not in the United States of America. They are in Brazil. Even the Africans in Brazil celebrate Ash Wednesday.

Because the United States of America is a largely Protestant country, however, the emphasis on Ash Wednesday is not that pronounced in those denominations where the largest numbers of African Americans are found.

I grew up in a Baptist church that observed Ash Wednesday, but all of my classmates, my playmates and my "partners" who went to other Baptist churches that were not of the American Baptist denomination did not celebrate Ash Wednesday.

To this day the vast majority of African American Baptists who are not a part of the mainline denominations do not celebrate Ash Wednesday in their congregations. I have found that to be an oddity since I got to be grown because African Americans are some of the hardest partyers for Mardi Gras and for Carnival! Mardi Gras and Carnival represent the "Feast of Meat" (Fat Tuesday) and the beginning of a period of denial and sacrifice that all believers engage in for a forty-day period preceding Easter. That day is the day before Ash Wednesday!

We celebrate Mardi Gras in the United States (especially in New Orleans), but those same celebrants skip the church services on Ash Wednesday. Because most of our members had come from other denominations that did not celebrate Ash Wednesday, it took many years for the Ash Wednesday Services to "catch on" in the congregation of Trinity United Church of Christ.

Maundy Thursday has been a special day on the Christian calendar since the first century in the Christian era. Like Ash Wednesday, however, Maundy Thursday is not celebrated by the vast majority of Blacks who are Baptist and Pentecostal.

Unlike those Blacks, however, I grew up in a congregation where Maundy Thursday Services were observed every year. Maundy Thursday is the day on which Jesus gave the "New Commandment" (*Mandatum* from which the word "Maundy" comes. *Mandatum* is the Latin word for "commandment").

Maundy Thursday is the night on which Jesus instituted the Lord's Supper after he had celebrated his last Passover Supper with His disciples.

When I started at Trinity we were celebrating the *Tennebrae* Service on Maundy Thursday. It is a European service that had absolutely no meaning for the members of the congregation who had not come out of the Catholic, the Anglican or the New England traditions.

Dr. Robert E. Wooten, Sr., and I had written a program for African American Christians for the celebration of Maundy Thursday entitled "Lest We Forget." We wrote that program during my first year as Assistant Pastor of the Beth Eden Baptist Church in Morgan Park (in 1969). I wrote the script and Mr. Wooten suggested the songs that would be used to observe the last night that our Lord spent with his disciples.

For the two years that I was at Beth Eden Church we celebrated "Lest We Forget" with the Wooten Choral Ensemble. As soon as I came to Trinity, we began to celebrate "Lest We Forget" with the music department of our congregation.

As the congregation began to grow by leaps and bounds in the years 1979, 1980 and 1981 Easter became a nightmare in terms of having Worship Services on Easter Sunday to accommodate our growing membership.

There is an old saying in the Christian church about "tangential" members, members who do not come to church every week and members who only show up three times a year. They are called "C.M.E. Christians." That means that they attend church on Christmas (**C**), Mother's Day (**M**) and Easter (**E**)!

That joke puts many a smile on the faces of those who understand how true the saying is; but the reality of trying to accommodate the "faithful" who only come out on Easter Sunday got to be unwieldy. If you will recall we were already at three services a Sunday in the early '80s. Adding a Sunrise Service relieved some of the crowd pressure, but it did not put a dent in trying to accommodate three and four thousand worshippers in a space that only sat 900!

As a result we moved from having our Sunrise Service at six, our seven-thirty service and our eleven o'clock Easter Sunday Services (plus our Hour of Power) to having just a Sunrise Service at 7:00 a.m., and the eleven o'clock service at the DuSable High School. We chose DuSable High School because it was a school in the Black community.

We chose DuSable High School for our 11:00 a.m. Easter Sunday Services because DuSable could seat 2200 persons. We thought that serving 900 persons at six o'clock and then 2200 at eleven o'clock would a blessing to the church and a relief on the nerves of cranky members who were jostling for position and trying to get seats in their own Sanctuary while being crowded out by people who would not be back to church until the next year's celebration of Easter!

What we did not take into account, however, was the cost of having services at DuSable High School. Renting a public school meant renting that school for a four-hour block of time. Renting DuSable for worship services also meant renting a Hammond B3 organ and renting risers for the choir. Moving the Services of Worship down to DuSable also meant moving the pulpit furniture every year after the Sunrise Service. When Easter fell on a First Sunday, moreover, it also meant moving all of the Communion trays and the Communion down to DuSable High

School, so that we could serve Communion to the 2200 people who came to worship at DuSable High School.

What we also did not take into account was the fact that many of the persons who went to DuSable were persons who were spending lots of money on Easter outfits and were not bringing their offerings to the Lord on Easter Sunday. Our Easter Sunday offerings showed no increase whatsoever when we moved to DuSable High School. If anything they even dipped lower than a normal Sunday in our own Sanctuary—especially a First Sunday in our Sanctuary!

As I have indicated over and over again and as God has providentially continued to show me throughout my ministry, God shows up in some surprising ways! God showed up in the person of Bishop Charles Blake and the West Angeles Church of God in Christ to give me an answer to our seating problem on Easter Sunday. I got to see what Bishop Blake did at West Angeles Church of God before they built their present cathedral.

At "West A" in their old Sanctuary, Bishop would have services every Sunday at six, eight and ten in the morning, twelve noon and then at six in the evening. Each of the services at six, eight and ten were one-hour services and the worshippers would exit through the front of the Sanctuary leaving their offerings as they left. The worshippers coming for the eight, ten and twelve noon services would be lined up and ready to come into the Sanctuary through the rear doors as the worshippers at the previous service left through the front doors. The twelve o'clock service was a regular two to two and a half-hour service.

I came back to our church and excitedly told our officers that we should try that.

I reasoned with them that Worship Service in a school auditorium was not the same as members of a congregation being able to worship in their own Sanctuary. I told them that members had shared with me what I was feeling which is that it does not feel like "church" to be in an auditorium with an orchestra pit and all of the stage accoutrements for a high school drama spectacles, for plays, for concerts, etc.

They agreed to try my suggestion for the following year and when we started out that next year having five services on Easter, the trustees sent me a note after the second service telling me that it was not working. They said to me that we needed to go back to lifting the Offering during the middle of the service and not at the end of the service as I had seen in Los Angeles and as I was suggesting for us. I sent a note back downstairs to the trustees telling them to have faith. We only had two services under our belt and we had three more to go. For me the "math" was simple.

An early morning service which seated 900 and an eleven o'clock service that seated 2200 was 3100 bodies. Five services at 900 apiece was 4500 persons! That provided 1400 more persons the opportunity of bringing their tithes in, bringing their Easter gleaners in and worshipping in their own Sanctuary. By the end of the fifth service my math and my faith proved me right. Our offerings started doubling on Easter Sunday simply because we could double the number of persons being served from the days when we used to go down to DuSable High School. We never went back to DuSable after starting our five services on Easter Sunday.

There was an "upside" to the Easter Services at DuSable, however. Many persons who had never heard of Trinity United Church of Christ and who could not get into their own Sanctuaries on Easter Sunday started coming to DuSable to worship with us.

Over 200 new members were added to the rolls of our congregation because of the Easter Sunday at DuSable services during the five years that we had services at DuSable.

Every Sunday when I would talk to my mother and father at the end of the Lord's Day, my mother would ask me, *"Any souls for the Lord?"* My mother always wanted to know how many people had joined church. She always wanted to know how many persons had confessed Christ. She always was interested in how many new converts there were because of the preaching of the Gospel.

For many years I found it a genuine blessing to be able to tell my mother that there were ten souls for the Lord. There were twenty souls for the Lord. There were fifty souls for the Lord. One Sunday we had over 100 souls for the Lord!

Our different kinds of Worship Services, our different kinds of worship experiences and our trying to "reach the masses" through culturally-relevant expressions of faith, and through being authentic and genuine as African Christians caused thousands of souls to be added to the Lord. For that I give thanks to the Lord and say, *"To God be the Glory for the things God has done!"*

Building Another Worship Center

In 1998, when the congregation had grown to the point that we were having four Worship Services on the weekend—three on Sunday and one on Saturday night with worshippers standing in the aisles for every service, the congregation voted to build a new worship center. That vote not only pushed several of our long range plans to the backburner—including our African-centered Christian school, that vote also caused us to have to grapple with several serious problems.

The first problem that we had was locating a site on which to build. The City of Chicago has strict laws about the size of public auditoriums. After a fire at Holy Angels Church back in the 1960s, the city passed an ordinance saying that every public auditorium had to have at least one parking space for every twelve seats in that auditorium seating capacity. That meant for a Sanctuary to seat at least 2,000, we needed 240 parking spaces.

To move out into the suburbs and build, or finding a site in the suburbs on which to build would have been no problem. There was lots of land in the suburbs! The number of Black churches that are now mega-churches out in the suburbs proved that point. Our congregation, however, had an additional factor that we had to weigh in and keep in the equation. We had made a commitment to stay in the city.

We had made a commitment to serve the community in which we sat. We had made a commitment to be in the *"heart of the community, ever seeking to win the community's heart."* To run to the suburbs seemed to us in 1988 as we would be abandoning the community in which we sat. We would be abandoning the inner city for the luxury and comfort of a church out in the suburbs. We began to look, therefore, for a site on which to build in the city and preferably somewhere near where we were located at 95th and Parnell. That was a frustrating (and at times a futile) exercise.

Even after we got our new Sanctuary built (and this is getting ahead of the story just a little bit) and even after we finished the entire 400 West 95th Street facility, we were still confronted with the issue of staying in the city or moving to the suburbs.

One of the very rich businessmen in Chicago who is not a member of our church asked for an appointment to talk to me about our church. Because our membership had grown to such an extent that the pastoral staff of ten was sharing counseling sessions with me, my office had the responsibility of juggling "members only" for the counseling sessions that I could accommodate. This nonmember, however, was insistent. What he did to get an audience was contact several other ministers in the city (including Rev. Jesse Louis Jackson) to have them contact me to let me know that he was legitimate and that he was not about anything frivolous. My office made an appointment for him to see me.

He walked into my office and said to me that he wanted to give our church twenty-two acres of land! (in Tinley Park, Illinois) He wanted to give us the property—not sell us the property. He wanted to do it, however, for a very personal reason. He said he had worshipped with us several times and he and his family had never been able to get a seat inside the Sanctuary. They always had to sit in the Atrium. He said to me that our church was too small for the size congregation that we had and I was too old to be preaching three services on a Sunday.

He wanted to give me the land and give our church the land in Tinley Park with the understanding and written agreement that we would build the new Sanctuary in Tinley Park on that land that could accommodate 5,000 worshippers or more. That way he would be guaranteed a seat. What we did with the balance of the property was entirely up to us, but he wanted us to sell the 400 West 95th Street property and use that money to build a new Sanctuary in Tinley Park.

Once again we were faced with the decision as to whether or not we were going to serve the community in which we sat or whether or not we were going to "run to the suburbs." We decided to stay in the city!

While we were trying to find a site to build a new Sanctuary back in the 1980s, we did find an old Jewel Food Store at 105th and Emerald. The store was abandoning that property and the property covered an entire block. It only went back as far as the alley between Halsted St. and Emerald Ave., however. Through our Long Range Planning Ministry and our buying the taxes on pieces of property we had also purchased a plot of land between 107th and 108th and Halsted. A Jiffy Lube company outfoxed us on that piece of property and that evaporated as a possibility for the site of our new worship center.

We had finally settled on the property down the street from the 532 West 95th Street Sanctuary - - the plot of land that ran between Normal and Eggleston on the south side of the street. There was this one problem, however. There was a building that sat halfway down the block between two empty parcels of property. The owner of that building found out that we wanted that entire block for our new Sanctuary, so the owner told us that he would sell it for $100,000!

South Shore Bank came and appraised the piece of property we were looking at and that building was appraised at $28,000! Our architect said to me, "*Reverend, the bricks and mortar that make up that building are only worth $28,000. The building is worth a million to you, however!*"

By that, he meant that if we could buy the building, raze the building and put our new Sanctuary up on that site, the increased revenue we would experience as a congregation, the ability to do ministry in a much less cramped facility than the 532 West 95th Street facility and the service we could provide to thousands would be "worth a million." The benefits would far outweigh the rip-off the owner was trying to pull off on us!

We were poised to go on and give the owner of that building the $100,000 he asked for when God stepped in again! The property where the church now sits at 400 West 95th Street became available! The irony of that property becoming available really deserves a separate chapter all on its own! Let me give you the summarized version of that irony, however.

In July of 1973, the then owner of that property was a Black pharmacist. There sat on the property an old A&P Supermarket. A&P had left the city, abandoned the ghetto and sold its property to a Black pharmacist. The pharmacist opened a Rexall Drug Store on the site and the A&P grocery store sat vacant.

The pharmacist walked down to the 532 Church Building to talk to me in the summer of 1973. This was five years before we built our first extension at 532 West 95th Street. He asked me if I had about thirty minutes to spare. With a congregation that was only slightly over 100 active members back then, I had tons of time on my hands! I told him yes and he asked me if I would walk back down the street with him to his pharmacy.

I went with him and he then showed me all of his inventory. I kept wondering to myself why is he showing me Avon products and Revlon products, pantyhose and toothpaste. What in the world did that have to do with anything was the question that was on my mind.

After showing me all of his inventory, the pharmacist pulled out his financial records to show me that the complete inventory was worth $25,000. That did not include any of the prescription drugs that he had on the premises. He then said to me that he was in trouble with the Internal Revenue Service and that he needed $15,000 cash before July 15th. It was July the 2nd when he and I talked.

He told me he would sell me all of the property, the A&P store, the two acres of land, the fast food store and the drugstore for $15,000. He said once I sold off the inventory, with the exception of the prescription drugs which were not for sale, the church would be ahead of the game by $10,000. We would own the property and he would be out of trouble with the Internal Revenue Service.

I was ecstatic! I could not wait for the trustees of the church to get off from work and come home, so I could share the good news with them. I called the Chairman of the Board and he called an emergency meeting of the trustees. I excitedly shared with them the good news and the offer made to us by the pharmacy. They quickly told me no! That call meeting did not last thirty minutes.

They explained to me that A&P did not want that piece of property. They explained to me that the property sat next to the projects. They explained to me that the gang problem and the proximity of the property to the railroad tracks and to the projects made it worthless. After all, they told me, that is why A&P left! I had to tell the pharmacist, "**No**."

We could have had the property on which our church now sits for $15,000 in 1973. By 1988, another Black businessman had bought the property from the pharmacist. He gutted the A&P grocery store and turned it into a skating rink. He gutted the pharmacy and turned the pharmacy and the store next to it into a fast food store and a junk food store.

His roller rink was making hundreds of thousands of dollars a year and he had intended to turn that business of his over to one of his children. He was a wealthy Black businessman and he had several other pieces of property throughout the city of

Chicago. The child to whom he was going to turn over his roller rink, however, did not want it and he was putting that piece of property up for sale. God stepped in!

We quickly called the bank and the bank appraised the Roller Rink property at $484,000. Remember! We could have had the buildings, the two acres of land and the drug store inventory for $15,000. It was now appraised at $484,000. There was another problem, however. The owner wanted one million dollars! The bank was not going to loan the church one million dollars, so we had to come up with a way to get the property while closing the gap between what he was asking and what the bank would loan us. The Long Range Planning Ministry negotiated a solution to our problem.

We borrowed the $484,000 from the bank and we gave the owner of the property that money as a down payment. It was more than "earnest money," however. It was money that closed the deal. We now had title to the property, but the provision was that the owner could continue to run his skating rink for two years rent-free!

He stayed on the property and made up the difference between the cash we were able to offer him and his asking price by allowing him to realize nothing but pure profits from that skating rink for two full years. That two-year period gave him enough income to close the gap between the $484,000 that we gave him and the one million dollars that he was asking for the property! Sometimes doing things like trying to build a worship center for God's people is much more involved than what the outside observer can see!

At the end of two years we razed the roller rink and the fast food place. We cleared the land and we got excited about building our new worship center. We had been raising monies for two years to construct our new facility. We had gone through the entire process all over again that we had been through in the mid-'70s.

We had all of the reports and all of the requests from all of the departments of the church. We had all of the "askings" from the Christian Education Department, the Music Department, the Fiscal Department, the Church Office staff, the clergy and all of the auxiliary ministries that helped to make our weekly ministry a reality. The architect took our askings in the late 1980s just as he had back in the mid-1970s.

Mr. Wendell Campbell came up with an awesome design for a worship center that gave us a Sanctuary "in the round." His design was phenomenal. There was no seat in the Sanctuary that blocked the pulpit with a post or a pillar. He designed a Sanctuary that would seat 2200 persons with the furthest seat from the Pulpit being no more than eighty feet away!

The square footage of the Sanctuary was determined (once again) by the size of the parking lot, the number of parking spaces that we could provide and the city ordinances that required 200 parking spaces for a Sanctuary that size.

We had purchased the land across the street (with the exception of that one building blocking our two parking lots) and we had purchased the 421 West 95th Street Building. We cleared the lots on the other side of the street and made them parking lots; and we busily prepared to break ground and begin constructing a worship center to the Glory of God at 400 West 95th Street.

Our Capital Stewardship Campaign to raise financial resources for the construction of God's church was going well. The people of God had a mind to work. The congregation was excited and we were on our way—so we thought.

The soil test borings had not shown us what we quickly ran into once we broke ground. Once we broke ground we found out that 400 West 95th Street was sitting on Lake Michigan! All of the land on 95th Street from 95th and Ashland over to Lake Michigan was once Lake Michigan! Where our church sits is on landfill! Where the old Fun Town Amusement Park used to sit on 95th Street and Stony Island Avenue is on landfill! Where Chicago State University sits is on landfill!

The water level, because of Lake Michigan, was so high that we could not build a new worship center to seat 2200 people or a facility of 100,000 square feet without doing something special to prepare the soil because the soil as it was could not sustain a building of that size. The ground preparation for pouring the foundation of the church cost us one and a half million dollars!

All of the construction plans had to stop while we sank caissons and prepared a platform on which to pour the concrete to form the foundation on which our church now sits—all to the tune of $1.5 million dollars. Our entire building at 532 West 95th Street had only cost $1.5 million and here we were spending that kind of money just to pour a foundation. That was the first major obstacle we ran into in building the third Sanctuary for the congregation of Trinity United Church of Christ

The second problem that we ran into was the problem of financing. For our first building at 532 West 95th Street, the Illinois Conference of the United Church of Christ had purchased the property and when I started as Pastor we were paying them back. We had a $90,000 mortgage on March 1, 1972. That mortgage, however, was held by the Illinois Conference of the United Church of Christ.

When we built our second Sanctuary at 532 West 95th Street, we paid off that $90,000 mortgage and we then had a $1.5 million dollar mortgage with South Shore Bank. By the time we were ready to build the 400 West 95th Street Building, we had that $1.5 million dollars down to next to nothing and were about to enter into a new construction period that was going to be in the "mega-millions" neighborhood. The drawings that we had from the architect and the bids that we had from the contractors showed us that our new worship center was going to be in the neighborhood of eight million dollars!

The Building Committee decided that going the conventional loan route was not going to work. It was not going to be easy. It had been difficult enough to get monies from local banks to build our second unit. Going after eight million dollars in or through a conventional bank loan was going to be an impossibility! We decided, therefore, to build by going the Bond route. We were going to sell Bonds to finance the construction of our third worship facility.

We "shopped around" for bonding companies. We found the best deal we could find and we entered into a contractual relationship with a bond company out of Amarillo, Texas. They began to sell Bonds and the money began to flow quickly. For a while we even had a few members who were buying Bonds.

We soon found out, however, that members buying Bonds, which is really a savings instrument and they were making money off the interest of their Bonds, was somehow confused in their minds with giving sacrificially to the Building Program! Rather than give sacrificially, those members bought Bonds, not realizing or thinking about the fact that they were not giving anything to the building of a new worship center. They were making an investment and getting a huge return on their investment. They were making money off of the church. They were not giving to the church!

We stopped pushing the Bond sale notion among our members because it was hurting our Capital Stewardship Campaign efforts. Our Capital Stewardship Campaign was raising money to pay for the Bonds and some of our own members were purchasing those Bonds. That meant we were raising gifts to pay our own members who were not giving anything in the Capital Stewardship Campaign!

While we were busy selling Bonds and while the money was coming in, construction was moving along at a phenomenal pace. Once we got the steel beams up to support the structure of the Sanctuary and the adjacent offices and classroom facility, we ran into another "hitch."

One of the national tabloids (I believe it was the *Star Magazine*) came out and took pictures of our steel beams. They put their pictures on the front page of their paper with the headlines that Oprah Winfrey was building a church, so she could marry Stedman! Members of the congregation started slacking off on their giving.

They reasoned that if Oprah was paying for the construction of the church, then why should they give to the church! It took weeks and weeks of notices in the bulletin, announcements from the Pulpit and even references in the weekly sermons to try to get the truth out to the members and the general public. We could not entirely change that kind of thinking among our members, however. Once a "lie" gets out there in the public's eye, people are quicker to believe that lie than they are to believe the truth.

The lesson that we learned while trying to build that Sanctuary came in handy or at least prepared us for large numbers of people believing the lies of the media many years later when Barack Obama decided to run for the highest office in the land!

While slowly battling the media lie about Oprah's building our church, we continued to build. We continued to work. We continued to sacrifice. We continued to give and then the bottom fell out! We ran into our second major hitch.

The bonding company that was selling our Bonds nationally (and internationally) for the construction of the new worship facility was put into receivership. A nationally famous white televangelist needed some money from the bonding company for some work that he was doing and instead of writing up a Bond issue which was the legal thing to do, the bond company just loaned him the money.

They had written several Bond issues for this evangelist prior to that and he had made good on all of them. Rather than go through the tedious paperwork of pulling together another Bond issue for that small amount of money, the bond company just lent him that money because they knew he would pay it back quickly.

The bank regulators, however, in the State of Texas were watching our bonding company carefully. Banks watch bonding companies carefully all of the time (except when Wall Street implodes as it did in the years 2008 and 2009). Bond companies are not allowed to loan money. They are bound by law to only issue Bonds, to sell Bonds and to do their financing through the sale of Bonds.

When the banking regulators saw that our bond company had loaned some money, they shut that company down! They put the company into receivership and all Bond sales stopped.

We had in our hands a plan for an eight million dollar worship center. We also had in our hands a plan that was designed to sell eight million dollars worth of Bonds. The bonding company had only sold six million dollars when it was put into receivership and the sale of Bonds stopped!

Among the dozens of problems that caused the two primary problems were: how were we going to make up the difference between the six million dollars sold and the eight million dollars needed to finish construction?

The second major problem caused by the bond company being put in receivership was that all the construction draws now had to go through a federal court in the State of Texas. When the contractors had finished a certain amount of work and submitted their requests for money, that request had to go to Texas, go to the lawyers in Texas who submitted it to the judge in Texas, who then approved of the work that was going on at 400 West 95th Street and that slowed the building process down to a snail's pace. Once the six million dollars was used up, moreover, that caused all construction to stop!

The third major hurdle we then faced as a congregation was: how were we going to get construction started again? How were we going to get the additional two million dollars to finish construction? How were we going to get the people of faith not to lose hope or to give up because construction had stopped? Add to that the fact that the money had run out because of the bonding company's problems: the fact of the "gossip mill," the "rumors" and the "word on the streets" and you have a major problem on your hands. It is a problem with which I was forced to live daily for two years!

The Porsche 928-S that I had leased in 1984 became the reason (on the street) that construction had stopped in 1989! The word on the street was that I had a new Porsche. In fact, the word was that I had a red Porsche! The truth of the matter is that I had the same 1984 Porsche 928-S that I had had for over five years, but the "word on the street" was that I was taking the money that the people had given for my personal use and that is why construction had stopped. That Porsche rumor was one of the nicer rumors that hit the streets that the members of the congregation heard and that affected their confidence in our ministry and in our attempts at being faithful to the Word of God and the Will of God.

There was no work going on at the new site for a full two years. For a full two years we were in conversations with local banks trying to get a local bank to pay off the bond company in Texas and to loan the congregation the balance of the money needed to finish the construction at 400 West 95th Street. Over a two-year period of time, incidentally, the cost of construction was constantly elevating.

The cost of steel and the cost of materials were going up dramatically. Labor costs were going up at an incredible rate and what we found out two years later was that our estimated eight million dollar Sanctuary was now going to cost somewhere in the neighborhood of fourteen million! It looked as if our dreams for building to the Glory of God had been dashed by the Adversary of God!

God stepped in once again, however.

South Shore Bank did not have the kind of loan portfolio that would allow it to loan us the monies we needed to finish construction. They would have to partner with another bank and no other bank was willing to partner with a Black church on the Southside of Chicago that was doing new construction next to the projects known as Governor Lowden Homes or "Princeton Park."

The banks that were closest to our church turned a deaf ear to our pleas and once again I found myself and we found ourselves like Ralph Ellison's ***Invisible Man***. Every bank just kept us running. No bank would help us at all! God had a member of our congregation, however, named Nate Cash. Mr. Cash was a loan officer at the First National Bank of Chicago.

After I had reported to the congregation for the sixth time that we had been turned down by yet another bank (this time Beverly Bank was the sixth bank that turned us down), Nate Cash came up to me at the end of the Congregational Meeting and asked me if he could float our loan past his people at his bank. I said, "*Absolutely!*" Mr. DeNye and the members of the Building Committee advised me not to say anything to anybody, however, and to keep what Nate Cash was doing on the "DL" (down low). Every time we announced what bank we were in negotiation with for the new facility, the loan would "mysteriously" fall through. Somebody on the inside of our church was messing us up on the outside of our church!

I did not say a word about Nate Cash or about his efforts to get First National to fund us. I made no public announcements about what was going on behind the scenes. I followed the advice of Mr. DeNye and the members of the Building Committee and not only did God show up. God showed out!

Nate Cash got the officers of First National Bank to agree to loan us four million dollars to finish construction of the Sanctuary. They would not loan us all of the money to finish the construction of the facility, however. They reasoned that if we got the Sanctuary completed, we would get enough people in our Sanctuary every Sunday to pay them their money back and to get the monies that we needed to complete the rest of the 400 West 95th Street Building Project. They loaned us four million dollars with the stipulation that we had to pay it back within two years!

God saw to it that we paid them back in eighteen months!

Because we had done so well in finishing off the Sanctuary and paying off the Sanctuary in such a record time, banks lined up from the Roseland community all of the way to California, offering to loan us the rest of the money to finish the project at 400 West 95th Street.

We moved into the new Sanctuary on the third Sunday of December in 1994 and we continued to raise money through our Capital Stewardship Campaign and the City of Chicago put every thing past the Narthex on "lockdown." We were not allowed to go past the barriers that the contractor had to put up to keep some unsuspecting worshipper (or some child) from wandering into the unfinished part of the building.

We leaned upon our most faithful banking partner, the **Shore Bank of Chicago**, to put together the loan package for the rest of the construction at 400 West 95th Street and we were able to dedicate the entire facility on the third Sunday of May in 1997. Dr. Samuel DeWitt Proctor preached his last sermon in life from the Pulpit of Trinity United Church of Christ on the Sunday that we dedicated our third worship center.

My father and mother flew out to Chicago for the dedication of the 400 West 95th Street facility. Dr. Walter Scott Thomas preached our eleven o'clock service, but for my family, the early service was the high service of the day. That is so because of the fifty-plus years of affiliation that my family had with Dr. Samuel DeWitt Proctor and his family. Dr. Proctor's family members were members of the Bank Street Baptist Church of Norfolk, Virginia. My mother's brother, Dr. John B. Henderson, had served as the Pastor of Bank Street and the Pastor of the Proctor Family for over three decades.

Dr. Proctor had been my primary professor when I entered Virginia Union University. He had given me five-hour lessons in Homiletics as he drove me from Virginia Union University to Philadelphia every weekend that he would go there to preach. Dr. Proctor had eaten in our home and when my parents had come to Richmond, Virginia, they ate at Dr. Proctor's home— the home of the President of Virginia Union University.

My mother's oldest brother, Dr. Thomas Howard Henderson was Sam Proctor's best friend. When you read Dr. Proctor's autobiography, *The Substance of Things Hoped For*, he mentions traveling around the country with Thomas Henderson to try to raise monies for Virginia Union University. Dr. Henderson succeeded Dr. Proctor when Dr. Proctor left Virginia Union University to go and become the president of North Carolina A&T College. His friendship with the Hendersons, however, remained intact and because of that closeness, he had stayed a part of my family all of my life! When I asked Dr. Proctor if he would come preach our Dedication Services he canceled an engagement that he had to come and be with us.

My parents flew in for the Dedication Weekend and they fellowshipped lovingly and enjoyably with their friend of over half a century. Mrs. Marie Cary was a graduate of Virginia Union University. Mrs. Marie Cary is the wife of our Conference Minister Emeritus, Dr. W. Sterling Cary. They were members of the congregation at the time and Mrs. Cary knew Dr. Samuel DeWitt Proctor because of her Virginia Union University experience and because of Dr. Proctor's close relationship with her father, the Reverend Porter Phillips. (Reverend Proctor preached Reverend Phillips' eulogy.)

The Carys and my parents had breakfast with Dr. Proctor on that Dedication Sunday after he had preached our first Service of Dedication and in the course of that breakfast amidst laughter, joking and remembering, Dr. Proctor told me he wanted to change his ticket. He was scheduled to fly out to Coe College in Iowa later that Sunday evening. He told me wanted to go home and spend the night with his wife, Bessie. He said that he could get to Coe College in plenty of time on Monday, but he wanted to spend that Sunday evening with his wife.

My parents and the Carys laughed and kidded him about why he wanted to go home to be with his wife, but he deflected their jokes by reminding me that changing that ticket was going to cost me some money! I told him it was no problem whatsoever.

We changed Dr. Proctor's ticket on Dedication Sunday. He flew home to be with Mrs. Proctor. He flew to Coe College the next day; and two days later while teaching his class, he slumped over in the classroom and he never regained consciousness!

On Dedication Sunday, he had specifically requested that we sing "Glory, Glory, Hallelujah! Since I Laid My Burdens Down." When the Women's Chorus had finished singing he said to me and to them, "*I want to hear the verse: 'I am going home to live with Jesus!*'" We sang that verse enthusiastically, not knowing that Sam was, in fact, going home to be with Jesus that very next week.

Stained-Glass Windows

When one walks into the 400 Building today, one of the most impressive sites is the stained-glass windows which depict our stories as Africans from the days of Moses up until the days that I started my pastorate in March of 1972. On the day that we dedicated the 400 Building, however, those stained-glass windows were not there!

As we wrestled with how to pay for the construction of the rest of the facility after having been in the Sanctuary for two years, we decided that we had to take the stained-glass windows out of the contract. The stained-glass windows were going to cost $465,000!

As we finalized the loan from First National Bank for the four million dollars to complete the Sanctuary, we had to cut out a lot of the "frills" in the contract and things that we wanted in order to stick with things that we needed. The stained-glass windows that we wanted were cut out of the building process!

From the founding days of the Association of Black Psychologists back in the 1960s, one of their most powerful points about miseducation when it came to Africans and persons of African descent was the issue of false images and the pictures from the Renaissance which became religious icons in the minds of persons of the Christian faith all over the world.

Because of the paintings of Rembrandt, Michelangelo, Leonardo da Vinci and other Renaissance artists, from the 1500s on, Christians all over the world thought that Jesus looked like Italian models in those paintings. They thought that the disciples looked like the Italians that they saw on the pictures of the Italian artists. Movable print came into existence during the Renaissance and those European pictures of Jesus and the disciples—and all of the Bible characters—went all over the world because of movable print.

Christians of every culture, every country and every creed were shown pictures of white Biblical characters and that became for them what the people in the Bible looked like. Of course, Charlton Heston and Hollywood did not help matters when all Americans came to identify Moses with that Hollywood character!

The Association of Black Psychologists argued that those images were teaching African Americans how to hate themselves. For a little Black boy or girl to want to be like Jesus meant they wanted to be like the white person that they saw in those pictures!

Because of my studies as an historian of religions, because of my work in the sacred music of Africans, because of my studies at The University of Chicago Divinity School and my knowledge of the history of Christianity, I knew that the white pictures were wrong. I wanted our children to grow up "*Unashamedly Black and Unapologetically Christian*," while not confusing in their minds what it meant to be a Christian!

Being a Christian did not mean they wanted to be white. It meant that they wanted to be all that God made them to be while confessing Christ as Lord! Confessing Christ, however, was problematic because since the 1700s many Africans in America thought that Christ was white! Those thoughts were reinforced all over this country (and all over this world) by what worshippers saw in their sanctuaries as they went to church each

Sunday. I knew that and I wanted to do something about that for unborn generations.

I also wanted to use a Black company to do something about it. I wanted a Black company to do our stained-glass windows and I wanted our stained-glass windows to be a perpetual reminder to our toddlers, our youth, our young adults and our adult worshippers of every race of what biblical characters really looked like and what Jesus, the Word who became flesh, looked like once God took on a human form in Northeast Africa in the first century of the Christian era!

I had been to churches all over this country and had seen Black stained-glass windows. I had seen Black artists' portrayals of historic figures. I had seen in churches such as the St. Luke Community Church in Dallas, Texas, and the Allen Temple Baptist Church in Oakland, California, pictures of Richard Allen, pictures of Absalom Jones, pictures of Harriet Tubman and pictures of Sojourner Truth.

I asked the pastors at the churches where I visited and I wrote the pastors whom I had heard had black stained-glass windows across the country for recommendations for a Black stained-glass window company, so that we could have stained-glass windows as beautiful and as powerful as those I had seen around the country.

I was given the name of Mr. Phillips who owned a stained-glass company in Cleveland, Ohio. He and I began corresponding with each other. We emailed each other. We faxed pictures and ideas back and forth to each other.

I told Mr. Phillips I wanted our stained-glass windows to show the story of our centrality in the Jewish faith and the Christian faith from the days of Moses (and before the days of Moses) up through the days of Jesus and on into the "New World" as we developed the faith that ended up being Trinity United Church of Christ sitting on 95th Street in the 20th and 21st centuries! We signed a contract with the Phillips company and Mr. Phillips threw himself wholeheartedly into the task!

Mr. Phillips corresponded with the Vatican. Mr. Phillips corresponded with church historians and art historians in Italy, in Africa and in England! Mr. Phillips really did his homework and he would send me different pictures and different sketches of pictures that showed who the early church fathers were as Africans. They showed what second century pictures of Jesus looked like in Northeast Africa and much, much more!

It broke my heart to have to tell him that we could not afford the $465,000 to get our stained-glass windows, however. We had gotten so far in the process that he would send me a copy of every character he was putting in our windows and he would send it for my approval. After my approval he would begin to construct the windows, to fabricate each panel and ready it for installation. All of that had to stop once we took the stained-glass windows out of our contract.

The stained-glass windows got put way on the backburner as we wrestled with paying off First National Bank's four million, worked through getting an additional two million for Wright Hall, the Atrium, the church offices, the counseling suite, the classrooms and the boardrooms. Two years after we were in our completed facility, I got a letter from Mr. Phillips' wife. She started off her letter by saying to me, "*I guess you wonder why you have not heard from me!*"

I smiled to myself because I was not wondering why I had not heard from her. I had said clearly that we would get back in touch with her company once we found $465,000!

With all of the change orders and all of the furnishings carrying our new worship center up over the sixteen million dollar mark (Remember? We thought it was going to cost eight million.), stained-glass windows were the last thing on my mind! In fact, they were not even on my mind! Nor were they on the minds of the members of the Building Committee.

Mrs. Phillips went on to explain that we had not heard from her because her husband had died! She pointed out, however, that he died with the Trinity Church project being the most important project of his career. He talked about it everywhere he went. He wrote about it to his friends and to his associates. He was looking forward to being able to install the stained-glass windows for us that he and I had talked about, dreamed about and worked towards for over a four-year period.

Mrs. Phillips said that she had been busy for the past few years in terms of burying her husband, settling matters in terms of his estate and finishing stained-glass window projects that he had been in the process of completing when he died. Mrs. Phillips had worked beside her husband in the stained-glass building for over forty years.

She said to me that she would like to complete the work that he did in honor of his memory. She would like to complete our stained-glass window project as a tribute to her husband's hard work and as a way of honoring his commitment to us and our commitment to him to do in a stained-glass window presentation that which was without equal anywhere in the United States of America. She said she would be willing to work with us price-wise and not make any requirements on us financially that we could not meet.

She said we could work out a payment plan and money was not the issue. Getting his work up and installed was all that was on her mind. She wanted the world to see what her husband's biggest dream was.

His dream was making our dream come true and depicting in stained-glass, the untold story of the African presence in the faith that Moses shared, the faith of Jesus, the faith of Dr. Martin Luther King, Jr., of Ida B. Wells and of the congregation of Trinity United Church of Christ.

I was excited as I read her letter and her offer. My excitement, however, turned to amazement when I got to the last few paragraphs of her letter.

She said in closing her letter to me that there was one thing she thought I should know and that one thing probably would affect my decision. She wanted me to know that she was white. She knew I wanted to go with a Black company. She knew I had chosen her husband because he was Black and his company was Black. Now that he was dead, she was completing his work, but she was not Black. She was a white woman.

She said she understood if I should choose to go with some other company or the congregation should choose to go with a Black company because she was not Black. She would like to finish her husband's work, but she would understand if we went with an all-Black company.

She then went on to say that she and her husband had two children and that they had raised their children as African

American children. Their children had attended HBCU's and had graduated and they were proud of their children just as she was proud of her husband's lifelong work. She would understand if we rejected her offer, but she did want us to know that her passion matched her husband's passion in wanting to complete that work to the Glory of God! We chose to go with Mrs. Phillips!

Mrs. Phillips not only fabricated each panel of our stained-glass windows. She came herself and personally climbed up on the ladders and the scaffolding to install every inch of that stained-glass presentation. Our stained-glass windows show the Egyptian (Kemetic) background which framed the monotheism under which Moses was raised.

They continue with the story of the Egyptian presence in the Old Testament and they move up through the ministry of Jesus and God becoming flesh to end oppression.

The stained-glass windows tell the story of the early church fathers' centrality in the Christian faith—African men who shaped the theology of the Christian faith; and they come up through our experience as Africans in the Diaspora. They capture important historical figures such as Cinque (his African name was Sengbe, the leader of the Amistad revolt), Toussaint L'Overture, Dessalines, and other important historical figures in the African church in the Caribbean and the African church in the United States of America.

Mrs. Phillips installed each panel and saw to it that her husband's work was finished and that our story as Africans and Africans in Diaspora was captured forever in the stained-glass windows at the 400 West 95th Street Building on the Southside of the City of Chicago!

Look where God has brought us.
Look how far we've come!
We're not what we ought to be.
We're not what we used to be.

Thank you, Lord. Thank you, Lord...
For what you've done!

Building the Kwame Nkrumah Academy

As the congregation was making its final payments on the mortgage for our 400 West 95th Street Building, the Providence of God began to "kick in" once again and God began to put together "pieces of the dream" that we never could have imagined!

The Strategic Planning Committee had given us a mandate to take the school off of the backburner and get the school up and running. The congregation had voted the strategic plan in year 2003 and Dr. Iva Carruthers and her Education Committee had begun to work feverishly to try to bring about the African-centered Christian school about which we had prayed, dreamed and worked since 1979.

The land banking that we had begun through our Long Range Planning Ministry and Reverend Donald Fairley's efforts had not put together any parcel of land large enough to hold or house our school, so the Long Range Planning Ministry set about the task of trying to find us the land for the school while the Education Committee began putting the final touches on its plans to open the school.

The Education Committee focused on crucial questions such as *"Should we be a charter school?"* or *"Should we be a contract school?"* They wrestled with questions such as *"Should we be a part of the Chicago Public School System through its Contract School Programs, its Renaissance 2010 Program?"* or *"Should we try to go strictly independent and hope that the financing will come through real estate ventures being put together through our Long Range Planning Ministry?"*

While the Education Committee wrestled with those questions, the Long Range Planning Ministry's land acquisition division was out feverishly looking for a site on which to build the school. The Education Committee was wrestling with *"How do we do this?"* The Long Range Planning Ministry was wrestling with *"Where do we do this?"* God stepped in once again!

Deacon Brenda Vance was on the Land Acquisition Sub-Committee of the Long Range Ministry. She was a realtor and as a realtor she became aware of parcels of land long before the average parishioner would ever become aware of such possibilities. Brenda Vance came to me and told me that Mr. Ed Gardner (of **Soft Sheen** fame) was interested in selling his property at 95th and Cottage Grove. Mr. Gardner had twenty-two acres at 95th and Cottage Grove. The site was known for the House of Kicks that Mr. Gardner had put up. The House of Kicks was a giant play station and indoor amusement park for children who were toddlers and children from the inner city who needed a safe place in which to be children!

Mr. Gardner was approaching retirement and he had closed the House of Kicks. He wanted to sell his property and he wanted to make sure that something worthwhile took place on that property. He just did not want an outside developer to come in and make money off of the Black community while not putting anything back into the Black community.

Because the church had had such a longstanding relationship with Mr. Gardner and because I had a personal relationship with him for over twenty years, Mr. Gardner decided that he wanted to sell his twenty-two acres to Trinity United Church of Christ.

Chicago State University, under the direction of Dr. Elnora Daniel, was desperately trying to get Mr. Gardner's property. Chicago State University offered Mr. Gardner almost twice what it was the church could afford to pay him, but Mr. Gardner decided that he wanted to go with the church. As he explained to the university personnel, he had had a long-term relationship with the church. Several of his employees and several of his personal friends were members of Trinity United Church of Christ. He knew the ministry of Trinity United Church of Christ. He knew the mission of Trinity United Church of Christ.

He knew of Trinity United Church of Christ's commitment to the Black community and he felt that Trinity Church through its Long Range Planning Ministry would do on that property what Chicago State would never be able to do for the Black community—especially since the university was a State university and could not publicly affirm any commitment to anything Black and still continue to receive State funding!

When Mr. Gardner learned that we were trying to build a school he said to us that the House of Kicks would be ideal for our school. Conversations with Ed Gardner proceeded at an intense, sincere and prayerful level until the deal was consummated! Simultaneously the Long Range Planning Ministry brought one of our members who had grown up in the church into the picture.

Zeb McLaurin, a well-known and highly successful developer in the City of Chicago had grown up at Trinity United Church of Christ. Dr. Karanja brought Mr. McLaurin's portfolio and persona into the project and Mr. McLaurin immediately began assembling additional lands adjacent to the twenty-two acres that we were negotiating with Ed Gardner to purchase. Mr. McLaurin's negotiations with **Timken Steel** and **Best Buy** took the contiguous acreage area up to thirty acres of land and then we began negotiating with the City of Chicago for the additional ten acres that were contiguous to the thirty acres over which we had control. Chicago State would not back down!

Chicago State wanted to "land bank." They wanted to purchase the ten acres and keep them in their "bank" for future development and for their long range plan. Chicago State is funded by the State of Illinois and there were no funds for them to use the ten acres anytime within the next decade; but because of the "politics" in the City of Chicago, a flat "No" could not be given to Chicago State. We had to negotiate a "deal" which stipulated that the city would sell five of the acres to Trinity United Church of Christ and five of the acres to Chicago State University. Chicago State, of course, wanted the five acres that were closest to its campus—the five acres that faced Cottage Grove Avenue.

In accordance with Zeb McLaurin's development plans and the excellent architectural work done by Phil Johnson (another member of Trinity) and his architectural firm, the developed property on the site was to include single-family housing and moderate income housing. We argued with the City of Chicago that no one would want a house on that site looking at five acres of weeds, five acres of undeveloped land and five acres of "a wasteland" where dumping, rodents, snakes and empty whiskey bottles would be thrown.

The "compromise" was that if Chicago State had not done anything with its five acres within the time limitations statute provided by city regulations for developing land, then those five acres would be sold to the church and taken away from Chicago State University. With the contiguous five acres that Chicago State has control over (and it has less than a year left to develop according to the law) now, Trinity United Church of Christ (through one of its subsidiary corporations) had control of over forty acres of land!

The site as planned by Mr. Johnson and Mr. McLaurin and the site as approved of by the congregation at one of its quarterly meetings consisted of a healthcare center (where clinical services could be provided for citizens of the Southside of Chicago), senior-assisted living facilities, additional senior citizen buildings, apartment buildings, single-family homes, a sports facility for personal use, an Olympic-sized athletic facility for football, baseball, track and swimming (with a view toward the 2016 Olympics being held in the City of Chicago), and our long-awaited African-centered Christian school! We now had the potential for having our "forty acres and a school."

A state of the art school facility was estimated to be in the neighborhood of $23 million dollars to construct. Those figures were given to us by the Chicago Public School System based on the costs of construction for their new facilities in the year 2006. Mr. McLaurin and his team were instructed to go about developing the piece of property such that the retail entities on the property, the income from rental on the property and the monies from additional sources would cover the cost of construction and operation for the new school. In the meantime, the House of Kicks was to be rehabbed and configured internally to such an extent that the school could open long before the new construction began.

It was the original plan to open the school as quickly as possible with all of the requisite licensing in place and to start the instruction for the students in accordance with what we had been designing since 1979. We would start that school in the "House of Kicks" building which had been rehabilitated and built to meet Chicago Public School System regulations and the City of Chicago regulations for Early Childhood Education.

The plan was to start with kindergarten and first grade. The plan was to add a grade each year until the brand new state of the art school was built and then to move the school physically into the new building while either using the House of Kicks for some other aspect of the developed community or razing those buildings to accommodate the newly configured site with all of its plans (the health center, the sports facility, etc.).

Dr. Iva Carruthers and her team worked with the Renaissance 2010 people and the congregational decision was made to go with the Chicago Public School System in opening up our school. As Dr. Carruthers' committee worked feverishly toward August of 2008 and the dedication of the new facility, a discussion led by the Education Committee and the Long Range Planning Ministry ensued.

The discussion was about the naming of the new school which was scheduled to open in August of 2008. It was the Education Committee's unanimous decision to name the school after me— The Reverend Dr. Jeremiah A. Wright, Jr. School. I objected strongly.

It was my thinking that for twenty-five years we had been trying to put up an African-centered Christian school. An African Christian who exemplified for me what it was we were trying to do was the African Christian (a Presbyterian!) Osagyefo Kwame Nkrumah. President Kwame Nkrumah was not only a Presbyterian who was an African. President Nkrumah was a graduate of Lincoln University in Pennsylvania. President Nkrumah was not only a committed Christian and an elder in the Presbyterian church. He was also the first African to lead his country to independence!

Since the Berlin Conference which carved up the continent of Africa so that the European powers could take over the entire continent and rape it of its resources, the continent of Africa had been under European control. The French took Cote d'Ivoire, Senegal, Burkina Faso, Benin and other countries. The Germans took Togo and Cameroon. The Spanish took Angola. The Portuguese took Mozambique. The British took Nigeria, Ghana and South Africa, and the Native Africans were left with nothing just like the Native Americans were left with nothing when the Europeans took over this country!

From the Berlin Conference in the late 1880s up until 1957, Ghana had been a part of the British Commonwealth. Osagyefo Kwame Nkrumah, however, led his people to throw off British rule and to become independent in 1957! He did it without firing a shot! He did it without needless bloodshed. He did it without the kinds of "revolution" that the Europeans had staged and waged in Russia, in France and in the United States of America.

Kwame Nkrumah practicing nonviolent resistance to British rule exemplified Dr. Martin Luther King, Jr.'s principles across the Atlantic Ocean and the country of Ghana and he exemplified for me what it meant to be an African-centered Christian. I felt that our school should be named after Kwame Nkrumah. I used my thirty-five years of seniority to overrule the Education Committee and the Long Range Planning Ministry and the school was officially dedicated and opened as the Kwame Nkrumah Academy in August of 2008.

The multi-talented and gifted artist who is a Ghanaian, Mr. Samuel Akainyah, is also a relative of Kwame Nkrumah! As one of Kwame Nkrumah's relatives, Mr. Akainyah brought other family members from the Nkrumah family to the dedication. Mr. Ed Gardner sat on the dais with us at the dedication because he was responsible for us being physically in the location where the school was being dedicated, and Pastor Moss led the leadership of the church—including Blaine DeNye whose Long Range Planning Ministry had first conceived of the school in 1979 and Manford and Cherribelle Byrd who were Charter Members of the congregation—in putting into the time capsule artifacts of memory and artifacts of hope as we officially opened our African-centered Christian school two months after I retired as Senior Pastor.

In its first year of operation, the Kwame Nkrumah Academy has been absolutely phenomenal. It is a record-setting model of African-centered education based on the principles established by Dr. Asa Hilliard and Dr. Iva Carruthers. It is an academic tribute to the "best models" alternative schools set up by Haki Madhubuti. Dr. Madhubuti, incidentally, sat on the dais on the day of dedication and deposited an artifact in the time capsule.

In a temporary space inside the old House of Kicks building, Dr. Nadine Headen, our first principal, and her staff have done a phenomenal job with the children who were the first students at the Kwame Nkrumah Academy. Additional grades are being added each year as we await the construction of the state of the art facility on the 95th and Cottage Grove site. When one steps back, however, and looks at how God worked through Blaine DeNye, Iva Carruthers, Thelma Hogg, Sydneye Wilson, Carol Edwards, Keith Bevans, Sokoni Karanja, Ed Gardner, Phil Johnson, Zeb McLaurin, Manford Byrd, Haki Madhubuti, Asa

Hilliard and "Momma Elaine" all one can say is, "*Look where God has brought us! Look how far we've come!*"

As Dr. Carruthers said during the Dedication Services for the computer school in Saltpond, Ghana, "*Gye nyame!*" (The Akan maxim: "**Nobody but God!**")

Chapter 6
The Plan of Succession

*I*n 1979 when our Long Range Planning Ministry began to do its work in earnest, one of the questions that we raised was: *"**How do you build an institution in the Black community that will last for generations**?"*

We wanted to know how to build a church that was built around the personality of Jesus Christ and not the personality of any one pastor or individual. We wrestled with how to build a congregation (in terms of our long-term vision), so that the congregation would not be built around the personality of Ken Smith, Willie Jamerson, Jeremiah Wright or any person other than the person of Jesus Christ of Nazareth!

As we reviewed the institutions in the Black community that had a long and proud history, we agonized over the fact that almost all of those institutions had died. We once had Black institutions like the ***North Star***. We once had Black newspapers. We once had Black banks.

We knew what had happened to the Black business community in Tulsa, Oklahoma, when the race riots hit in the 1920s, but short of the race riots and outright destruction of Black businesses, we wrestled with what it was that those other Black businesses did that caused them to go out of business! That ongoing and long-term assignment became one of the tasks for our Long Range Planning Ministry and we worked faithfully, quietly and "below the radar" on the task of addressing that question for a number of years. We wanted to put in place a God-centered and Godly-anointed plan of succession for our church that would guarantee its success and reduce the risk of failure.

While we were working on our long term plan of succession we saw Black banks in our neighborhood changing hands from Black ownership to white ownership. We saw Independence Bank leave Black hands and we watched in amazement as we lost one of our oldest Black institutions on the Southside of Chicago. We had an outstanding relationship with a white lending institution, The South Shore Bank of Chicago, which later became ShoreBank, but we wanted to know why that could not be replicated with a Black bank. We even tried to have a Black church-owned bank on the Southside of Chicago.

I worked with Ron Gryswinski in trying to pull off that unheard of feat. Ron was the moving force and the guiding hand behind the creation of South Shore Bank. Ron had purchased South Shore Bank when it had assets of $32 million dollars and had taken the assets up over $100 million dollars by 1977. Ron was winning awards for South Shore Bank's being a nationally acclaimed Community Reinvestment Bank. Ron and I worked together on the Boards of Center for New Horizons and the City Colleges of Chicago. Ron and I had extensive conversations about the need for a Black church-owned bank in the city of Chicago.

Ron showed me how he and I (and the United Church of Christ and other denominations) could together purchase Union Bank in Roseland (which was for sale) for $1 million in cash. We got the denominations to agree and we were on our way to having a Black church-owned bank only to discover that the deal had been "queered and killed" by a leading Black businessman who sat on the Board of the Union Bank of Roseland.

This prominent Black businessman was the only Black person sitting on Union Bank's Board so his white colleagues asked him who I was. They knew Ron Gryswynski. Ron had pulled off the miracle of South Shore Bank. They did not know me, however, so they asked their one Black board member who I was. Our leading Chicago Black businessman told his white colleagues that I was not "a player" and that they should not enter into any dialogue with me about purchasing their bank! That was the end of that project!

Our Long Range Ministry kept on working, however. We looked across the nation and we looked across the years at the stories of the Black institutions that had gone out of business and we decided that none of those businesses had planned to fail! None of them sat down in a Boardroom somewhere, some day and said, "*On January the 1st of such-and-such a year, we will fail. We will go out of business. We will shut our doors.*" What we discovered was that they had not planned to fail. They had failed to plan!

So many of the Black institutions at which we looked as we wrestled with our long-term goal had no long-term plans. They had no long range goals. They had no strategic plan in place to ensure the continuity and longevity of their institution.

It was while wrestling with those realities that we came up with our endowment program. It was while trying to do something about our church fifty and sixty years in the future when all of us sitting around the table would be dead and buried in our graves, that we put together a financial program that would sustain the ministry of Trinity United Church of Christ well into the 21st century. We still grappled, however, with the spiritual future of Trinity United Church of Christ. We wanted to know how to build a church that was not "personality-centered," (unless that personality was the personality of Jesus Himself!).

We looked at other churches in terms of their long range planning and their plans of succession. We saw what worked and we saw what did not work and we began to structure our ministries, our Worship Services and our being around those churches that had "best practices." We found out that excellent worship was one of the keys to success.

Of course Luke had already said that in Acts 2 and Dubois had repeated it in the *Souls of Black Folks* but very few churches that we could find paid any attention to Acts 2 or Dubois. Excellent worship became our goal and mantra!

I stressed continually to Mr. Radford and to his music staff that every Sunday the services had to be excellent! Every Sunday that God gave us to stand before the people of God, to minister to the people of God, and to work in the house of God, was another opportunity for us to demonstrate excellence in our preaching, excellence in our teaching and excellence in our music.

At one point, Mr. Radford complained to me saying, *"Rev, you want perfection!"* I told him I did not want perfection, I wanted excellence. God demanded excellence and we should not be content at any point ever to offer anything but excellence to God and to the people of God who gathered in the house of God on the Lord's Day.

I playfully told Mr. Radford one week that I expected him to be seven days better than he was the last week because God had given him seven more days to live, seven more days to work at his craft, seven more days to hone the gifts that God had given him into a sweet-smelling sacrifice that he should offer to God the following Sunday—and the Sunday after that, God expected him to be seven days better than he was the last week—and so did I.

We taught the principle of "excellence" to all of our staff ministers. We tried to teach it in every ministry and we tried to exemplify it in all of our work. We wanted all three services every Sunday to be of such an excellent nature that it did not matter which choir was singing or which preacher was preaching, the music would be top-notch and the sermons would be of the highest quality humanly possible. We developed that strategy to such a point that I could miss any Sunday on the calendar out of fifty-two Sundays and the congregation would not falter. The Offerings would remain the same, the music would be just as good, the spiritual food served to the people of God would be excellent and the faithful souls would leave nourished with new souls being saved.

The question of succession, however, and the question of "how do we keep this going when you are not here, Reverend Wright?" kept surfacing. Across the years we slowly crystallized our thinking on the matter and began to put in place some structure for how the Plan of Succession would proceed. One of the first things we did was to explain to every new minister who came aboard the staff that his or her tenure at the church was contingent upon the Senior Pastor's tenure.

Every minister who was brought aboard the staff of Trinity United Church of Christ on my watch understood that he or she was only on my staff for as long as I was the Pastor of the church. The day that I died, the day that I was fired, the day that I accepted another Call to another ministry or the day that I left was their last day on the Pastoral Staff of Trinity United Church of Christ.

From 1975 until 2005, there was no problem with that understanding among our Pastoral Staff. There was no major concern in any of our clergy staff's minds because I was young. I was healthy. I was not going anywhere and nobody had to worry about finding something else to do in ministry unless they were like Reverend Paul Sadler, Reverend Ozzie Earl Smith, Reverend Don Fairley, Reverend Susan Smith and other ministers who were actively seeking to pastor somewhere else in God's vineyard as they worked on our staff.

Actually five years before the year 2005, the matter of "What do I do now?" became an issue that started to loom larger and larger in the minds of the Pastoral Staff of Trinity. That was because in the year 2000 when we had our twenty-year review, the Long Range Planning Ministry not only put together the Strategic Plan for the next twenty years of the church. The Long Range Planning Ministry and the strategic planners started talking about the "Pastoral Plan of Succession" and how the pastoral leadership of Trinity United Church of Christ would look within the next few years.

The minister we hired to lead our strategic planning process, incidentally, wanted to form a sub-committee to work on the Plan of Succession for our pastoral leadership. We assured him that we had that under control, however, and that was not why he had been hired. We told him to "stick to the script" and lead our members in the strategic planning for the congregation.

The Long Range Planning Ministry and the Pastoral Relations Committee would handle the pastoral succession of the strategic plan for the next twenty years.

It was here once again that Iva Carruthers became an invaluable asset to the ministry of our church. Like hundreds of other volunteers who work in ministries at the church for no salary, Iva threw herself totally into the process of putting together my retirement package and the "Call Package" for the incoming successor. Working along with Barbara Bell, Iva and the Pastoral Relations Committee began doing the "nuts and bolts" work of putting together two plans that would ensure a successful transition, a smooth transition, a retirement package that would care for me and my family and a plan that would make the Calling of my successor as painless as possible in the lives of those who had only known me as Pastor for thirty-six years.

It was during those years between 2001 and 2005 that we began to look earnestly for a pastor to succeed me in leading the flock of God known as Trinity United Church of Christ. Because of my age (I was no longer a young man), I was not as familiar with the younger clergy across the country as I once had been. I, therefore, asked my younger sons and daughters in the ministry for names of clergypersons whom they knew who were serious about the Gospel of Jesus Christ. We were looking for somebody who loved the Lord with all of their hearts, their souls and their minds. We did not want anybody coming into the congregation who was playing with the Gospel or playing God's people, pimping them or trying to get over on them!

I told my sons and daughters in the ministry that we were looking for somebody whose head was on straight, somebody who loved Black people, and somebody who understood that we were

Africans living in the Diaspora, somebody who understood our commitment to the people of Africa and to people of African descent. Gardner Taylor's words haunted me in terms of our not being guilty of turning our back on Africa in the 21st century as the African church in America had done in the 20th century.

We were looking for somebody who was an excellent preacher. We were looking for somebody who had administrative skills. We were looking for somebody who had some pastoral experience and we were looking for somebody with integrity and honesty stamped all across their resumes and their spiritual DNA! As we looked for that person and looked over a long list of names, we did several other things in terms of our Plan of Succession.

We looked at other churches that had had a Plan of Succession. We looked at what worked in those congregations and we also looked at what did not work in those congregations. We saw what mistakes they had made and we learned from their mistakes. We saw what they had done right and we saw what they had done wrong and we patterned our Plan of Succession after a model that was put together from the "best practices" of other congregations.

Prayer bathed the entire process. We prayed as we looked at what other churches had done. We prayed as we saw the mistakes that other churches had made. We prayed as we learned from the steps and missteps other churches had taken. I prayed as I asked my sons and daughters in ministry to give me possible names. I prayed as I talked with other Senior Pastors. I prayed as I talked with retired pastors. I prayed with Iva Carruthers as she did the "nuts and bolts" groundwork to put together a Succession Plan. As the old folks used to say, "Prayer works!" The "model" that we put together included the following:

1. **Beginning a series of personal pastoral interviews with the possible successor.**

   Those interviews would explain to the candidate the history of the church, the intention of the succession plan, the thinking behind the succession plan and the prayerful hopes of the people of God who were looking for a person to carry on the mission of ministry of Trinity United Church of Christ. During the interviews the candidate would be expected to share his or her heart, to see whether or not the vision of the church and the vision of the candidate for ministry seemed compatible and to address any and all concerns about the "what-ifs?"

   If the candidate was already serving a church, married with a family and settled in, in another city the tough questions had to be addressed like "*What if* this does not work? *What if* I get to Chicago and do not like it? *What if* my family has problems adjusting? *What if* the congregation does not like or want me?" Iva Carruthers carefully crafted that section of the Succession Plan to ensure the health and wholeness of the congregation and the potential successor and his or her family.

   The interview process was designed to try to answer all of those tough questions and determine whether or not the process should move past the interview stage. If the interview stage was successfully completed and both parties felt comfortable then we would move to the second part of the process.

2. **The preaching and the practical.**

In this phase of the Succession Plan the design was for either the Pastor or members of the Pastoral Relations Committee to visit the candidate's church and see him or her in that natural element.

It was also the design to bring the potential candidate to Trinity Church, to have them preach in the congregation of Trinity Church and to prayerfully gauge the congregation's response to the preaching of the candidate. At this point in the process the congregation was not to be made aware of the potential succession. The congregation was coming to be fed and it was our intent to see if spiritual feeding was taking place as the candidate preached from the unsearchable riches of the Gospel of Jesus Christ.

Simultaneously as the preaching phase was under way, the Pastoral Relations Committee under the guidance of Dr. Iva Carruthers was taking care of the practical matters. Iva Carruthers and Barbara Bell headed up the process of looking at the issues of financial remuneration, the potential financial package, the benefits, a comparison of what the candidate was making, where he or she was serving and what would be a fair amount to offer as they left that work and came to serve the congregation of Trinity United Church of Christ.

The practical also included investigating whether or not the candidate lived in a church parsonage where he or she was serving, if they were serving a congregation, to see what the price of the home was in which they lived if it was their own home and to look at comparable pieces of property in Chicago should the candidate and his or her family choose to purchase their own home in Chicago rather than live in a church parsonage.

Of course the practical also included mundane issues like healthcare, health insurance coverage and dental coverage for the potential pastor and his or her family. Dr. Sokoni Karanja, Mrs. Barbara Bell and Iva Carruthers crafted a caring document that ministered to both the congregation of Trinity United Church of Christ and the potential successor to the Senior Pastor of Trinity United Church of Christ.

The practical phase of the succession plan also included bringing the pastor's spouse to the city, so that they could look at potential places for housing, potential schools for their children and an environment in which they would be living that was comparable to where they were living at the time of the Call should the Call proceed to take place.

Long after we got past the "model phase" and got into the actual Call phase, Mrs. Monica Moss came to the city of Chicago and was hosted by my daughters, Janet and Jeri, as she looked at different neighborhoods and investigated the different schools for the Moss children, Elijah and Mikayla. Mrs. Moss' visit also included some time to sit with the Pastor. That time together allowed her to share her heart and it allowed me to share my heart.

It also gave Mrs. Moss some parameters in terms of timelines and time frames for the move from Augusta, Georgia to Chicago, Illinois.

3.   **The Trial, Transition and Training Period.**

If the succession plan succeeded to the next phase, the potential candidate would be issued the official Call on paper and then move his or her family to Chicago to begin a two-year period of "trial, transition and training." During that two-year period the candidate would get an "up close and personal" view of what the ministry of Trinity United Church of Christ was all about. He or she would learn what all of the fifty-plus ministries of the church were doing. He or she would learn the "flow" of the Worship Services three times a Sunday and throughout the week.

He or she would learn the church calendar, be a part of the services of the congregation from Ash Wednesday through Maundy Thursday, through Good Friday, through Easter Sunday, through Women's Week, through the Annual Church Revival, through the Youth Revival, through Men's Week, through *Umoja Karamu*, through Christmas, Kwanzaa and the Watch Meeting Services on New Year's Eve.

The successor would learn what each of the ministries and official bodies of the church did. He or she would attend deacon meetings, trustee meetings, Stewardship Ministry meetings, Christian Education Ministry meetings, usher meetings, youth meetings, married couples meetings, singles meetings, active seniors meetings and so forth.

He or she would be expected to participate in the special Worship Services and the conferences where applicable such as the First Friday Services, the Feasting at the Throne Worship Services in the Loop that are held every Friday of the year, the Married Couples Worship Services, the Singles Worship Services, the Youth Retreats, the

Married Couples Retreat, the Men's Retreat and/or the Men's Conference and the Married Couples conferences.

These two years of trial, transition and training would also include learning the affiliate corporations that were spun off of Trinity United Church of Christ across a thirty-six year period. The successor would become a member of the Board of the Trinity Childcare Program, the Senior Citizens Housing Corporations (Trinity Acres and Trinity Oaks), the Higher Education Corporation, the Trinity United Church of Christ Healthcare Corporation/Amani and the Community Development Corporation.

The successor would also learn the work of the Federally-Charted Credit Union during the two-year trial, transition and training period.

All of this would give the successor an opportunity to see what the ministry of Trinity United Church of Christ was all about while simultaneously giving him or her and the congregation a chance to see if the "ministerial marriage" was working!

4. The Vote of the Congregation

The congregation would be asked somewhere during this process to take an actual vote on the potential successor and vote him or her in as Pastor. What we learned from other churches was that an official vote such as this would cut down on competition and "factional" fighting within the congregation once the Senior Pastor stepped aside.

5. Senior Pastor/Pastor

A mentor and mentee program for the two-year period was also a part of our thinking in terms of the Plan of Succession. The Senior Pastor would have had over three decades of experience with the members of the church and the ministries of the church. The incoming Pastor would need to be mentored by the Senior Pastor in terms of learning as much as was humanly possible to learn about a congregation within a two-year period. The mentor/mentee process would include every aspect of the pastorate from hospital visitations through administration.

The administration of a corporation the size of Trinity United Church of Christ was not like the administration of other churches around the country. Overseeing a multi-million dollar church budget, caring for the benevolence aspect of the church's annual budget, overseeing fifty-plus ministries, being the CEO of affiliate corporations and learning how to wear several different hats in the course of a month and sometimes in the course of just one week would require a training program that involved the oversight of the Senior Pastor who knew where the pitfalls were, who knew where the landmines were and who knew what the incoming Pastor needed to know. It was the design to have this mentor-mentee program make the transition as smooth as possible with the incoming Pastor having as much knowledge under his or her belt as was needed, so that when the Senior Pastor stepped aside the succeeding Pastor would be off and running at full speed!

A part of the practical piece that had been put together by the Pastoral Relations Committee covered the "what if" questions that would have been raised during the interview phase. The Pastoral Relations Committee also addressed some of the problems that we had learned about while looking at other congregations and their succession plans. A keen insight we gained from two other churches in the country was as follows: A clause was to put into the official Call Package to cover the possibility of the "ministerial marriage" not working!

In two other congregations in the country we learned of the tragic stories where the proposed successor left his or her work in ministry and moved to another city, moved their families to another city and began to work in the new congregation—only to discover that the "ministerial marriage" was not working. In those instances the proposed successor was just released. There was no financial consideration for him or her and their families after being released!

They had been transplanted from one city to another and then they suddenly found themselves without employment, without housing, without income and without any consideration of their children who were in school in a new city; and that was *not* a scenario we wanted to have to deal with as the people of God.

To cover that exigency and that possibility the Pastoral Relations Committee put into the Call Package the understanding that if the marriage did not work and if either party decided that it would be best not to pursue the pastor/people relationship any further, the potential successor would be paid for two years at the same rate that he or she was being paid while working full-time at Trinity United Church of Christ.

That two year "grace period" would give the potential successor an opportunity to find a new ministry, to receive a Call from some other congregation and to move on with his or her life and the work to which God had called him or her while not having their family suffer needlessly or thoughtlessly because the congregation seeking a successor had not taken those crucial considerations seriously.

6. Preaching Transitions

The next phase of a smooth transition moved from the administrative/business side of the equation to the worship side of the equation. How to integrate the new Pastor into the three services of Worship each Sunday and how to do that smoothly became the next "hurdle" we had to address. What we designed was as follows:

A. For the first six months of the transition period during the succession process, the new Pastor would preach every Sunday when the Senior Pastor was away.

B. Starting at the 7th month of the transition the Senior Pastor would no longer preach all three services on a Sunday. For a full year he would preach two of the three services every Sunday and the new Pastor would preach the third service on that Sunday.

C. The new Pastor would also preach during that next twelve-month period on the Sundays when the Senior Pastor was away from the church.

D. In the last six months of the transition period, the preaching assignments would shift from "two to one." That is to say that the Senior Pastor would no longer preach two sermons every Sunday with the successor preaching just one sermon. The Senior Pastor would only preach at one of the services each Sunday and the successor would preach two sermons out of the three sermons preached every Sunday.

E. At the end of the two-year transition period the successor Pastor would move from two sermons a Sunday to three sermons a Sunday and the Senior Pastor would be in retirement!

After our twenty-year review of our Long Range Planning Ministry the Strategic Plan of the Congregation was put together over the course of a year and a half's work. The congregation voted to accept the Strategic Plan of the committee in 2001. The pastoral succession planning process began in earnest in 2001 and somewhere between then and 2003-2004, we had completed the *process.*

We had looked at other churches and had seen what they did and we had put down on paper what it was we wanted to do. By the end of 2003 and the beginning of 2004, we had "the plan" in place (the *process*). We had what we thought was a workable plan and we had it firmly fixed in our minds. The problem was that we had no *person!* We had a plan, but no person.

I had begun my unofficial search the year that my father died (2001). I had begun to ask my sons and daughters in the ministry for potential names and I had begun to look across this nation for a possible successor while praying about the matter and asking

God for some direction. I had shared with my Pastoral Staff from way back in 1975 up through 2005 that none of their names would be in the mix or in the process. As indicated a few pages ago, all of the Pastoral Staff understood that once I left, their jobs were over also. The thinking behind that decision was two-fold.

First of all, to consider one of the present Pastoral Staff for the pastorate would set-up a fierce competition and introduce the possibility of bitterness and envy among the Pastoral Staff. We were functioning under a spirit of cooperation and teamwork. We had been doing that since 1975, and I had no intention of disrupting that spirit of cooperation with the destructive reality of competition and having the staff pastors think that one of them might be chosen to be my successor at Trinity United Church of Christ! They all knew that once I retired, the new Pastor had no obligation to keep them on his or her staff.

That was the second reason behind that decision. I said to my Pastoral Staff that I would not shackle the new Pastor with persons who had been hired by me. I would not tie the new pastor's hands by giving him or her a team of clergy who had worked for me. The possibility was there that somebody on that team might have felt that he or she should have been called to succeed me and that would open up the possibility of that staff person undermining the new Pastor as he or she tried to carry out the vision that God had given them.

Prior to 2004 and 2005, however, that kind of talk, that conversation and those ideas were all in the abstract and they did not "hit home" at all. After 2005, however, when the succession plan became concretized, the pastors on the staff of Trinity entered into a season of soul searching, anxiety and in many instances stress! They did not know if the new Pastor would keep them, so they began to make plans to move on in their ministry.

There was some serious soul searching in terms of the Pastoral Staff having to begin to ask themselves some serious questions. They asked questions like: Has God called me to ministry or has God called me to Trinity? Is the ministry to which God has called me a ministry that extends into God's church universally? Or, is the ministry to which God has called me limited to the 95th Street community? What are my plans for ministry? What are God's plans for my ministry and for my life? Where do I see myself in ministry five years from now or ten years from now?

Our Pastoral Staff began to wrestle with those questions seriously in 2005. They were even asked to put their plans in writing, so as to be clear in their thinking and in order to share their prayerful preparation with their colleagues in ministry, so that together we might pray about what direction God had in God's mind for their lives and for their families. Once a person was found to fit the succession plan, several of the Pastoral Staff began actively looking for places to work in ministry other than Trinity United Church of Christ.

Several of the Pastoral Staff began actively seeking a Call to Ministry in other congregations. Once we had the "person" in our sights and the official Call was extended to Pastor Moss, other members of the Pastoral Staff who were not looking to pastor someplace else began to wait anxiously to see whether or not Pastor Moss would keep them on staff following my official retirement on May 31, 2008.

One of the names that kept resurfacing during the active search for a "person to fit the plan" was the name of Reverend Otis Moss III. Like the Queen of Sheba said, I had heard about him. I kept hearing about him. I had heard about him from members of Trinity Church who were from Augusta, Georgia. I had heard about him from other pastors and I had also heard about him from my sons and daughters in the ministry.

I had actually met Pastor Moss when he was a teenager. His father and I were classmates under Samuel DeWitt Proctor in the D.Min program at the United Theological Seminary in Dayton.

His father had asked me to preach for him in Cleveland and while I was there I met Pastor Moss who was then not a Pastor or even a minister. He was a teenager! I had run into Pastor Moss later in life after he was out of college and while he was a student at the Yale Divinity School. I had not been to his church in Augusta, however, and I did not know anything at all about what he was doing in ministry other than what I kept "hearing" from all over the country.

I invited Pastor Moss to come and preach our Youth Revival in August of 2004. Once again I felt like the Queen of Sheba. After hearing him preach and seeing our congregation's response to him, I felt as the Queen said, "*The half has not been told!*"

I went before the Lord and asked the Lord if this was the answer to my prayer. I asked if this was the answer to our prayers! I checked with my sons and daughters in the ministry and they told me that Pastor Moss was doing an awesome work at the Tabernacle Baptist Church in Augusta; and he probably would not leave. I shared with my wife. I shared with my Executive Minister and I shared with Reverend Frederick Douglas Haynes III that I was going to ask Otis if he would consider being my successor.

Reverend Haynes asked me if I had talked that matter over with his father, Otis Moss, Jr. I told him I had not and he suggested to me that I had better do just that! He pointed out that Otis and I had been classmates in the doctoral program and that I might not want to risk losing a friendship over something this important. He also pointed out that Otis, Jr., probably wanted his son to succeed him as Pastor of the Olivet Baptist Church in Cleveland! He suggested strongly that I talk with Otis, Jr., before mentioning anything to his son.

At Pastor Haynes' suggestion I called Otis, Jr., and after we chatted for a few moments I asked him pointblank if he wanted his son to succeed him at Olivet Church. Pastor Moss, Jr., said that he wanted what was best for his son in ministry. He wanted God's Will for his son in ministry and that was his primary concern.

He added his own personal reflection by saying that he, of course, would love to see his son follow him as the Pastor of Olivet Church. He did not think that would happen, however, because his son had a very strong and positive ministry going on in Augusta and he probably would not leave that work to come to Cleveland. He then asked me pointblank, "*Why do you ask?*"

I then went on and shared with him our Plan of Succession and I shared with him my thinking and my feelings concerning his son. I told him that I thought God had answered my prayer and he said to me that it was a high honor to hear his son thought of and spoken of so highly. It was awesome to think that his son was being offered the possibility of succeeding me at Trinity; but on a personal level the answer to my question was, "*Yes.*" He would want his son to succeed him at Olivet should he choose to leave the work he was doing in Augusta, Georgia.

I then thanked Pastor Moss and invited him and his wife to
come and hear their son as he preached for our Youth Revival.
A tragedy, however, suddenly hit the Moss Family right before
the Youth Revival. A sudden and unexpected death of their
teenage grandson caused Otis, Jr., and Edwina not to be able to
come that year. Monica and the children did not come either.
Otis came to Trinity by himself.

On the last night of the Youth Revival I shared with Otis what I
had said to his father and what my thinking had been. I shared
with Otis what his father had said to me. I shared that
conversation as I took him back to his hotel. He thanked me
and said goodnight. He thanked me for inviting him to the Revival
and he wished God's blessings upon me. He never responded to
anything I said about my conversation with his dad or my
thinking about his becoming my successor.

One of the things that fifty years of ministry has taught me is
how God steps in in some surprising ways over-and-over again.
God stepped in once again. Because Otis' age puts him in the
age bracket as my oldest two daughters, they formed a "second
generation preacher's kids" bond while he was here and they
continued to dialogue after he had left our Youth Revival.

It was somewhere between that August when the Youth Revival
was held and that following Christmas that my daughters started
teasing Otis about his "dissing" me. He did not know what they
were talking about. My daughter, Janet, said to him, "*Daddy
offered you the position of becoming his successor and you just
dissed him. You did not even respond to what he said to you in
one way or the other!*"

When Pastor Moss called to wish me Season's Greetings during
the following Christmas season he said to me, "*You weren't serious
about what we talked about in the car. Were you?*" I asked him

if he meant what I said to his daddy and he said yes. I asked him why in the world he thought I would talk to his daddy if I was not serious.

He then asked me if we could talk some more about that possibility and I said gladly. We agreed to talk about it during the Samuel DeWitt Proctor Pastor's Conference in February of 2005. During the Conference he came to my room and we talked extensively about our succession plan and where or how if in any way he fit into what it was we had in mind in terms of him being the person to succeed me. Otis had dozens of questions and I tried to answer all of them.

He then asked me if he and Monica could pray about it during Lent and I said, "*Of course.*" Once again the entire process was bathed in prayer. We had been praying on our end. The Pastoral Relations Committee had been praying. Freddy Haynes and I had been praying. Those who put together the Succession Plan had been praying. Ramah had been praying. Janet and Jeri had been praying and now Otis and Monica were going to pray throughout the period of Lent.

Lent came and went. Easter passed and I heard nothing from Otis. As the members of Trinity United Church of Christ have known for the past quarter of a century, Reverend Frederick Douglas Haynes III and I talk every Sunday night (when the Dallas Cowboys have not been whipped!). On Easter Sunday night and on two or three Sunday nights succeeding Easter, Freddy Haynes asked me if I had heard from Otis. I told him, "*Not a word!*" It seemed as if no news was bad news. It seemed as if he and Monica had prayed about it, talked about it, sought the Lord concerning it and the answer was obviously "*No!*"

During the Memorial Day weekend, Pastor Moss called me to wish me a Happy Holiday. After a brief period of salutations and inquiries about our family members he said to me, *"How does the word 'Yes' sound to you?"* I asked him what he meant. He said he meant that the answer to his and Monica's prayer was yes. The answer to the prayer that he and Monica had been praying was yes! God had said yes. I was ecstatic!

Otis and I then began to talk about the next phase of a succession plan, putting together the package, having Monica come to the city to look at housing and schools and all of those kinds of details. He was scheduled to preach our Youth Revival once again that year.

As I shared my enthusiasm with Pastor Haynes sometime during the month of June, once again, he asked, *"Have you talked to Otis' father?"* I reminded him that I had talked with his dad the year before and he reminded me that the year before things had not gotten serious. At this point as we were talking package, and talking about moving and talking about his actually coming to the city of Chicago, I needed to talk to his father to keep the air clear and to keep the friendship intact! I then called his daddy once again.

Of course his father knew of his decision. They had already talked about it. They had prayed about it and his father was not the happiest kid in camp! I invited his father to the Youth Revival for the second time. I reminded him of the tragedy that kept him from coming the year before and told him that the invitation still stood. I assured Pastor Moss that we would pay for him and Edwina to come and fellowship with us during the Youth Revival and to enjoy the preaching of their son in the congregation that would be calling him to succeed me. I assured him that he and

I would talk face-to-face and man-to-man once he got to Chicago.

Pastor Moss, Monica and the children came to the Youth Revival. His father and mother also came and I got the chance to talk to his dad and to his mom about Otis III's succeeding me during that year's Revival.

On the last night of the Revival, Pastor Moss and Monica stayed in my office to meet with Ramah and me, and we decided that they would remain in Augusta until the end of the school year in May of 2006. Elijah had just started school and Elijah needed to complete that first year in school.

That would also give Pastor Moss the opportunity to share his decision with the members of the Tabernacle Baptist Church of Augusta, Georgia. It would give them some time to prepare to look for a successor for him and it would give his family adequate time to put their house on the market, to pack things up and to move to Chicago.

I shared the good news with the leaders of the church. I shared the good news with the officers of the church. At the October meeting of the Board of Directors for Trinity United Church of Christ, the Board of Directors voted to extend the Call to Otis Moss III to succeed me. We held our breath between October and January when the congregation would hold its Annual Meeting.

We expected word to leak out in the congregation. If it did, no one ever said anything to me. People from other parts of the country, however, were calling me and congratulating me, and saying how proud they were of our decision to handle the succession in such a powerful, unique and unheard of manner.

At the Annual Meeting of the Congregation in January of 2006, I announced what the Board had voted at its October 2005 meeting. I explained to the members of the congregation in my Annual Report to the Congregation how our succession plan had been put together, how it had worked and how God had provided the person to go along with the plan.

We made that portion of my Annual Report a separate CD, so that members could purchase that verbal account of our Succession Plan and have it for themselves, their children and their neighbors to counter any rumors and any misinformation that would start circulating about the process. Copies of that CD are still available.

Pastor Moss and his family moved from Augusta to Chicago and he started to serve on June 1, 2006.

One of the first things we did to ease his moving and his transitioning into the family life of Trinity United Church of Christ was to have eight sessions of "Meet the Mosses."

Four of the sessions were held during the daytime and four of the sessions were held in the evening for members of the congregation who worked during the day and could only come to meet the Mosses during the evening. The "Meet the Mosses" sessions consisted of a twenty to thirty-minute presentation by Otis and Monica which was followed by an hour of questions from members of the congregation. Following the hour-long question and answer period in the Sanctuary, members of the congregation went into the Atrium for an informal fellowship, for light food and for informal dialogue with Pastor Moss, Mrs. Moss and their children.

I was in Revival out of town during the first daytime "Meet the Mosses" session. Our Media Department under the direction of my daughter, Jeri, made the wise decision of video streaming those sessions. Video streaming the "Meet the Mosses" sessions gave the nation an opportunity to see a congregation learning about, embracing and loving its new Pastor and his family. It also gave members of the congregation who were not able to get to the sessions an opportunity to see, to hear, to learn and to listen.

I watched that first session of the "Meet the Mosses" from my hotel room in Detroit. I was impressed. I was excited. I felt good and I was blown away! I was blown away because the first question to come to Pastor Moss (or the first statement) after his presentation came from Camille Robinson. After Pastor Moss and Monica had finished saying who they were and how they got to that point on their spiritual journey, the members of the Host Committee turned the session over to the congregation for their questions and/or comments. Camille Robinson was the first person at the mic.

Camille Robinson is the "middle daughter" of Reverend Wayne Robinson who had been on my staff in the early 1980s. Camille Robinson is also the daughter of Mrs. Lola Robinson who had worked with our Women's Chorus and worked as a part of our Ministry of Music team for over a decade. Many of our members know Natasha Robinson as the attorney who directs the Sanctuary Choir. She is the conductor who followed Donald Young's tenure as the Sanctuary Choir conductor. Camille is Natasha's sister.

Camille stepped to the mic and said that she was almost born in Trinity United Church of Christ. She came to Trinity United Church of Christ when she was in elementary school. She had been raised in Trinity United Church of Christ. I had been the only Pastor that she knew all of her life! When she heard that I was really leaving she was hurt. When she heard that I was retiring, she said, "*When Daddy J goes, I go!*" She was determined that she was "out of here!"

With tears in her eyes and a lump in her throat, Camille choked up and said in a half-talking, half-sobbing voice, "*But, if Daddy J says you are going to be our Pastor, then Pastor Moss, I am saying to you that you are going to be my Pastor too!*"

Camille was married and the mother of three. Here was a young woman who grew up in the church who was married by me, whose children were blessed by me and who said that I was the only pastor she knew. Her public embrace of Pastor and Mrs. Moss, however, caused the congregation to break out in thunderous applause. People were crying and hugging her and loving this new couple who had come to serve us because of prayer. God showed up and God was still at work in some surprising ways!

During the last "Meet the Mosses" sessions, I was in the Sanctuary. It was a night session and the Sanctuary was jammed pack. We followed the same format. I introduced the Mosses and then Otis and Monica talked for just about twenty minutes. The question and answer period, however, went on well past the one-hour time slot that had been allotted. The size of the crowd caused the question and answer period to be lengthy.

When I saw that we were way past the allotted Q and A hour and I knew that we still had the informal hour of food and fellowship in the Atrium, I got in line behind the person who speaking at the mic and I said to the persons behind the member who was asking their question that the Mosses had young children. The Mosses had to go home. We still had a whole hour ahead of us for informal conversation in the Atrium and I was asking would they please take their seats and reserve their questions for the fellowship session back in the Atrium. They all graciously thanked me and took their seats.

I stood behind the speaker at the mic to whom Pastor Moss was addressing his response. While Pastor Moss responded to that member Mrs. Ethel Jordan came up to me and pulled my sleeve. Ethel, you will remember, was the wife of Val Jordan - - the man whose entry into my home on December 31, 1971 changed my life forever! Mother Jordan was in her early eighties. She said to me, "*Reverend Jerry, can I say something?*" The answer was an obvious, "*Yes, Ma'am.*"

When Pastor Moss finished his response, I took the mic and said I had announced that the previous speaker would be the last person to ask a question, but Mrs. Jordan had requested permission to say something. I handed one of my "other mothers" the mic and literally held my breath because I had no idea what she was going to say. Mrs. Jordan put a spiritual bookend on that "Meet the Mosses" session to match the opening affirmation that had been given by Camille Robinson seven sessions previously!

Mrs. Jordan said:

"*Young man, Val and I have known 'Reverend Jerry' longer than anybody else in this congregation. My husband met him before the Search Committee met him. Reverend Jerry has been our Pastor for thirty-five years. He is more like a son to us than our minister. We love him as if he were our own child.*

"*What I need to say to you, young man, is this: If Reverend Jerry trusts you enough to turn over his life's work to you. He has been here for over half of his life; and if he trusts you enough to turn*

*this ministry over to you, then you are going to be our Pastor
also!"*

Once again the congregation erupted in thunderous praise! The
hour of fellowship back in the Atrium was anticlimactic for me.
God had put an exclamation point on the succession plan in
that Sanctuary through the words of a woman who had become
like my mother in the faith.

In the thirty-six years that I served as the Pastor of Trinity United
Church of Christ, I had never taken a sabbatical. Blaine DeNye
and members of the Board of Directors had offered me the
opportunity to take sabbaticals from the earliest days of my
ministry. Val Jordan kept pressing me to take some time off, to
take some time away, to refresh, to renew and to regroup in the
loving and graceful arms of our God. I always stayed too busy to
take a sabbatical and I never did take the sabbatical that the
church offered me.

As a matter of fact, I accumulated over five periods of sabbatical
leave which is a total of fifteen months that I could have taken
away from the pulpit and away from the pressures of pastoring.
I decided that I would finally take a sabbatical starting on the
day of my 36th anniversary as the Pastor of Trinity United Church
of Christ. Rather than take fifteen months, however, I took
only three months of sabbatical, so that I could retire on May
31, 2008.

I preached my last three sermons on the second Sunday in
February of 2008. According to our succession plan we had
moved into the final phase of the preaching transition. We were
in that third phase where Pastor Moss was supposed to preach
two of the three services when I was in town and I was to only

preach one. That was to have been the format for my last Sunday in the Pulpit also.

I started catching flack from everywhere, however, when I indicated that I would only be preaching one sermon that Sunday just as I had only preached one sermon for the other Sundays that I had been in the Pulpit since we entered phase three of the preaching transition! The flack I was catching was from members who did not know at which of the three services I would be preaching my last sermon.

Some of the members of the church went so far as to contact Freddy Haynes and urge him to stress to me the importance of preaching all three services on my last Sunday in the Pulpit. They argued (and Freddy became their spokesman) that it would be unfair to the members who worshipped at seven-thirty in the morning if I preached at eleven and did not preach my last sermon while they were in attendance. The same was true, they argued, for persons who only came at six.

Whichever service I chose to preach at, they said to me, would put the members who worshipped at the other two services in the position of not having been able to hear my last sermon on my last Sunday as the preaching Senior Pastor of their congregation. I gave in and preached all three services on my last Sunday in the Pulpit.

I had been working on a series of sermons in the Book of John as the final series of sermons that I would preach in the Pulpit of the place where God had placed me for thirty-six years. I started that John series in the fall of 2007. I had mapped out sermons and planned my preaching schedule up through the second Sunday in February staying in the Book of John. Having to preach three different sermons on that Sunday, however, caused my plans to be abandoned.

I preached the first service from the Book of Exodus. I preached the second service from the Book of John and I preached the 6:00 p.m. service from the Book of Philippians. Those were my last three sermons as the Senior Pastor of Trinity United Church of Christ.

On the third Sunday in February, and on the fourth Sunday in February, we had guest ministers who came in to preach in honor of my thirty-six years of service. Between the fourth Sunday in February and the first Sunday in March, we had preaching services each night with different ministers who came in to honor my thirty-six years of service and to preach in celebration of my retirement.

On the first Saturday in March (the day before my 36th anniversary), an all-day symposium was held with guest lecturers and guest panelists who focused in on my work in Ethnomusicology and my work as an African American deeply and inextricably tied into the work of the church of Jesus Christ on the Continent of Africa.

A news reporter from the *New York Times*, incidentally, was at both of those Saturday sessions and hounded me trying to get me to talk about Barack Obama when I was trying to celebrate thirty-six years of ministry as the Pastor of Trinity United Church of Christ!

Even after having been in church all day, when the final session was over, that reporter who refused to hear the word "no" followed me all of the way upstairs to my office and security had to turn her around and get her out of the building. Her obnoxious behavior, however, was simply a "preview of coming attractions!"

On the first Sunday in March, as I celebrated my 36th anniversary and my last Sunday as Senior Pastor, Reverend Lance Watson preached the 7:30 a.m. service. Pastor Moss preached the eleven o'clock service and then we went over to Christ Universal Temple for the final Service of Celebration at six o'clock in the evening. Reverend Frederick Douglas Haynes III flew in from Dallas to preach that service. Richard Smallwood joined all of our choirs and our dance ministries in a Service of Celebration and a farewell to their Senior Pastor of 36 years.

A reception at the South Shore Cultural Center followed that final service and the memories of that Sunday will live forever in my heart and in my soul.

I have tried to serve the congregation of Trinity United Church of Christ to the best of my ability. I offer this *Sankofa* moment to help new members, non-members and future members know something about the road over which God led us - - from the ten years prior to my being Called to serve, up through my last Sunday of service when Pastor Moss took over the reins and began to lead us as God would lead him.

I have not been successful in everything I tried. I have made mistakes. I have fallen. I have disappointed members. I have not lived up to the expectations of many. I have been misunderstood. I have hurt people and I have been far from perfect. I have tried, however, and any success that God has given me has simply been because of God's grace and God's mercy. I thank God for the way that God kept me and used me in spite of me.

As I rapidly approach the "magical year" of seventy, I often think of my father's favorite song. I believe it was sung by the Banks Brothers. Its words are:

> *I have never reached perfection, but I've tried.*
> *Sometimes I have lost connection; but I've tried!*
> *Lord, I've tried!*

I have tried to be faithful to God. I have tried to be faithful to the people of God. I have tried to be faithful to the vision that the people of God gave me in March of 1972. I have tried to be faithful to the Black Value System that the congregation put together for itself in 1981. I have tried to preach with integrity. I have tried to pastor with compassion. I have never reached perfection, but I have tried!

I have turned over my life's work to a gifted young man. I have left our congregation in the hands of God.

I enter this new phase of ministry with hope and with confidence.

I offer this *Sankofa* reflection to you to help you get a better glimpse of what God has been up to (to use Reverend Barbara Heard's phrase) in my life and in the life of this congregation.

It is my hope as I offer these pages to you and offer my life's work to God that I will get to hear Him say one day, "*Well done, thou good and faithful servant!*"

Lovingly yours,

Reverend Dr. Jeremiah A. Wright, Jr.
Pastor Emeritus

Afterword
God's Hope for the World

You have just read a fascinating history of a local church that has made an impact, not only on its city, but on the world. Dr. Gardner C. Taylor, the "Dean of Black Preaching" in the United States of America for the 20th century and the Pastor Emeritus of the Concord Baptist Church of Christ in Brooklyn, New York, had this to say about the Pastor Emeritus of this local church and its impact nationally and internationally:

> *People who love the Lord and who embrace the noblest concepts of our democracy will enthusiastically applaud the establishment of the Reverend Dr. Jeremiah A. Wright, Jr. Lectureship. The Lectureship appropriately salutes the Pastor and mentor who prepared President Barack Obama for the role of President of the United States.*
>
> *Mr. Obama had hardly any grasp of the meaning of being a Black person in the United States. By example and exhortation, Reverend Dr. Jeremiah A. Wright, Jr., cured that deficiency, sending to Washington a President qualified to give America a chance to actually become a democracy!*

Dr. Taylor sent those words of encouragement as the Center for

African American Theological Studies inaugurated its Annual Lecture in honor of the preaching and ministry of Reverend Dr. Jeremiah A. Wright, Jr.

In 1903, Dr. W. E. B. DuBois said that the Black church needed three primary ingredients in order for it to be a church. Those ingredients were and are: its preaching, its music, and the Holy Spirit!

Because Dr. Wright realized that preaching was and is such a crucial part of the ministry of Jesus Christ, he preached the Gospel of Jesus Christ faithfully for thirty-six years. It is that preaching to which Dr. Gardner Taylor refers when he says Pastor Wright "prepared Barack Obama to be the President of the United States."

It is that same preaching that led not only President Obama to Christ, but also led over 8,000 souls to Christ over a thirty-six year period. That preaching stressed the importance of individuals having a personal relationship with Jesus Christ and also the importance of them being a part of a congregation which served Christ daily!

Perhaps, you, in reading this brief history, are a person who has never developed a personal relationship with Jesus Christ, the Head of the church. If that is the case, this "Afterword" is for you.

The focus of the ministry at Trinity United Church of Christ was to introduce Christ to a people and a community who had known the horrors and ugliness of slavery, the Transatlantic Slave Trade, white supremacy, segregation, Jim Crow and who now experience what Tim Wise calls, "Racism 201."

How to get Christ a "hearing" in that context and how to get people to hear the good news of the Gospel as separated from the bad news of American culture was the ongoing task of the preacher who stood for thirty-six years proclaiming the Gospel in spite of the context in which the hearers of that Gospel lived.

In many ways what Pastor Wright tried to do was what the Apostle Paul tried to do as he wrote to a people under Roman oppression. The Apostle Paul sought to present Christ to a people under Roman oppression in spite of the harshness of their Roman oppressors. Paul was faithful in his context and Pastor Wright was faithful in his context.

How does that pertain to you? Here is how: You too can know that same Christ today if you have not already developed a relationship with Jesus Christ.

You do not have to be a Black person living on the Southside of Chicago to know and accept Christ and develop a personal relationship with Him. You do not have to be a Black person at all to do that. The Gospel of Jesus Christ is preached to all persons of all colors, all nations, all cultures and all ethnicities. Pastor Wright preached that Gospel and persons from four different continents became followers of Christ because of that preaching.

You can become a follower of Christ also; and you don't have to wait until the Lord's Day to do so. You can accept Jesus Christ today—right where you are, *just* as you are! You can ask God for salvation wherever it is you are as you read this book!

If you understand clearly that Jesus Christ died for you, you can become a Christian today! If you confess with your mouth that Jesus is Lord; if you believe in your heart that God has raised Jesus from the dead; and if you accept God's gift of grace through faith, then you can be saved right now!

If you accept the fact that God loves you unconditionally, that is the first step toward receiving God's grace. God wants nothing but the best for you. God made you in His image and He has a purpose for your life.

If you accept those basic principles and pray right now for God to come into your life, then God's Word says "You shall be saved!" You can follow through with your personal commitment and your private commitment by becoming a part of the Body of Christ called the church as quickly as possible.

Our faith is a communal faith. Our faith is a faith that is practiced and made to "come alive" in community. God sent Jesus to save a community. He saves individuals, yes; but it is in the community of faith called the Church that God works in wondrous ways!

It is our prayer that you will accept Christ today as your personal Savior and that you will become a part of a local congregation as quickly as possible.

Lovingly yours,

—The Grace of God, NFP
Hazel Crest, Illinois